THE HEART OF LEARNING

PRAISE FOR THE HEART OF LEARNING

"This book is an act of courage. Fascinating and at times exhilarating, *The Heart of Learning* asks us to imagine an education grounded, yes *grounded,* in spiritual inquiry. The unfolding conversation within these pages reveals the outline of an educational reform movement that emphasizes intuitive understanding and place-based knowledge. Glazer's effective weaving of such disparate voices only strengthens the book's ultimate message: restore the heart to education, return our gaze to our own homeground, dwell artfully and joyfully within the essential mystery of life."

—LAURIE LANE-ZUCKER, MANAGING DIRECTOR,
THE ORION SOCIETY

"A contemplation of what we are doing, and what we are called to do as educators . . . provides clear, incisive and compelling pictures of everything from the nature of knowing, to the wisdom of myth, to the design of ecologically sustainable architecture."

—*INDUSTRIAL EDUCATION REVIEW*

"I find in *The Heart of Learning* much that is healthy, and that seems to regard spirituality as our inborn need to contact the Really Real. It is a book—and this is highest praise—that is unlikely to do harm, and that is bound to stimulate thought without denying feeling."

—FREDERICK FRANCK, ARTIST, TEACHER, AND AUTHOR OF
THE LITTLE COMPENDIUM OF THAT WHICH MATTERS

"Steven Glazer's *The Heart of Learning* illuminates the dark side of our educational process, the assumption that learning is solely about the transmission of knowledge. Chapter by chapter, each contributor clarifies the place wisdom and compassion have in the development of a society that is open, loving, supportive, and tolerant. This is a book that contains the seeds for healing and nourishing an ailing planet and its people."

—JOHN DAIDO LOORI, ROSHI, ABBOT
OF ZEN MOUNTAIN MONASTERY AND AUTHOR
OF *TWO ARROWS MEETING IN MID-AIR*

This *New Consciousness Reader* is part of a new series of original and classic writing by renowned experts on leading-edge concepts in personal development, psychology, spiritual growth, and healing. Other books in this series include:

The Art of Staying Together
EDITED BY MARK ROBERT WALDMAN

The Awakened Warrior
EDITED BY RICK FIELDS

Creators on Creating
EDITED BY FRANK BARRON, ALFONSO MONTUORI, AND ANTHEA BARRON

Dreamtime and Dreamwork
EDITED BY STANLEY KRIPPNER, PH.D.

The Erotic Impulse
EDITED BY DAVID STEINBERG

Fathers, Sons, and Daughters
EDITED BY CHARLES SCULL, PH.D.

Gay Men at the Millennium
EDITED BY MICHAEL LOWENTHAL

Healers on Healing
EDITED BY RICHARD CARLSON, PH.D., AND BENJAMIN SHIELD

In the Company of Others
EDITED BY CLAUDE WHITMYER

Meeting the Shadow
EDITED BY CONNIE ZWEIG AND JEREMIAH ABRAMS

Mirrors of the Self
EDITED BY CHRISTINE DOWNING

The New Paradigm in Business
EDITED BY MICHAEL RAY AND ALAN RINZLER
FOR THE WORLD BUSINESS ACADEMY

Paths Beyond Ego
EDITED BY ROGER WALSH, M.D., PH.D., AND FRANCES VAUGHAN, PH.D.

Reclaiming the Inner Child
EDITED BY JEREMIAH ABRAMS

Sacred Sorrows
EDITED BY JOHN E. NELSON, M.D., AND ANDREA NELSON, PSY.D.

The Soul Unearthed
EDITED BY CASS ADAMS

Spiritual Emergency
EDITED BY STANISLAV GROF, M.D., AND CHRISTINA GROF

The Truth About the Truth
EDITED BY WALTER TRUETT ANDERSON

To Be a Man
EDITED BY KEITH THOMPSON

To Be a Woman
EDITED BY CONNIE ZWEIG

What Survives?
EDITED BY GARY DOORE

Who Am I?
EDITED BY ROBERT PRAGER, PH.D.

Founding Series Editor: CONNIE ZWEIG, PH.D.

THE HEART
OF LEARNING

Spirituality

in

Education

EDITED BY

STEVEN GLAZER

JEREMY P. TARCHER/PUTNAM

a member of

PENGUIN PUTNAM INC.

New York

Most Tarcher/Putnam books are available at special
quantity discounts for bulk purchase for sales
promotions, premiums, fund-raising, and
educational needs. Special books or book
excerpts also can be created to fit specific needs.
For details, write Putnam Special Markets,
375 Hudson Street, New York, NY 10014.

Jeremy P. Tarcher/Putnam
a member of
Penguin Putnam Inc.
375 Hudson Street
New York, NY 10014
www.penguinputnam.com

Library of Congress Cataloging-in-Publication Data

The heart of learning : spirituality in education / [edited by]
Steven Glazer.
    p.   cm.—(New consciousness reader)
    "This book grew out of the Spirituality in Education
Conference hosted by the Naropa Institution in Boulder,
Colorado, during the summer of 1997"—Introd.
    Includes bibliographical references.
    ISBN 0-87477-955-3 (alk. paper)
    1. Education—Aims and objectives—Congresses.   2. Spiritual
life—Congresses.   3. Educational anthropology—Congresses.
4. Learning—Congresses.   I. Glazer, Steven.   II. Spirituality in
Education Conference (1997 : Boulder, Colo.)   III. Series.
    LB41.H353   1999   98-43266   CIP
    370.11—dc21

Printed in the United States of America
10   9   8   7   6   5   4   3   2   1

This book is printed on acid-free paper. ∞

BOOK DESIGN BY JENNIFER ANN DADDIO

"Lover and beloved, union of love sublime"

This book is dedicated to

the life, work, and memory of

Lex Hixon,

friend, inspiration, and teacher

December 25, 1941–November 1, 1995

CONTENTS

Introduction   1

Part I: Sacredness: The Ground of Learning   7

1. The Grace of Great Things: Reclaiming the Sacred
   in Knowing, Teaching, and Learning
      PARKER J. PALMER   15

2. Educating for Mission, Meaning, and Compassion
      RACHEL NAOMI REMEN, M.D.   33

3. Buddhist Education: The Path of
   Wisdom and Knowledge
      THE DZOGCHEN PONLOP RINPOCHE   51

4. Unlearning to See the Sacred
      JEREMY HAYWARD   61

Part II: Identity   77

5. Education and the Human Heart
   HIS HOLINESS THE DALAI LAMA   85

6. Commitment and Openness: A Contemplative
   Approach to Pluralism
   JUDITH SIMMER-BROWN   97

7. Embracing Freedom: Spirituality and Liberation
   BELL HOOKS   113

Part III: Relationship and Community   131

8. Reassembling the Pieces: Architecture as Pedagogy
   DAVID W. ORR   139

9. Education and the Western Spiritual Tradition
   JOHN TAYLOR GATTO   151

10. Learning as Initiation: Not-Knowing,
    Bearing Witness, and Healing
    JOAN HALIFAX   173

Part IV: Tradition and Innovation   183

11. Holistic Education for an Emerging Culture
    RON MILLER   189

12. Spirituality and Leadership
    DIANA CHAPMAN WALSH   203

13. Spirituality in Education: A Dialogue
    RABBI ZALMAN SCHACHTER-SHALOMI
    AND HUSTON SMITH   217

14. Where Do We Go from Here?
    VINCENT HARDING   233

Conclusion: The Heart of Learning   247

Acknowledgments   251

Notes and References   255

Bibliography   259

O irrevocable
river
of things:
no one can say
that I loved
only
fish,
or the plants of the jungle and the field,
that I loved
only
those things that leap and climb, desire, and survive.
It's not true:
many things conspired
to tell me the whole story.
Not only did they touch me,
or my hand touch them:
they were
so close
that they were a part
of my being,
they were so alive with me
that they lived half my life
and will die half my death.

—PABLO NERUDA
"ODE TO THINGS"

INTRODUCTION

Steven Glazer

IN THINKING ABOUT SPIRITUALITY in education, perhaps the first thought that crosses our minds is, "Well, what about prayer in schools?" Slogans like "prayer in schools" or "separation of church and state"—heavily politicized, divisive, and dangerously electric—arise like fiery titans in the mind with the mere turn of a simple phrase: spirituality in education. These slogans—and others like them—flash quickly and decisively, dividing contemporary society into sides: believer versus nonbeliever; conservative versus liberal; right versus left; fundamentalist versus moderate; spiritualist versus materialist. Call the sides what you like, but in our towns, our country, and our time, a real and painful battle is being waged: one with many casualties. The struggle comes down to a split about how to deal with (or heal) a very human, very personal sense of disconnection: one that threatens to tear apart not merely individuals, schools, and communities but the living fabric of our world as well.

Joining the voices of world-renowned teachers, visionaries, and spiritual leaders, *The Heart of Learning: Spirituality in Education* responds with a powerful message that will speak to educators, parents, students, and lifelong learners—indeed everyone interested in growing and learning. The book articulates an approach to integrating spiritual development and learning rooted neither in church, state, religion, nor politics. Instead, the heart of learning is revealed *within* each one of us: rooted in the spirit. By moving inside to the core of our experience—and working out from there—the apparent duality of "sides" is pierced; the hyperbole and sandbags can deflate; and the real work of integration and healing can begin.

Why are some people so afraid of prayer in schools? The fear of.

prayer in schools is the fear that education will be rooted in imposition. People are afraid of the indoctrination of particular beliefs, values, and habits on themselves or their children. They are afraid of the imposition of identity: the filling up with *beliefs about* prior to having *actual experience*. Imposition is disrespectful: it denies and taints the quality of experience. In place of freshness and receptivity are placed preconceptions and judgments.

Out of this fear of imposition, however, a great tragedy has taken place in our public schools: the wholesale abandonment of the inner world. This fear has allowed us to ignore in our classrooms (and lives) the existence of the inner realm, the realm of spiritual formation, of spiritual identity. This is a crucial mistake. By not pointing out the inside, the doorway to awareness, self-knowledge, and wholeness is lost.

Once we forget how to look to our inner experience as a resource for knowledge and understanding, we lose resourcefulness, connectedness, our sense of well-being, and confidence. Feeling broken or incomplete, we begin a potentially endless, exhausting search outside for something that in fact can only be found within. Unsure of what or who we are, we become hypersensitive, even defensive. Having lost our basic identification with wholeness, we begin to wobble back and forth between bipolar experiences of hope and hopelessness.

The Heart of Learning calls on us to begin to look inside—but without forcibly filling inside up. It beckons us to move away from the conceptual poles of fundamentalism and nihilism (or perhaps more accurately, spiritual and secular materialism) and back into our direct experience. The book is neither about religion, indoctrination, nor compulsion. Spirituality in education is about intimacy with experience: intimacy with our *perceptions*—the experience of having a body; our *thoughts*—the experience of having a mind; and our *emotions*—the experience of having a heart. Spirituality in education is rooted in experience. Spiritual identity arises as an expression, not from indoctrination; it arises out of our unique, particular mingling of awareness, experience, and expression.

The question of spirituality in education is a timely one. There is a renaissance of interest in paths of the heart and spirit, and this resurgence of spiritual values crosses racial, ethnic, political, cultural, and class lines. At the same time, there is a strong resurgence in fundamentalism, sectarianism, and religious politicking. To a great extent, both of these "movements" result from (or are an outgrowth of) the same single, pervasive dis-ease: the experience of the loss of meaning in our culture.

The spirituality movement in general can be seen as one approach towards dealing with anxiety or meaninglessness. Fundamentalism, too, can be a strategy for coping with dis-ease. Regardless, at a basic personal level, the loss of meaning can be touched, felt. Often it is experienced as anxiety, fear, or distrust: in oneself; in one's experience; in others; and especially in the coming unknown. Unfortunately, this feeling—a feeling of disconnection—is born in our schools: in the way we are taught to perceive, understand, and interact with the world.

The Heart of Learning shows us how education can serve as the core of a lifelong journey towards wholeness, rather than merely an accumulation of facts, figures, or skills.

"Sacredness," the first section of the book, examines how what we believe affects the quality of our experience; affects how and what we learn. This section includes chapters by master teacher Parker Palmer, medical educator Rachel Naomi Remen, Tibetan Lama Dzogchen Ponlop Rinpoche, and science educator Jeremy Hayward. Each of the contributors articulates how we, in some very fundamental ways, do not fully recognize or appreciate who and what we are. The contributors offer practical advice towards reclaiming our senses, sense of place, and sense of spirit: claiming the view of the sacred.

The next section, "Identity," explores a central dilemma of education: given the cultural and religious diversity of students, how can we cultivate spirit and other inner qualities? How do we nurture spiritual identity in the pluralism of modern America? "Identity" focuses on the fact and experience of diversity: chapters offer advice on approaching difference and consider topics like indoctrination, sectarianism, and objectification. "Identity" joins chapters by His Holiness the Dalai Lama of Tibet, religious studies professor Judith Simmer-Brown, and author/cultural critic bell hooks.

In the third section, "Relationship and Community," environmental educator David Orr, former New York City public school teacher John Taylor Gatto, and anthropologist Joan Halifax address ways of being in relationship: with others, with the larger community, and with the living ecological systems that sustain us. This section is rooted, to some degree, in Ken Wilber's articulation of "holons": the idea being that the world isn't made up of separate things, but rather wholes, which are in turn part of other wholes—all the way up and down. "Relationship and Community" articulates how education can take the experience of wholeness—the fact of an interconnected world—more fully and usefully into our classrooms and lives.

"Tradition and Innovation," the final section, explores the need to balance our past—our history and traditions—with a continuous openness to the present and the needs of the future. Included are chapters by holistic education scholar Ron Miller, Wellesley College president Diana Chapman Walsh, and theologian Vincent Harding, and a dialogue between two elder statesman of American spirituality—Huston Smith and Rabbi Zalman Schachter-Shalomi. "Tradition and Innovation" examines the strategies available to us in facing an unknown future; looks at obstacles to openness, intimacy, and collaboration; and review the challenges of *embodying* spirituality in education. The book closes with an extensive bibliography on the subject.

This book grew out of the Spirituality in Education Conference, hosted by The Naropa Institute in Boulder, Colorado, during the summer of 1997. Each day of the conference focused on a particular theme. The four conference themes make up the main divisions of the book. Days featured keynote presentations; selected, edited, and revised versions of these presentations make up the majority of the chapters.

The main objectives of *The Heart of Learning* are to: (1) establish the understanding that true learning requires openness to the unknown, to mystery; (2) establish awareness and wholeness as important, necessary goals of education; (3) help people understand learning as a process of transformational growth that requires—in addition to conceptual and physical mastery—dynamic interpersonal (and interactive) work; and (4) offer tools, information, and resources to make spirituality in education a viable, rewarding approach.

Not a scholarly book intended solely for educators or specialists, this is the first contemporary, popular book arguing that education—whether public or private, institutional or informal—must engage and nurture the spirit. *The Heart of Learning* offers a vision that acknowledges the centrality of the place of the spirit, and practical advice on how to discover spirit in our lives, our classrooms, and culture.

I. SACREDNESS

The

Ground

of

Learning

WHAT IS the ground of learning? Ground is what is underneath; it is where things come from. The ground very much affects the type and quality of plant life, habitat, or culture that arises.

American education has become grounded in disconnection, in particular, the separation between the spiritual and the material. The *Oxford English Dictionary* defines *sacred* as "set apart for or dedicated to some religious purpose, and hence entitled to veneration or religious respect." We, as a culture and as individuals, are taught to understand the sacred as set apart, as special, apart from ordinary life. Public and higher education have drawn a bold line between the world we experience and share, and the sacred. As a result, the ground of learning— the foundation of our worldview—has become one in which the world is flat. "Flatland," Ken Wilber and others have called it. Our worldview has been deflated to the point at which all that remains for us is the knowledge of surfaces, and belief in the material.

In our schools, we learn to approach the world as an assortment of separate objects, rather than as an interconnected whole. We learn to see things at face value; as fixed; as in and of themselves. We learn and share in a cultural mythology that the world is made up of matter, and that matter is free to be owned, manipulated, and consumed. Plants, animals, and elements are all considered to be merely "substance," with no spirit, no feelings—and certainly no inherent rights or liberties.

In this culture, what we want or need is always an object outside of us, "other" than us. We are driven from a feeling of lack—which is really a feeling of separateness—towards consumption. We learn to consume information and ideas just as we do so-called consumer goods. We learn that more is better, and that with more comes power.

In learning to see in this way—and live with this view—we have developed an entrenched sense of disconnection. We feel apart from others. We learn to live in abstraction and conception, and to ignore our intuition and experience. Along the way, we have lost basic appreciation for ourselves and respect for others. It is no accident that in our time we are experiencing unprecedented rates of alcohol and drug abuse, depression, violence, and suicide—and environmental destruction. With the separation of the sacred from our world and experience comes not merely disconnection but also the desecration of the world.

Across America, we can see the impact and faces of this disconnection. Sometimes disconnection manifests as nihilism (i.e., generation X). Other times it manifests as despair (adolescent suicide). Disconnection can manifest as single-mindedness (substance abuse and other addictions), mindlessness (random violence), selfishness, or narcissism. *The Heart of Learning* begins to resolve this disconnection by establishing *sacredness as the ground of learning*. Sacredness is not understood within a particular religious framework but instead as growing out of two basic qualities of our experience: awareness and wholeness. Awareness is a natural, self-manifesting quality: it is our ability to perceive, experience, and know. A sense of awareness can be cultivated (or enhanced) through mindfulness or attentiveness. The development of awareness enables us to bring a greater and greater sense of presence to the repercussions and meaning of our lives.

Wholeness is the inherent, seamless, interdependent quality of the world. Wholeness, indeed, is the fact of the matter: the things of this world (including us) are *already* connected, are already in relationship, are already in union. Wholeness, however, can be cultivated within us by *experiencing* this nondual quality of the world. Through experiences of awareness and wholeness, we begin to establish the view of the sacred.

Sacredness as the ground of learning asks us to consider the possibility that the sacred is here and now. It challenges us with the questions: Can we see this world as sacred? Treat everything and everyone as worthy of respect? Can we open our minds wider, and our hearts wider, too? If we can revise our definitions of sacred and spiritual—to nest them in this world—we can begin to experience the world differently, indeed experience a very different world. Understanding the world as sacred does not require the adoption (or the repudiation) of a particular religious faith or allegiance.

In bringing the sacred into our experience of the world, the call to moral or ethical behavior becomes stronger and stronger. Merely by seeing the writing on the wall—the traces of our causes and effects—our path in life can be illuminated. What is required is not code, law, or force but instead a scale, intimacy, and ethic where call and response—cause and effect—can be witnessed, experienced, understood.

Unfortunately the current trend is towards the opposite: towards exponentially increasing scale and globalism, towards the increasing distance between causes and effects, the increasing hiddenness of cause and effect. As Jerry Mander makes clear in his book *In the Absence of the Sacred,* the proliferation of materialism, technology, conceptuality, and abstraction—all various methods of distancing from direct experience—is undermining sacred perspectives worldwide. Hiding effects and relationships behind veils of concept, language, and physical distance, the sum total of that which is "entitled to veneration" in our world is becoming smaller and smaller. Further, as we lose genuine contact with each other—and direct, unmediated physical experience—the intimacy through which compassion is naturally engendered is quickly and easily lost.

So, then, what is sacredness? Sacredness is the practice of wholeness and awareness. It is approaching, greeting, and meeting the world with basic respect. What is sacredness as the ground of learning? It is rooting education in the practices of openness, attentiveness to experience, and sensitivity to the world. Spirituality in education begins with questions: What is my experience? What is my effect? What are the interrelationships between myself and others? Are these being attended to?

As Shantideva asked: With my actions today, is spirit growing? If it is not growing, has it at least been maintained? If it has not been maintained, has it been depleted? One can ask the same questions in a different way: Are individuals healthier, happier, more aware as a result of education? Are families healthier, happier, more aware because of education? And what of communities? The planet? Unfortunately, contemporary education doesn't get a great review when evaluated from this perspective. In his book *Earth in Mind,* David Orr tells us that

> *if today is a typical day on the planet Earth, we will lose 116 square miles of rain forest, or about an acre a second. We will lose another 72 square miles to encroaching deserts, the result of human mismanagement and overpopulation. We will lose 40 to 250 species. . . . It is worth noting that this is not the work of ignorant people. Rather, it is largely the results of work by people with B.A.s, B.S.s, LL.B.s, M.B.A.s and Ph.D.s.*

The chapters in "Sacredness" articulate an alternative course for education as well as for individuals and modern culture. Quaker educator Parker Palmer begins by articulating that our entire learning process must acknowledge inwardness and model the practice of respect. Dr. Rachel Naomi Remen, a medical educator and author of *Kitchen Table Wisdom,* reveals the dangerous materialism inherent in our highly prized concept of objectivity. She asks us instead to root education in the intimacy of our experience. Dzogchen Ponlop Rinpoche frames the entire process of learning within the context of waking up students—no, *all* of us—to inherent, inner positive qualities. He articulates an educational vision rooted in revealing knowledge rather than acquiring it. Finally, Jeremy Hayward makes clear that this transformation—remembering the spiritual—is serious, difficult work. This work requires each of us to examine and move beyond harmful, deeply embedded preconceptions. Taken together, these chapters articulate a truly progressive vision of education: education as the doorway to the sacred.

THE GRACE OF GREAT THINGS: RECLAIMING THE SACRED IN KNOWING, TEACHING, AND LEARNING[1]

Parker J. Palmer

Parker J. Palmer is a writer and traveling teacher who works independently on issues in education, spirituality, and social change. In a 1998 survey of eleven thousand American educators, Dr. Palmer was named as one of the thirty "most influential senior leaders" in higher education and one of ten key "agenda setters" of the past decade: "He has inspired a generation of teachers and reformers with evocative visions of community, knowing and spiritual wholeness." His latest book is *The Courage to Teach: Exploring the Inner Landscape of a Teacher's Life*. Parker lives in Madison, Wisconsin.

WE ALL KNOW that what will transform education is not another theory, another book, or another formula but educators who are willing to seek a transformed way of being in the world. In the midst of the familiar trappings of education—competition, intellectual combat, obsession with a narrow range of facts, credits, and credentials—what we seek is a way of working illumined by spirit and infused with soul.

This is not romanticism. Recently, I saw a remarkable documentary called *The Transformation of Allen School*.[2] Allen School is an inner-city school in Dayton, Ohio. For many years it was at the bottom of the list in that city by all measures: there were fifth-graders who had parole officers, and the dropout rate was saddening. The failure of those students in every aspect of their lives sickened the heart.

Then, along came a new principal. He brought the teachers together and said to them, in effect: We must understand that the young people with whom we work have hardly any external substance or support. They live in dangerous neighborhoods. They have little food to eat. They have parents who are on the ropes and barely able to pay attention to them. The externals with which American education is obsessed will not work in this situation. But these students have one thing that no one can take away from them—they have their souls. From this day onward, we are going to lift those souls up. We are going to make those souls visible to the young people themselves, to their parents, and the community. We are going to reground our students' lives in the power of their souls. But this task will require us to recover the power of our own souls, remembering that we, too, are soul-driven, soul-animated creatures.

Over a five-year period, the Allen School rose to the top of every dimension on which it had been at the bottom. It happened through good group process, through hard, disciplined work—and through attentiveness to the inward factors that we are here to explore. Attention to the inner life is not romanticism. It involves the real world, and it is what is desperately needed in so many sectors of American education.

As we proceed, let us remember one thing about the human soul: it is like a wild animal. It is tough, self-sufficient, resilient—and exceedingly shy. If we go crashing through the woods, screaming and yelling for the soul to come out, it will evade us all day and night. We cannot beat the bushes and yell at each other and expect this precious inwardness to emerge. But if we are willing to go into the woods and sit quietly at the base of a tree, this wild thing will, after a few hours, reveal itself. Out of the corner of our eye, we might glimpse something of the wild preciousness we all are looking for.

What are we seeking when we seek "spirituality" in education? I think, at heart, that we are seeking to find life-giving forces and sources in the midst of an enterprise which is too often death dealing:

education. It may seem harsh to call education death dealing, but I think we all have our experience of that sad fact.

We should be saddened by the fact that this country, which has the most widespread public education system in the world, has so many people who walk around feeling stupid, feeling like losers in the competition we call "teaching and learning." If the competition doesn't do us in, too often we go to schools where learning is made so dull that, once we get out, we don't want to learn again. Too many children have their birthright gift of the love of learning taken away from them by the very process that's supposed to enhance that gift—a process that dissects life and distances us from the world because it is so deeply rooted in fear.

So we are here to seek life-giving forces and sources in the midst of a system that is too often death dealing. Everyone has had an encounter with the forces of death—be it with racism, or sexism, or justice denied. My face-to-face encounters with the forces of death include two prolonged experiences of clinical depression, passages through the dark woods that I made when I was in my forties, devastating experiences when it was not clear from one day to the next whether I wished to be alive, or even *was* still alive.

This depression was partly the result of my own schooling, partly due to the way I was formed—or deformed—in the educational systems of this country to live out of the top inch and a half of the human self; to live exclusively through cognitive rationality and the powers of the intellect; to live out of touch with anything that lay below that top inch and a half—body, intuition, feeling, emotion, relationship.

A therapist and spiritual guide said words that eventually helped me get back on the road to wholeness. He said, "You seem to keep imaging your depression as the hand of an enemy trying to crush you. Why don't you try imaging it as the hand of a friend trying to press you down to ground on which it is safe to stand?" That image has stayed with me—an image of moving from the world of abstraction, the hot-air balloon that education so falsely represents as the good life,

17

down to the ground of our being. Unlike the airy and scary heights, this is ground upon which it's safe to stand *and* safe to fall, ground that will hold you, support you, and allow you to get back up again.

At some point during my depression, a friend gave me some words from an extraordinary novel by T. H. White, *The Once and Future King.* In this passage, the young Arthur, king-to-be, is in the midst of his own dark night of the soul, so he seeks counsel from Merlin, the magician. In response, Merlin speaks wonderful words that created a spark of light for me in the midst of that death-dealing episode of my life:

> *The best thing for being sad is to learn something. That is the only thing that never fails. You may grow old and trembling in your anatomies. You may lie awake at night listening to the disorder of your veins. You may miss your only love. You may see the world around you devastated by evil lunatics or know your honor trampled in the sewers of baser minds. There is only one thing for it, then: to learn. Learn why the world wags and what wags it. That is the only thing which the mind can never exhaust, never alienate, never be tortured by, never fear or distrust, and never dream of regretting. Learning is the thing for you.*[3]

"Learning is the thing for you." As I read those words, I began to understand that in the midst of death, there is life in learning. I could not do much in the darkness of my depression. I couldn't work, I couldn't connect with other people. But I could grope around in the darkness and start to learn what, and who, was in there—and those of you who have been in that place know that part of what I found and learned about there was what Thomas Merton calls "true self."

What Merlin knew is that education at its best—this profound human transaction called teaching and learning—is not just about getting information or getting a job. Education is about healing and wholeness. It is about empowerment, liberation, transcendence, about renewing the vitality of life. It is about finding and claiming ourselves and our place in the world.

The question we must wrestle with is why, in our culture, there is so little life-giving power when we use the words *education, teaching, learning.* Why are these words and the things they point to so flat, dull, so banal when compared with Merlin's understanding?

Of course, there are many answers to this question: an industrial model of schooling that is our inheritance from the nineteenth century, the diminishments of "professionalism" in teacher education, the way education has devolved into political rhetoric serving the purposes of power.

The answer I want to propose, however, is different. I propose that education is banal because we have driven the sacred out of it. Merlin, the magician, understood the sacredness at the heart of all things, and, for him, life-giving learning was a natural derivative of that insight. I want to explore what it might mean to reclaim the sacred at the heart of knowing, teaching, and learning—to reclaim it from an essentially depressive mode of knowing that honors only data, logic, analysis, and a systematic disconnection of self from the world, self from others.

But as I launch into this inquiry, I want to remind all of us that the marriage of education and the sacred has not always been a happy one. It has not always produced creative offspring. Ask Copernicus or Galileo. Ask anyone whose family or friends were devastated by the Nazis' murderous attachment of the sacred to blood, soil, and race. There are real dangers in this enterprise when the sacred gets attached to the wrong things. There are real dangers when the sacred gets institutionalized and imposed on people as one more weapon among the objectifying forces of society.

But we need to have the courage to jump into the midst of that mess. The Nazi story, the murderousness of the Third Reich, is not only about the attachment of the sacred to the wrong things by a system of political power; it's also about German higher education refusing to get involved with those issues, distancing itself from life, clinging to logic and data and objectivism as a way of staying disengaged from the social reality of its time.

We can no longer afford a system of education that refuses to get engaged with the mess. We must be willing to join life where people live it—and they live it, we live it, at this convoluted intersection of the sacred and the secular.

What do I mean by the sacred? I still remember my first yearning for the sacred. At first it was only a word for me, a word I heard in church when I was young. Later on, in college, I ran across a book by Rudolf Otto called *The Idea of the Holy*.[4] Otto has a remarkable description of the sacred in which he uses terms like *numinosity* and *mysterium tremendum*. I laughed as I was preparing these remarks, recalling that title—*The Idea of the Holy*. At the time, I could have only an *idea* of the holy because I had no conscious experience of it. And over the years, I've struggled to move from the abstract level of idea to the groundedness of embodied experience.

I remember a night in the middle of one of those devastating depressions when I heard a voice I've never heard before or since. The voice simply said, "I love you, Parker." It was not a psychological phenomenon, because my psyche was crushed. It was the numinous. It was the *mysterium tremendum*. But it came to me in the simplest and most human way: "I love you, Parker."

That experience opened me to the definition of *sacred* that I want to explore. It is a very simple definition: *The sacred is that which is worthy of respect.* As soon as we understand this, then we see that the sacred is everywhere. There is nothing—in its undistorted form, rightly conceived and understood—that it is not worthy of respect.

I once had a rare experience of the numinous, and I treasure it. But I do not have a steady flow of numinosity in my life, so I cannot count on such experience to be my sustaining daily reminder of the sacred. But I *can* practice respect every day, minute by minute—especially towards those things that arouse my anger, my ire, my jealousy, my contempt, or any other strong ego reaction that should remind me of my potential for violence and my need to reach deep for respect.

How it would transform academic life if we could practice simple respect! I don't think there are many places where people feel less respect than they do on university campuses. The university is a place where we grant respect only to a few things—to the text, to the expert, to those who win in competition. But we do not grant respect to students, to stumbling and failing. We do not grant respect to tentative and heartfelt ways of being in the world where the person can't think of the right word to say, or can't think of any word at all. We do not grant respect to voices outside our tight little circle, let alone to the voiceless things of the world. We do not grant respect to silence and wonder.

Why? Because in academic culture, we are afraid. Academia is a culture of fear. What are we afraid of? We are afraid of hearing something that would challenge and change us.

The German poet Rilke has an amazing line which says, "There is no place at all that is not looking at you. You must change your life."[5] There is no place at all that is not speaking to me. I must change my life. But I don't want to hear those voices because I am afraid of change. So in academic culture, I carefully wall myself off, through systematic disrespect, from all of those things that might challenge me, break me, open me, and change me. It is a culture rooted deep in fear.

We need to remember the counsel at the heart of every great spiritual tradition: "Be not afraid." These words demand careful reading. They do not say you're not supposed to *have* fear. I have fear. I have fear as I stand here before you. How am I doing? Do they like me? Am I delivering on all the preparation I've put into this talk?

I am fearful. I *have* fear. But I don't need to *be* my fear as I speak to you. I can approach you from a different place in me—a place of hope, of fellow feeling, of journeying together in a mystery that I know we share. I can "be not afraid" even while I have my multiple fears.

If we could reclaim the sacred—simple respect—in education, how would it transform our knowing, teaching, and learning? I would like to suggest several answers, but I want to preface them by telling a story, not from the world of religion, not from the world of education, but from the world of science—because there is much for us to learn from the world of science about the very things we care about most. Science is not the enemy of this quest to reclaim the sacred, certainly not great science.

My story is about a great scientist. Her name was Barbara McClintock. She died a few years ago in her early nineties. Her obituary was on the front page of *The New York Times* in the space usually reserved for heads of state. She was probably the greatest American biologist of the twentieth century and arguably the greatest American scientist of the twentieth century.

As a young woman, Barbara McClintock became fascinated with genetic transposition. She wanted to know how genes carried their messages from one place to another. In her day, there were none of the instruments and chemical procedures that my biologist son works with as he works with DNA. There were only hunches, hypotheses, clues, and the powers of human imagination—the mystical capacity to identify with the other and still respect its otherness.

In her obituary, she was eulogized by one of her colleagues, a geneticist from the University of Chicago, as "a mystic who knew where the mysteries lie but who did not mystify."[6] That is part of *our* task, if we wish to deepen the spiritual dimension of education—to be mystics who know where the mysteries lie but who do not mystify.

McClintock exercised her mystical capacities in pursuit of genetic puzzles, but the price she paid was to be marginalized by her profession. Her work was scorned and distrusted. She could not get grants, she could not get articles published, she could not get laboratory space—could get none of this, that is, until she won a Nobel Prize in science. Then her dance ticket started filling up!

Another scientist named Evelyn Fox Keller came along when McClintock was in her early eighties and said, "I would like to write your intellectual biography, your story as a scientist. Tell me," she said, "how do you do great science?"

McClintock—who was one of the most precise empirical observers and one of the most rigorously logical thinkers in American science—thought for a moment and said, "About the only thing I can tell you about the doing of science is that you somehow have to have a *feeling* for the organism."[7]

Keller asked her question again. "Tell me, how do you do great science?" McClintock—who was at that age when all that's left is to tell the truth—thought for a moment about those ears of corn that she had worked with all her life, because they were cheap and plentiful, and she said, "Really, all I can tell you about doing great science is that you somehow have to learn to lean into the kernel."

At that point, Keller, herself a physical chemist, wrote a sentence that I regard as brilliant and luminous. She said, "Barbara McClintock, in her relation with ears of corn, practiced the highest form of love, which is intimacy that does not annihilate difference."[8]

When I read that, tears came to my eyes. McClintock had a relation with ears of corn that I yearn to have with other people! She knew it was possible to have that kind of relationship with all creatures and all forms of being because she understood their sacredness and approached them with simple respect. Here was a scientist—a Nobel Prize winner, a key source of the genetic breakthroughs with which we live in the late twentieth century, an intellectual heroine—who practiced the highest form of love in the doing of science itself.

I think this story stands on its own. But let me reflect on a few dimensions of it that would transform education if we could embody in our own knowing, teaching, and learning, this simple sense of the sacred that McClintock brought to her work with ears of corn.

First, if we could recover a sense of the sacred in knowing, teaching, and learning, we could recover our sense of the *otherness* of the things of the world—the *precious otherness* of the things of the world.

One of the great sins in education is reductionism, the destruction of otherness that occurs when we try to cram everything we study into categories that we are comfortable with—ignoring data, or writers, or voices, or simple facts that don't fit into our box, lacking simple respect for the ways in which reality is other than we want it or imagine it to be. This fear of otherness comes in part from having flattened our intellectual terrain and desacralized it: people who know the sacred know radical otherness, but in a two-dimensional, secularized culture, we don't possess that sensibility anymore.

When we teach about Third World cultures in ways that confine them, make them measure up to *our* standards of what greatness or excellence are supposed to be like, we ignore their powerful richness. These cultures have more to teach us than we have yet to understand about real values—about community, about respect, about the sacred. Yet they come out, by our measures, as shabby, dirty, dusty, lacking in merit. Through that reductionist model, too many students have developed a trained disrespect for the otherness of the great cultures of the world.

We do this with great literature too. The story itself may convey a powerful message about the human condition, but because the story's author does not measure up to current tests of rightness or righteousness, the text often gets dismissed. David Denby has shown the hubris of this posture itself: it gives us, teachers and students alike, feelings of superiority to the text, thus depriving us of the chance to learn anything from it—except how superior we are.[9]

So the first thing that a people who know the sacred would know in education is the precious otherness of the things of the world, an otherness that probably will not confirm conventional wisdom.

The second thing that such a people would know is the precious *inwardness* of the things of the world. McClintock respected ears of corn in their integrity as an "alien nation," as having a selfhood that was other than her own, an otherness that she needed to respect if she was to do good science. But that selfhood is also an inwardness, the idea that corn has its own mind, if you will; I am told that McClintock once said, "I needed to learn to think like corn." She didn't use that insight to mystify but to clarify. She built on that intuition and used it to enter the "mind of corn" in a way that led to her breakthrough discoveries.

But we often don't respect the inwardness of the things we study—and we therefore do not respect the inward transformation that may be in store for us when we have a deep encounter with those things.

I have thought often and painfully about my own education in the murderous history of the Third Reich, an education received at some of the best colleges in this country. Though I was taught by well-trained historians, I was taught that history in a way—and I've never known quite how to say this—that made me feel as if all of those horrors had happened to another species on another planet.

My teachers were not revisionists. They weren't saying it didn't happen. They taught the statistics and the facts and the theories behind the facts. But they presented those data at such objective arm's length—just the facts and only the facts, obsessed with the externalities of history—that they never connected with the inwardness of my life, because the inwardness of those historical events was never revealed to me. Everything was objectified and externalized, and I ended up morally and spiritually deformed as a consequence.

There are two things I failed to learn from those history courses that I should have learned—and had to learn painfully the years after college. One was that the very community I grew up in, on the North Shore of Chicago, had its own fascist tendencies. I grew up as a Protestant Christian in Wilmette, Illinois. But if you were a Jew who lived in that area in the 1950s, you didn't live in Wilmette, and you didn't live in Evanston, and you didn't live in Kenilworth. You lived in a gilded ghetto called Glencoe because there was a fascism at work that said, "People like me don't want to live with people like you."

I should have been taught that. My little story and the inwardness of my life should have been connected with the inward dynamics of that big story in a way that would have helped me understand my own time, my own place, and my own involvement in the evils of fascism—because until I understood all that, I could not grow morally.

The second thing I didn't learn—and this takes me even more deeply inward—is that there is within me, in the shadow of my own soul, a little Hitler, a force of evil. When the difference between me and thee becomes too great, so great that it challenges some value or belief that I am clinging to, I will find some way to kill you off. I won't do it with a gun or a gas chamber, but I'll do it with a category, a dismissal, a word of some sort that renders you irrelevant to my universe and to my life: "Oh, you're just a _____." It is a form of dismissal that we manage with such facility in academic life as to render each other and each other's truth irrelevant to who we are.

A few years ago I spent two semesters as a visiting professor at Berea College in Kentucky. Some of you will know this remarkable institution devoted to the young people of Appalachia, where they charge no tuition because they serve so many students whose families have no money. I taught a course in which I attempted to rectify the wrongs in my own education, paralleling the big story I was teaching with the little stories of my students' lives in order to connect and interweave the two.

At the first class, I assigned my students some brief autobiographical essays connected with the core concepts of our distinguished text. I wanted them to see their own little stories through that big story for the sake of illumination. And I wanted their little stories to correct the way the authors of this particular text had written the big story, because the whole Appalachian experience had been omitted from this book on "American life."

At the end of the first session, a young man came up to me, and he said, "Dr. Palmer, in these autobiographical papers that you want us to write, is it okay to use the word *I*?"

It was a tense moment: I knew that I might crush his spirit if even my body language said "What a stupid question!"

So I said, "Yes, of course, it is. I invite you to use the word *I*. I don't know how you would be able to fulfill the assignment if you didn't. But help me understand why you needed to ask the question."

And he said, "Because I'm a _____ major, and every time I use the word *I* in a paper, I'm downgraded one full grade."

This dismissal of the subjective self goes on all the time in higher education. Recovering the sacred is one path towards recovering the inwardness without which education as transformation cannot happen.

Third, by recovering the sacred, we might recover our *sense of community* with each other and with all of creation, the community that Thomas Merton named so wonderfully as the "hidden wholeness."[10] I have become increasingly convinced that this recovery of community is at the heart of good teaching.

Good teaching isn't about technique. I've asked students around the country to describe their good teachers to me. Some of them describe people who lecture all the time, some of them describe people who do little other than facilitate group process, and others describe everything in between. But all of them describe people who have some sort of *connective* capacity, who connect themselves to their students, their students to each other, and everyone to the subject being studied.

I heard about one young woman who said she couldn't possibly describe her good teachers because they were all so different from each other, but she could easily describe her bad teachers because they were all the same: "With my bad teachers, their words float somewhere in front of their faces like the balloon speech in cartoons." Here is an extraordinary image which tells us that bad teaching involves a disconnect between the stuff being taught and the self who is teaching it.

Throughout the secularized academy, there is a distance, a coldness, a lack of community because we don't have the connective tissue of the sacred to hold this apparent fragmentation and chaos together. Merton is right: there's a wholeness in our lives, but it's a *hidden* wholeness. It's so easy to look on the surface of things, especially in the academy, and say there is no community here at all—never was and never will be. But if you go deep, to the depths you go when you seek that which is sacred, you find the hidden wholeness. You find the community that a good teacher evokes and invites students into, that weaves and reweaves our lives, alone and together.

This community goes far beyond our face-to-face relationship with each other as human beings. In education especially, this community connects us with what the poet Rilke called the "great things" of the world, and with "the grace of great things."[11]

We are in community with all of it: the genes and ecosystems of biology; the symbols and reference of philosophy and theology; the archetypes of betrayal and forgiveness and loving and loss that are the stuff of literature; the artifacts and lineages of anthropology; the materials of engineering with their limits and potentials; the logic of systems and management; the shapes and colors of music and art; the novelties and patterns of history; the elusive idea of justice under the law. We are in community with all of these great things, and great teaching is about knowing that community, feeling that community, sensing that community, and then drawing your students into it.

I had a teacher at Carleton College who changed my life by bringing me into this community, even though he lectured nonstop. We would raise our hands and try to get a word in edgewise, and he would say, "Wait a minute. I'll get to that at the end of the hour." But he didn't get to it at the end of the week, or the month, or the year. Now it's thirty years later, and my hand is still up—which means I'm still engaged with what he said.

What was this magic that made me feel so deeply related to the world of social theory that my teacher taught, even though he was a shy and awkward person who didn't know how to connect with his students on the social level? I remember vividly how he would make a strong Marxist statement—then a puzzled look would come over his face, and he would step to one side, turn back to where he had been, and argue with himself from a Hegelian viewpoint. It wasn't an act: he was genuinely confused!

Years later, I realized what the magic was: this man didn't need us to be in community! Who needs eighteen-year-olds from the North Shore of Chicago when you're hanging out with Marx and Hegel and other really interesting people? But he opened a door to me that had never been opened before, the door to a world of imagination and thought that I had no idea existed, and it was an enormously gracious act. He was an amazing man who carried community within himself, an invisible host of great people and great thoughts, and he gave me a community that is part of my life to this day.

Fourth, if we recover a sense of the sacred, we will recover the *humility* that makes teaching and learning possible. Everybody in academia knows what Freeman Dyson meant when he said, about the development of the nuclear weaponry that threatens to destroy the earth, "It is almost irresistible, the arrogance that comes over us when we see what we can do with our minds."[12] That arrogance prevents us from knowing reality on its own terms. It is only with humility—the humility that comes from approaching sacred things, like life on earth, with the simple quality called respect—that genuine knowing, teaching, and learning become possible.

A few years ago, James Watson and Francis Crick, who discovered the DNA molecule, celebrated the fortieth anniversary of that momentous event. Those of you who have read *The Double Helix,* the book about their discovery, know that it portrays all of the antivirtues of academic life: competitiveness, ego, greed, power, and money.[13]

But when Watson and Crick were interviewed forty years after their first encounter with DNA, Watson said, "The molecule is so beautiful. Its glory was reflected on Francis and me. I guess the rest of my life has been spent trying to prove that I was almost equal to being associated with DNA, which was a hard task."

Then Crick—of whom Watson once said, "I have never seen him in a modest mood"—replied, "We were upstaged by a molecule." By the grace of great things, humility can be induced in the least likely of places![14]

Finally, if we recovered a sense of the sacred, we could recover our capacity for *wonder and surprise,* essential qualities in education. Unfortunately, we all know what normally happens when we are taken by "surprise" in a competitive academic setting: we reach for the nearest weapon and try to kill the surprise, or its source, as quickly as we can, because we are scared to death that we are about to lose some war.

I will never understand why some people so devoutly believe that competition is the best way to generate new ideas, because I know from experience what happens under those conditions. In competition you do not reach for a new idea, because a new idea is risky—you don't know how to use it, you don't know where it's going to lead, you don't know what flank it may leave open. In competition, you reach for an old idea that you know how to wield as a weapon, and you smite the untruth as quickly as you can.

Why are we startled into fear when something pops up to surprise us? Secularism has flattened our intellectual landscape. The objectivist terrain in higher education is so flat, so lacking in variety, so utterly banal that anything that pops up and surprises us is instantly defined as a threat. Where did it come from? It must be from the underground!

But the sacred landscape has hills and valleys, mountains and streams, forests and deserts. It is a place where we learn to live with surprise because in it, surprise is our constant companion—and a capacity for surprise is an intellectual virtue beyond all telling. We might recover that virtue, and much else of value, if we were persistent in trying to recover the spiritual dimension of education and of our own lives.

A final word about the journey toward recovering the sacred in education, about getting from here to there: I do not believe that we can rightly or hopefully ask our educational institutions to manifest the qualities of the sacred that I have been talking about. I don't think institutions are well suited to carry the sacred. Indeed, I think distortion is a great risk when the sacred gets vested in an institutional context or framework.

Institutions have their utility. They have jobs to do. As individuals, we all have important vocational decisions about whether to be inside or outside institutions. But I don't believe that the qualities we are talking about here are going to be carried institutionally by the Roman Catholic Church, or the Religious Society of Friends, or the University of Colorado at Boulder, or The Naropa Institute. I believe these are qualities *we* carry into the world in our hearts, through solitude and through community.

I have been doing a small study of social movements that have transformed the human landscape: the women's movement, the black liberation movement, the gay and lesbian identity movement, the movement for freedom in Eastern Europe and in South Africa. I will not trouble you with all of the details of how movements evolve. I just want to say a word about the starting point of social movements as I understand it.

Movements start when individuals who feel very isolated in the midst of an alien culture come in touch with something life-giving in the midst of a death-dealing situation. They make one of the most basic decisions a human being can make, which I have come to call the decision to live "divided no more," the decision to no longer behave differently on the outside than one knows one's truth to be on the inside.

I call it "the Rosa Parks decision" because she is emblematic of the historic potentials of a decision that might seem to be "merely inward." Of course, Rosa Parks was prepared for that day on the bus in Montgomery, Alabama, December 1, 1955, prepared in many ways. She had gone to the Highlander Folk School where Martin Luther King, Jr. also learned strategies of nonviolence. She was the secretary of the NAACP; she had a community.

But in the moment when she sat down at the front of the bus, she had no assurance that the theory would work, that the strategy would succeed, or that the people who said they were her friends would stand with her in the aftermath of her action. It was a lonely decision being made in the inwardness of many people's lives for which Rosa Parks became the icon and exemplar—and it was a decision that changed the lay and the law of the land.

I've often asked myself where people find the courage to make a decision like that when they know that the power of the institution is going to come down on their heads. How do they find the courage to live "divided no more" when they know that doing so could easily lead to loss of status, of reputation, of income, of job, of friends?

The answer comes to me through the lives of the Rosa Parks—and the Václav Havels and the Nelson Mandelas and the Dorothy Days—of this world. These are people who have come to understand that no punishment anyone might lay on us could possibly be worse than the punishment we lay on ourselves by conspiring in our own diminishment, by living a divided life, by failing to make that fundamental decision to act and speak on the outside in ways consonant with the truth we know on the inside.

As soon as we make that decision, amazing things happen. For one thing, the enemy stops being the enemy. When Rosa Parks sat down that day, it was partly an acknowledgment that, by conspiring with racism, she had helped to create racism. By conspiring with death-dealing education, we help to create death-dealing education. But by deciding to live divided no more, we help change all of that.

When the police came on the bus that day, they said to Rosa Parks, "You know if you continue to sit there, we're going to have to throw you in jail." Her answer is epic. She said, "You may do that," which is an enormously polite way of saying, "What could your jail possibly mean to me compared to the imprisonment I've had myself in for the last forty-three years, which I have broken out of today?"

I don't know exactly where you are on your journey. But I suspect that your journey, like mine, is towards trying to come into a deeper understanding of what it means to live divided no more. If we can come to a deeper understanding of what this decision might mean for us in the context of education, we will have done something well worth doing.

2.

EDUCATING FOR MISSION, MEANING, AND COMPASSION

Rachel Naomi Remen, M.D.

Dr. Rachel Naomi Remen is associate clinical professor of family and community medicine at the UCSF School of Medicine, the medical director of the Commonweal Cancer Help Program, and the director and founder of the Institute for the Study of Health and Illness at Commonweal. Her book, *Kitchen Table Wisdom: Stories That Heal,* published by Riverhead Books, was a *New York Times* bestseller and won the 1996 Wilbur Award for the year's outstanding work of spiritual nonfiction.

As a medical educator, I know little about education or educational theory. The only preparation that I have had for teaching is that I've studied medicine myself, and have been successful at practicing it. There is a certain arrogance in this: rather like saying that the only qualification a person might need to teach kindergarten is that they were successful at being a five-year-old.

This chapter is based on two curricula that I have designed and taught since 1991. One is a semester-long course for first- and second-year medical students at the University of California at San Francisco School of Medicine, called The Care of the Soul. The other is a postgraduate continuing medical education course accredited by the California Medical Association that I teach for physicians at Commonweal. The latter is a year-long curriculum entitled Relationship-Centered Care. The hundred physicians who have gone through this postgraduate course since it began are all traditional practitioners and academics: surgeons, internists, cardiologists, oncologists, emergency-room physicians, and the like.

Although designed for those at very different stages in a medical career, both of these courses focus on the individual's experience of compassion and meaning. The medical students' course might be seen as preventative, while the physicians' course, unfortunately, is often remedial. I have learned a great deal about the strengths and shortcomings of contemporary medical education from these two very different groups of learners, and would like to share some of this insight with you.

Compassion, of course, cannot be taught. Compassion is discovered, or perhaps simply remembered. So teaching a course on compassion is fairly audacious in and of itself. Compassion is not a behavior; neither is it an action. Compassion is a lived experience of profound connection from which all of the behaviors and actions that we might call "compassionate" emerge.

Most important, compassion is not an act of obedience. We do not act in a compassionate way because someone has told us to act compassionately, or even because we want to be good people. Such acts are not really compassionate. Compassion emerges from a sense of belonging: the experience that all suffering is like our suffering and all joy is like our joy. When we know ourselves to be connected to all others, acting compassionately is simply the natural thing to do.

True compassion requires us to attend to our own humanity, to come to a deep acceptance of our own life as it is. It requires us to come into right relationship with that which is most human in ourselves, that which is most capable of suffering.

By recognizing and attending to that basic humanness, our basic human integrity, we find the place of profound connection to all life. That connection then becomes for us the ground of being. It is only through connection that we can recover true compassion, or any authentic sense of meaning in life: a sense of the mysterious, the profound, the sacred nature of the world.

Recovering compassion requires us to confront the shadow of our culture directly. While relatively few people carry a gun, we all carry with us the values of the frontier, such values as self-sufficiency, competence, independence, and mastery. These are core values of our culture. We are a culture that values mastery and control. But in the shadow of these values lies a profound sense of isolation from our human wholeness. As individuals and as a culture we have developed a contempt for anything in ourselves and in others that has needs, and is capable of suffering. In our isolation, we also tend to develop a suspicion of anything beyond ourselves, anything that falls outside of our control. So we become separated, both horizontally and vertically.

Shadow is the wound that a culture inflicts on its people: a diminishing of innate wholeness through a collective judgment or disapproval. Every culture diminishes wholeness in its own way. All people born into a culture find approval for certain aspects of their own wholeness and suffer judgment for certain other aspects. It is only human to trade our wholeness for approval, and share in the collective wound. Some of us are more deeply wounded than others, but no one escapes.

Of all of the contemporary cultural institutions, education holds the greatest promise for healing the wounds of the cultural shadow. In some ways, education has historically held this responsibility. *Educare,* the root of the word *education,* means "to lead forth the hidden wholeness," the innate integrity that is in every person. And as such, there is a place where "to educate" and "to heal" mean the same thing. Educators are healers. Educators and healers both trust in the wholeness of life and in the wholeness of people. Both have come to serve this wholeness.

Now, as educators, we cannot heal the shadow of our culture by educating people to succeed in society as it is. We must have the courage to educate people to heal this world into what it might become. Medical education does not yet do this. The current charge of medical education is to create successful doctors and technicians, people who are held in great respect by society. Often, however, the most successful and admired members of a wounded society are those who carry the cultural wound most deeply. In my experience, many doctors embody the cultural shadow. In fact, we are trained to embody it.

As a student in medical school, I was rewarded for my woundedness and punished for my wholeness. My sense of cultural wound was actually deepened and reinforced by my experience of medical education. It took me many years to realize that medical education is not an education at all: it is a training. An education evokes wholeness and attends to integrity, while a training specializes, focuses, and narrows us. And in specializing, we disavow parts of our wholeness. We sacrifice our wholeness for expertise.

Many years ago when I was twelve years old I was taken to Quebec. During a visit to a historic graveyard I saw a tombstone which said: "Here lies George Brown; born a man, died a gastroenterologist." Now, I come from a medical family. In two generations of my family, there are nine physicians and so I was inspired by this epitaph. It never occurred to me that this was not a step up.

In the medical culture, we do not engage with our full humanity. In fact, authentic human connection—connecting to the humanness in yourself and in others—is actually seen as being something undesirable, unprofessional, even dangerous. We have become ashamed of our wholeness and may come to see it as a weakness. We are taught to fear connecting with our humanness, and especially our emotions, because this will destroy our scientific objectivity and mar our judgment.

Objectivity is seen as a requirement for those who wish to be good physicians. To this end, we are literally trained to distance, to expect that truth is best perceived at arm's length. We are taught that if we lose our objectivity we will make mistakes. Many physicians believe that keeping distance will protect them from making mistakes. After thirty-seven years as a physician, I think I would have to say that many more mistakes are made in medicine because of objectivity than were ever made because of knowing sick people too well.

Sir William Osler is often misquoted as having said that objectivity is the single most important trait of the true physician. He spoke in Latin and the word which is usually translated as "objectivity" is *aequinimitas. Aequinimitas* does not mean "objectivity," it means "mental stillness" or "inner peace." Inner peace is an important quality for anyone whose daily work puts them in contact with human suffering. But this is not the outcome of distancing oneself from life, rather it is about knowing life so intimately that one has become able to trust and accept life whole, embracing its darkness in order to know its grace.

One of the early things we do in the continuing medical education curriculum is help physicians to "unload the baggage" they carry from their training. We do this by asking them to tell their stories. Telling these stories to a group of physician colleagues is profoundly healing. Often it feels like freeing oneself from some sort of collective spell. At the close of one of the first storytelling sessions, one of the physicians said that he understood how the statue in Pygmalion must have felt when it was freed to come to life.

One of my own stories is typical of these kinds of stories. On the second day of my internship in pediatrics I went with my senior resident to tell young parents that the automobile accident from which they had escaped without a scratch had killed their child. When they heard this news, they broke down and cried. Very new to this doctor thing, I had cried with them over their loss. After it was over, the senior resident took me aside and told me that I had behaved very unprofessionally. "These people were counting on our strength," he said. I had let them down. As one of the only women in the training program, I desperately wanted to get it right and I took his criticism very much to heart. By the time I myself was senior resident, I hadn't cried in years.

During that year a two-year-old baby drowned in a bathtub. I directed a team which fought determinedly to resuscitate him but after an hour we had to concede defeat. Taking the intern with me, I went to tell these parents that we had not been able to save their child. Overwhelmed, they began to sob. After a time, the father looked at me standing there, strong and silent in my white coat, the shaken intern by my side. "I'm sorry, Doctor," he said, "I'll get a hold of myself in a minute." I remember this man, his face wet with a father's tears and I think of his apology with shame. Convinced by then that emotion was a useless, self-indulgent waste of time, I had become the sort of a person you could apologize to for being in agony. In many ways, medical training is like a disease; you need to recover from it. Fortunately this is possible: I am a recovering physician.

I'd like to tell you about beginning a program of recovery in the heart of a major training institution, the UCSF School of Medicine. It is a program whose goal is to enable people in the midst of their medical training to remember their wholeness, to attend to it in themselves and in others, to connect deeply with themselves and others, and hopefully to preserve a sense of compassion and meaning in their professional lives.

A course such as this can become a strategy for healing the collective wound of the medical culture. The wounds of the cultural shadow are very difficult for an individual to heal alone because they are reinforced everywhere. Every social interaction reinforces these wounds; every innuendo reinforces them; in expressing greater wholeness you see judgment in the eyes of everyone around you. Now, this is different from recovering from the wound inflicted by family shadow. Not everyone has grown up in your family. So when you leave home, you can find people who can offer you through their relationship a different perspective from the one you grew up with: a permission for greater wholeness. There are many healers of family shadow, but few healers of cultural shadow; we carry the cultural shadow collectively.

But just as culture wounds, culture heals. Healing the shadow of a culture may require the formation of a subculture of credible people who value that which has been devalued by the dominant culture. This subculture confers on its participants permission for a greater wholeness and heals them.

It is possible for a single course in a medical school to become such a subculture. The students in this course recognize each other. During the course they learn to share honestly with each other. They come to know and trust one another. They support each other's wholeness. Because a medical school is a relatively small community, these students will continue to associate with each other long after the course has ended. They see each other in elevators. They see each other in the halls. Sometimes they simply pass each other. Other times they talk with each other. But each time they meet, they create for each other a place of refuge from the cultural shadow, a reminding of a greater wholeness. The Healer's Art is an elective course that enrolls between fifty and sixty first-year medical students each year. It has been taught continuously for the past eight years. At this point, one out of every three medical students currently enrolled at UCSF has been through this course.

The UCSF catalogue does not say that The Healer's Art is a course in compassion and meaning but states that the purpose of the course is attending to human wholeness: one's own wholeness and the wholeness of others. The course is experiential rather than didactic and based on a discovery model. These sessions are each three hours long and take place in the evening, in the very large living room of the faculty/alumni house, an informal, homelike setting. By choosing this time and place, we change mental set from the very beginning; we take students out of the familiar physical environment and the customary time frame where the shadow dominates. Let me describe the first two sessions of this course.

That first evening, everyone arrives wearing masks. Masks of professionalism, masks of expertise, and masks of confidence and invulnerability. By their second year, many students have worn this mask so constantly that they may not realize or remember that they are wearing it.

Gathered in the room are the fifty to sixty students, and ten to twenty practicing physicians who are either graduates of our physician's training program in Relationship-Centered Care or favorite UCSF faculty selected by the student advisors to the course. These doctors—who represent all the major medical specialties—serve as course faculty and teach from a level playing field, sharing their own personal experiences, vulnerabilities, concerns, and satisfactions in the practice of medicine. This in itself is unique. Many students have told us that they have never before known a practicing physician personally, as a friend.

At the beginning, the room is not a comfortable place to be. As we sit together the first night, you can actually feel a certain wariness, the competitiveness between the students and their isolation from each other. And of course you can also sense fear, because isolation causes us to be vulnerable and afraid.

I begin that first evening by offering the students silence as a substitute for fear and isolation. Now, this itself is a very rare thing in a medical school classroom—having permission to be silent together. Yet silence is the way we connect, both to each other and to ourselves. I say a few words about the importance of silence and initiate a brief period of sitting in silence together. After fifteen minutes of silence, I ask the students a single question: "Is there a part of you that you are afraid you may forget in this process of becoming a doctor?" This question is a shock. It directly addresses a hidden fear shared by almost every medical student: the personal experience of the shadow of the medical culture.

I ask them to reflect upon this question first within the privacy of their own consciousness. Then I ask them to find a symbol or image for the part of themselves that is vulnerable to becoming lost, and to name its quality or qualities. I ask them how old this part is; how long it has been with them; and how precious it is to them. I ask them to consider what this part of themselves has added to their lives and what would it mean for a person who is ill to meet with this part. Finally, I ask them to write down their responses to the questions. There is such a taboo around these dimensions of the self that students often need to write their insights down first before they can openly discuss them.

Then we break into small groups. The students will be part of the same small group for the length of the course. Each group is made up of five or six students and a physician. The physicians facilitate the group as well as share their personal responses to the experiential exercises—in the same honest way that the students do. This is very important and quite powerful, as most of the students know physicians mainly as admired and seemingly infallible experts or as teachers who evaluate them. Over the course of the semester the students will get to know these doctors as genuinely as they will get to know themselves and each other.

The groups begin by sharing what they discovered in the exercise: at first very hesitantly, and then more and more openly as it becomes clear that, despite appearances, everybody has a part that they fear losing. The masks of control and professionalism fall away, and the students find an acceptance for personal aspects and concerns they have hidden because the dominant culture disavows them. The groups then develop and discuss ways to feed and nurture these parts of themselves, ways to attend to them. Very specific approaches—which may involve ritual, imagery, journal writing, poetry, music, and meditation—are designed by the students, shared with the small group, and validated.

Each small-group session ends with a healing circle exercise. This, too, involves sitting together in silence. The physician rings a bell, and then the student to his or her left says their name aloud. In silence, the group attends to the humanity of that student. They listen. They remember the part of their humanity that that particular student is struggling to preserve. And in perfect silence, they send strength: they believe in the student; they value their humanity; and they may even pray for it. They offer their silent support for each student's struggle to be whole.

After a minute or so the bell is rung again, and the next student to the left says their name. Everyone attends to this student for a minute; and we continue around the circle until the doctor has said his or her name and everyone has attended to him or her as well. As we do this exercise, the group moves into what might be termed a right relationship with each other for the first time, a supportive collegiality based on affirming the wholeness of every person in the group.

Now, I do this same closing exercise in our continuing medical education training with postgraduate doctors, but there is a difference. When I do a healing circle with a group of oncologists, radiologists, surgeons, internists, emergency-room doctors—middle-aged men who have lived with the cultural shadow for most of their professional lives—they are often moved to tears.

The first time I led this exercise, I was startled by its emotional power for the group. After the exercise was complete, one of the doctors explained this by saying, "I've never been wished well by another doctor before." The medical profession is a culture of profound isolation.

The second three-hour medical-student session is held two or three weeks later and is an exploration of loss, grief, and healing. Using the discovery model, I ask the faculty and the students to reflect on and identify their own style of dealing with loss, often a style learned from family and enforced by medical culture. We discuss all the things people do to manage loss, strategies such as denial, rationalization, busyness, substitution, spiritualization, and the like: strategies that numb pain but do not heal loss. I then present grieving as the way that loss can heal. Then, I teach them to grieve together.

Once a student stood at the close of this session, and said to me, "You know, we've already had two lectures on grieving from the psychiatry department." I was horrified to hear this and apologized, saying that had I known I would have chosen another topic.

"Oh, no," she responded. "This is different. Our lectures were focused on the grief of patients. They told us many of our patients would be grieving, and that we would need to make allowances for this. That their minds would not be functioning clearly because of their grief, and we would have to repeat things—often several times. We even learned the medications you can give to numb psychological pain. But they didn't tell us that we ourselves would have anything to grieve."

In a medical lifetime, a physician encounters a great deal of loss and disappointment, often on a daily basis. These range from small events such as discovering that a treatment is not working as hoped to the large blow of a patient's death. But as professionals, we are not supposed to be personally touched by any of this. This is a bit like walking through water and expecting yourself to emerge dry. After a lifetime of ungrieved loss it is not surprising that depression, cynicism, and burnout are so common in medicine. Grieving allows us to heal from loss, to risk closeness in situations where loss is a possibility, to be openhearted and present with patients. Grieving allows us to become close enough to feel compassion. So in this course, the students are given the opportunity to revisit one of their own personal losses and begin to heal it.

In the small groups, students will tell each other the story of one of their own losses. The students are asked to listen to each other's stories of loss with respect. They are told that many of the things they will hear about cannot be fixed, and are encouraged to listen without thinking about how to fix things. If you believe that your job as a physician is to fix everything, you may not want to hear about the things that cannot be fixed. But this is not about fixing: it is about witnessing and validating the feelings of others. I make it clear that fixing is often disrespectful to loss, and that it is a subtle form of judgment.

So they share their losses, and listen to the losses of others. They cry. They experience the healing which can happen when we simply attend to each others' losses. For many, this session will be a form of metta practice, an experience of authentic compassion. Students learn to see loss as simply one stage in a larger process of life, and to distinguish loss from brokenness. They hear about the hidden vulnerability in others who appeared to be less vulnerable than they knew themselves to be. They examine their own pain and discover what has begun to grow in the places of pain: what has been revealed or learned through loss and suffering. They discover what really matters. Most important, they have the chance to see the qualities of love, devotion, loyalty, and courage in the same people that they were competing with just four weeks ago.

By witnessing the commonality of loss, they come to see loss not as shame or weakness but as a natural part of life. They learn that things that cannot be fixed can still heal, and experience some of that healing personally. The body language often graphically reflects a change in the students' attitudes about loss. At the beginning of the evening, many students sit with their arms folded, often leaning back, away from the center of the circle. By the end, each small group is leaning so close together that their heads almost touch.

In this exercise, students move from an experience of isolation and judgment to an experience of compassion for themselves and each other. In this shift, they find a sense of acceptance, and of intimacy, which is very new. Students often write to us about this. They tell us how it felt to be listened to without judgment. They express surprise at the easing of their pain. They comment on how letting go of fixing the pain of others has enabled them to receive the feelings of their classmates in a new and caring way. They are surprised by the genuineness and depth of their caring. For the first time, they write, they truly want to hear how it is, and know how it feels for others. True compassion naturally arises out of this sense of openness and connection. Out of listening.

In the continuing medical education physicians' course, I do an exercise in listening which is actually a form of reflection and contemplation. I draw on the work of my friend and colleague Angeles Arrien for this exercise, but adapt it for physicians.

I suggest they spend a few minutes each evening, with a special bound journal just for this purpose, and ask themselves three questions about their day. The three questions are: What surprised me today? What moved me or touched me today? What inspired me today? The answers need not be long. What is important is to review the experience of the day for a brief time, looking at it in a new and different way.

A cancer specialist, a surgical oncologist, took this exercise on. He committed to spending five minutes a day considering and answering these questions. This was a very burned-out, profoundly cynical man whose basic attitude was: "You know, everybody dies anyway. What's the use?"

So the first night, he considered these three questions, and wrote in his journal: "Nothing, nothing, and nothing." The second night, he got the same results: "Nothing, nothing, and nothing."

After two more days of this, he called me up, and said, "What's the trick, Rachel? I don't like to fail at things." I said to him: "Pay attention from the heart. Look at your life experience as if you were a novelist or a poet, not a doctor."

Over time he has come to see his work very differently. "Rachel," he told me, "the most extraordinary people are in my practice!" He has gotten to know them; he has become close to them. He now feels himself enriched by the very same work that he had experienced as a terrible burden.

For most people there is a time gap between experience and perception. At first, people often do not see what's going on around them. After a while they see only several hours after they have lived through an experience. But in the privacy of their living room or their bedroom, in the company of a little journal, over time they begin to see again: to reconnect to their lives and to themselves.

As they do this journal practice—over and over, day after day—the gap diminishes until eventually people are inspired, surprised, moved in the very moment that life is happening within and around them.

Sometimes seeing differently comes spontaneously as a sort of grace. Another doctor found his eyes while he was delivering a baby in the emergency room. Now, emergency-room doctors are like Blue Angels; they're the fighter pilots of medicine. They deal with life and death daily, often at high speed. They rarely get to know anybody whom they treat in any depth. These doctors generally enjoy a sense of competence and mastery. This particular doctor is a man very much like this.

One evening, a woman came into the emergency room within

minutes of delivering a baby. The doctor realized that the woman's personal physician probably wasn't going to get there in time, and that he was going to get to deliver this baby himself. Now, this pleased him. In fifteen years of ER work he had delivered hundreds of babies and had always gotten a sense of satisfaction and competence doing it. He told the mother that her doctor was on the way, but if the baby came first he would deliver her. He assured her he had delivered many babies, and that she and her baby were safe. He had barely time to finish speaking when her birth began and he successfully delivered her baby, a little girl. Then, as he was suctioning out the infant's mouth and nose, suddenly she opened her eyes and looked deeply and directly into his eyes. In that moment, the doctor realized that he was the first human being that this child had ever seen. In this moment, something softened in him. Something that had stood between him and the meaning of his work. And he could feel his heart open to her in welcome from the whole human race. His sense of fatigue and cynicism dropped away, and he knew that no matter how foolish or undeserving we may be, the new ones keep coming and with them comes hope.

As he tells it, in this moment too, all his years of hard work—all the stress and all the sacrifices—were worth it. He felt a sense of the endless grace that life offers us, and a deep sense of gratitude at being there. Compared to this sense of gratitude, he said, the satisfaction that he had found through pursuing competence was nothing. This doctor had delivered hundreds of babies, but he feels he had never really been there as a human being before. He had been there only as a competent professional, an expert, and had missed something important. If you are willing to bring your human heart and eyes to the work of medicine, even the smallest patient will show you the meaning of your work.

Often genuine meaning comes to us as a sense of revelation. Since much meaning is carried in the unconscious mind, in these two curricula I use the unconscious mind as a resource. I use symbols, art, and even poetry. A renewed sense of meaning requires a kind of double vision. We know what we have come to do and we remember why we have come. We have not come to be experts, we have come to befriend life.

In times of crisis, meaning can be a source of strength: meaning enables us to endure and prevail through difficult times. Meaning heals us not by numbing our pain or distracting us from our problems but by reminding us of our integrity: of who we are, of what we are doing, and how we belong. Meaning gives us a place to stand: a place from which to meet the events of our lives; a way to experience life's true value and its mystery. Most of us live far more meaningful lives than we realize. It is possible for physicians to do profoundly meaningful work without ever experiencing a sense of meaning. Objectivity can make you blind.

Meaning is a practice. The recovery of compassion, the recovery of meaning is, in the words of Proust, a "voyage of discovery that lies not in seeking new vistas but in having new eyes." Recovering a sense of original mission and meaning in medical education has been my work for many years. Looking backward, I remember just when and where I recognized the need to recover something lost.

During my second year of medical school, I was invited to a formal dinner to honor one of our most famous professors, who was retiring. He was an elderly physician who had made a huge scientific contribution and had the highest international reputation for his medical research.

The occasion was a black-tie affair, and people came from all over the world to honor him. Everyone was invited, even we second-year medical students. During the evening, the professor gave a talk synthesizing the progress of scientific knowledge over the course of the fifty years that he had been a physician and pointing out the directions for future scientific research. The talk was brilliant, and he received a long standing ovation.

I and the other students were completely awed by him, by his life and work. He was the quintessential role model, the doctor we all wanted to become. So afterwards a little group of us went to talk to him for a minute, really just to be close to him. And one student asked if there was anything that he wanted to tell us now, at the beginning of our careers as doctors.

He looked at us. And an unreadable expression came over his face. In a quiet voice he said that he felt we should know that he didn't know one thing more about life now than he had at the beginning. "I am no wiser," he told us. "It has slipped through my fingers." Then he turned, and just walked away.

Now, we were all very young at the time. The other students thought that the old man had gone gaga. After all, he was sixty-five years old. I didn't think so, but I simply could not understand what he meant. Now, having been a physician myself for close to forty years, I think that I do, and my heart goes out to him.

He was one of the most outstanding alumni of his school. I am certain that his teachers were very proud of him. But I also feel that they failed him in the same way that my own teachers failed me. They did not recognize our need to remember and strengthen our humanness, they did not help us to seek and find the meaning of this work and to hold it close, so that at the end of fifty years of being a physician we might feel grateful for the privilege of living this life of service.

In putting together these thoughts, I remembered an incident that happened at the end of one of the physicians' workshops. I wrote a poem about it, which in closing I'd like to share with you.

A MALA FOR THE TEACHER

At the close of the CME curriculum,
a physician tells me, "I have a gift for you."
His eyes shining.
His face filled with an unaccustomed joy.

In his surgeon's hands he holds a mala of bone beads.
"To count your blessings," he tells me.
"To remember life's promise and its grace."

My mala is of different stuff,
My blessings known by heart:

A surgeon who has learned to pray;
An internist who has found he is a healer;
An oncologist who has remembered how to cry.
A cardiologist who once again hears the heart.

Like them, this physician is a blessing,
the giver far more precious than the gift.

3.

BUDDHIST EDUCATION:
THE PATH OF WISDOM
AND KNOWLEDGE

The Dzogchen Ponlop Rinpoche

The Dzogchen Ponlop Rinpoche is the director and main teacher of
Nithartha Institute at Gampo Abbey in Cape Breton, Nova Scotia.
He has received many important teachings of the Kagyu and
Nyingma lineages of Tibetan Buddhism, from such noted teachers as
H.H. Karmapa and H.H. Dilgo Khyentse Rinpoche. Ponlop Rin-
poche is known for his kindness, his ability to communicate directly
with Western students, and for his wonderful blend of intellectual
precision, humor, and warmth.

BUDDHADHARMA, the teachings of Shakyamuni Buddha, describes a path of wisdom and knowledge. As His Holiness the Dalai
Lama and other teachers have often pointed out, Buddhism is not
really a religion per se. It is rather a science of mind. It is a philosophy
for humanity, an inner science dealing with the mind and, in particular, with the fundamental state of consciousness.

According to Buddhadharma, the fundamental state of consciousness—the basic state of our minds—is completely pure. This basic purity is called Buddha nature. Thus, the ground, or basis, of learning in
Buddhism is the view that the nature of our mind, no matter who
or what we are, is fundamentally pure. The goal of Buddhist education is the bringing about of the full understanding and realization of
this basic mind: the mind which has been fundamentally pure and
fully awakened right from the beginning. Education is then under-

stood to be like a mirror that allows us to glimpse and recognize our own face: our true nature, our original purity. The practices of education, the various steps that we take, are simply the application of different tools, techniques, and studies that help us to reach this ultimate goal.

Along the path of uncovering this heart of enlightenment, there are many different processes that we go through. We deal with our ignorance. We deal with our emotions. We deal with all the negative aspects of our mind states. According to Buddhadharma, every experience that we go through is a creation of our mind. In this tradition, there is no outer creator who is responsible for our particular circumstances, situations, experiences—or even our liberation! Because of this, on the path of Buddhist education, there is no such idea of worshipping or relying on any kind of outer entity existing outside of mind.

Sometimes, when I'm driving my car, I see the little message printed on the side-view mirror. Have you seen it? This seems to me to be a very Buddhist message. It says something like this, "Objects in the mirror are closer than they appear." According to the perspective of Buddhism, this statement is true. The objects that we perceive as being outside of us are actually closer than they appear. They are not appearances outside of us, but instead reflections of our mind.

I have studied the teachings of the Buddha for a long time, and this seems to be one of the main messages. I see it everywhere. In fact, if you read the whole literature of the Buddhadharma, the direct teachings of the Buddha recorded in his words, you will never see any word referring to "Buddhism." There is no such word as Buddhism in this tradition at all! But indeed you will find a great deal written about this idea of "objects being closer than they appear."

Therefore, this tradition, while called Buddhism, is simply a path towards knowledge and wisdom. Knowledge and wisdom, of course, exist in many traditions. They are ultimately beyond tradition. The Buddha's teachings and insights do not necessarily conflict with other religious faiths or philosophical traditions. We can share and partake of this basic understanding of sacredness, and share our basic understandings of the path to knowledge and wisdom.

In terms of our actual experience, however—what and how we understand—this can be very individual. Very particular. Therefore, even within the so-called Buddhist tradition, there are many different traditions. I come from the background of the Buddhism of Tibet. But there is also the Buddhism of India, the Buddhism of China, the Buddhism of Japan, and the Buddhism of the Southeast Asian countries. There are many different schools within the Buddhist traditions of these countries as well.

The differences among them, if I may speak my understanding, are how, within their particular cultural and historical situations, they understand the Buddha's message. If we try to repeat what someone says, for example, to repeat what the Buddha said—his message—we each repeat it in a slightly different way. Since I come from a Tibetan cultural and psychological background, then the way I understand what the Buddha was saying is perhaps slightly different from a colleague who may be Chinese or Indian or American. When we each repeat the words of the Buddha, the message becomes slightly different. It's like the children's game called "telephone." One person whispers into the ear of another, and then another, and so on. And slowly, over time, the message changes. You know, it gets a little bit different each time. I don't necessarily mean worse. But different. Sometimes the message really comes back, but different, better: perhaps clearer to that particular speaker and listener.

While there are different traditions and schools of Buddhism in terms of educational style, spiritual discipline, or meditation practice, they are all actually the same in their nature. There is no difference in what they are trying to teach. The only difference is the way that we understand, the way that we repeat the words of Buddha.

For example, we have heard another presenter speak this morning. If we each try to repeat what his message was, then how I reflect on it will be different from how you do it. The differences may be slight or vast, because we come from different contexts of culture, language, psychology, tradition, and history.

But the basic nature of the Buddhadharma is just simply one: one teaching, one dharma. I usually compare it to water, genuine pure water. Water has no shape or color. Water is totally free from shape and color. But when you pour genuine pure water into a container, that container must have a shape. The container has a size, too, and sometimes a color, as well. The individual who holds or looks into this container of water also sees reflections in the water. His or her hands and face reflect in the water.

In a similar way, when we pour the genuine teachings, the genuine wisdom and knowledge, into different containers, they begin to take on different aspects. In the same way that the water adopts the shape of the pitcher and the size of the pitcher, the teachings take on different qualities. But if someone says, "Okay. You know, what I really want is just the water. I'm not interested in any containers—not interested in the Tibetan cup, not interested in the Japanese cup, not interested in the Chinese cup—I'm just interested in the water." Well, this is a reasonable request. This is what we all really want, and what we should be looking for. There's just one small problem. Water cannot be preserved without a container. Water cannot exist without the container. If you break the container, the water is gone. It's gone.

This raises a dilemma, a paradox. The genuine teaching of Buddha has no form, no color, which also means no culture and no language! It is beyond language and culture. It is beyond tradition. But it relies on culture, on language and tradition for its preservation and transmission.

Therefore, as we are gathered here from different traditions, different cultures, and different languages, we have the ability to understand the true wisdom teachings, the true spiritual path, without any cultural, philosophical, or linguistic clothing. Understanding teachings from this perspective is very important, especially in Buddhism. However, in terms of preserving and transmitting this knowledge and wisdom across time, across the centuries, this depends on the forms and practices of education. This depends both on the educational institutions, which store the knowledge in the particular clothing of cultural, historical, and social forms, and on the great wisdom teachers, the genuine practitioners. We depend on genuine masters to continue a living tradition of wisdom and knowledge.

Let me expand a little bit. What is being transmitted? What is knowledge? What is wisdom? Knowledge, in this case, is our understanding. Knowledge is our understanding, which is conceptual, which is intellectual, which is philosophical. It is insight which is very much connected to our brains. Wisdom, however, is the insight and understanding that comes from our hearts. Wisdom is compassion; it is genuine love, genuine caring.

When we talk about Buddhist education, we are basically talking about getting in touch with these two sources. Buddha had, and taught about, his sharp understanding. Buddha also had, and spoke of, compassion and love. Education, from a Buddhist perspective, is about developing these two qualities. And to develop these two is to uncover that which is deep within our hearts.

Buddhadharma, remember, teaches that there is no external deity who is responsible for us. Therefore, compassion is not outside; wisdom is not outside. We must recognize that we are not paying institutions to buy wisdom or to buy knowledge. Knowledge and wisdom can't be bought. They are not outside; they are already within us. Let me repeat: these things are not outside.

Buddha said this again and again in the sutras. Sutras are writings, the Buddhist scriptures. Buddha himself said that no matter how compassionate the Buddhas may be, they cannot give their knowledge, they cannot give their wisdom to us. We have to develop these within ourselves. This is one of Buddha's most important messages.

Therefore, we begin by recognizing that wisdom and knowledge are already within us, inside of us, part of us. Then we recognize that the educational institutions and the great masters are there to help us discover, uncover, and develop this knowledge and wisdom that we already possess.

In Buddhism, wisdom is sometimes called "self-secret." We have it but we don't know that we have it. The secret is not a secret kept from someone else. It's a secret that we ourselves don't know yet! When we finally realize that we have the thing that we're looking for "out there" somewhere, then it's no longer a secret. The secret—surprise!—is revealed to us by our own experience. What this means is that if we did not have the seeds of knowledge and wisdom within us, then the institutions wouldn't be able to give us anything. And a corollary to this is that the institutions, the spiritual masters, the books, and so on, are not there to do it for us, but to help us.

The traditional example we use to teach this point in Tibetan Buddhism is the example of gold ore. If you take gold ore and refine it, you will get gold. Now, if you take some other kind of rock, and you put it through the same process—the same machines, the same chemicals—try as you may, you'll never get gold. Why is this the case? In the gold ore, the essence of the gold was there from the very beginning. The gold's nature, its ore, was already present in the rock. The other stone, however, does not contain this same essence.

Therefore, if we did not already have knowledge and wisdom within us, there would be no way the great schools or masters could help us. But alas, there is no way that any institutions can just give us these two qualities. According to the teachings of Buddha, we must come to our own understanding, and this process is born from our realization: from actually seeing this true potential as already existing within ourselves, within our own hearts.

Buddhism teaches that this basic wisdom, Buddha nature, is in every being. No matter what their appearance to the contrary, deep in their hearts, there is a soft spot. No matter how aggressive, how ferocious they may appear, there is certainly a soft spot deep in their hearts. Compassion. Wisdom. The brilliant sharpness of knowledge. An ability to love called wisdom. These are the two main subjects of Buddhism. In Buddhist culture, the educational institutions of the past, all the way up to the institutions of the present, are basically there to teach us to rediscover ourselves, to rediscover this heart of enlightenment, rediscover the awareness which contains these two key qualities, knowledge and wisdom. This, in essence, is the entire foundation, path, and goal of Buddhism. It is the entire educational journey of Buddhism.

In some ways, it's like the American movie *Back to the Future*. The educational journey takes us "back to the future," back to enlightenment. We think of enlightenment as some time or some place out in the future, but actually we need to go back and meet our original state of mind. Our original state of mind is already a graduate student. Our original state of mind is already a Ph.D. More than that. It is a Buddha! The original state of our mind is Buddhahood. It is already fully awakened. The whole business of education is to bring us back to this original state.

While the basic goal of Buddhist education may be so simple, so to speak, that does not mean that there weren't great, highly complex institutions of learning. In India, there was a great institution, Nalanda University. At Nalanda, students explored many different languages, philosophies, and sciences, not only Buddhism but also astrology, psychology, medicine, and the other sciences of that time. In Tibetan Buddhism, we usually talk about the "five major sciences" or the "ten different aspects of knowledge."

Many great Buddhist masters came from Nalanda: Nagarjuna, the great philosopher of emptiness; Atisha, the great Mahayana teacher and master of Madhyamika, the "Middle Way"; the great scholar and practitioner Naropa, for whom The Naropa Institute is named. You can still see the ruins of Nalanda in India. Archeologists tell us that what they have found is perhaps only one-tenth of what was originally there. This was a huge Buddhist educational center in India.

In Tibet, as well, there were many different institutions: monastic institutions, academic institutions, hermitages. Now most of them have moved to India. But what is studied in all of these institutions is the balancing of these same two energies, so to speak. Balancing knowledge and wisdom. Knowledge and wisdom are very important factors. If you lose one of them, this can create a problem. If you lose the wisdom part, if you lose the compassion part, and simply develop the brain part—philosophy, knowledge, and understanding alone—this can create great problems. I don't have to tell you about these problems! On the other hand, if you are very intuitive with lots of compassion and genuine love, but are missing the intellectual part, this can cause problems as well.

In Tibetan Buddhism, we have two examples to show how important it is to have both of these factors. We say that having knowledge is like having a good eye. When you have good eyesight, you can see everything clearly. You can see the path clearly. You can see your destination. You have a clear mind, a sharp mind. But if you have perhaps some problem with your feet, there is a big problem. You can see what you want. You can see where you want to go, but you're not moving. You're not going anywhere. You can't get there. You're just sitting still. Or you're just talking about it—talking, talking, talking—and there's no movement. This is the example of having the intellectual knowledge alone, without wisdom, without compassion.

The compassion part is like having healthy feet. It's like having a healthy body. When you have the two together, you can see the road. Your destination is clear. At the same time, you can walk. You can proceed on the path. You can take the journey. Therefore, the combination of these two together is very important.

The importance of compassion should not be underestimated. In the sutras, Buddha taught that compassion, in the beginning of our journey—in the beginning of our education—is like a seed. It's like the seed of a fruit tree. Without this seed, we can't have fruit. Without compassion, nothing will grow. In the middle of our education—during the course of our path—Buddha said that compassion is like water. Once we have planted the seed, we need to water it. Without water, our seed won't grow. At the end, Buddha said, compassion is as important as the heat of the sun. The heat makes things ripen. It makes the fruit ripen. Without the heat, there is no fruit; and without the fruit, there is no nourishment. Here, "the end" is referring to the point where we come to fully realize our true nature, the heart of enlightenment, a fully awakened heart.

So for these reasons, the practice of compassion is always important—and always a part of the educational process. It seems to me that in the West, in comparison with traditional Buddhist education, the development of compassion is what is most missing from schools today. Perhaps it is that our teachers are not compassionate, or maybe it is the students who are not compassionate. But it is clear—something is wrong. We are not learning properly. I feel that we are not learning properly because we are not open to each other. Compassion, however, is what opens the heart.

Within our educational institutions, it is important that we develop more emphasis, more training, and more exercises for the development of compassion. Joining knowledge and wisdom is the most important part of education: not only within the Buddhist tradition but also, so to speak, for the great tradition of all sentient beings.

This is what I understand. Thank you very much for your patience. I pray for all of you: for your continued development on the spiritual path; for the deepening of your faith, whatever faith that may be; and for the education of our children for the future.

UNLEARNING TO
SEE THE SACRED

Jeremy Hayward

Jeremy Hayward received a Ph.D. in physics at Cambridge University in 1965. He conducted research in molecular biology at MIT for four years, was a high school physics teacher for two years, and then, in 1974, helped found The Naropa Institute. Jeremy served as vice president of the institute until 1984, has written four books, and coedited a fifth. These include *Gentle Bridges: Conversations with the Dalai Lama on the Sciences of Mind, Sacred World: The Shambhala Way to Gentleness, Bravery, and Power,* and most recently, *Letters to Vanessa: On Love, Science, and Awareness in an Enchanted World.*

WE HAVE perhaps been to wonderful ceremonies: evocations of spirit, of the light within and the light all-pervading, the evocation and invitation of Grandmother and Grandfather. But what do we really mean by these ceremonies? What is actually going on, or what do we believe is going on? Sometimes it is helpful to pause and question the words that we use to describe our so-called reality.

Let's really think about these things. And ask some questions: What do we mean when we say everything is sacred? What do we mean by the *inwardness* of other? What do we mean when we say everything is mind? Whose mind are we talking about?

Please look at the chair nearest to you, and ask, "Is this chair sacred? In what sense is the chair mind?" Look carefully. Please, really look! My question is this: Do we *feel,* in every cell of our body, that everything is sacred? Or do we just *think* it's sacred?

Suppose you go for a walk next week, say Monday at five o'clock, after you leave work. Go for a walk, stop in front of a rock, and ask yourself, "Is this rock sacred?" Your thinking might say, "Of course. I agreed with everything in that nice little book." But what will your body say? What will the cells of your body say? How will your body vibrate to that rock? How will your heart *feel* the rock? This is the real question.

Now, if we do this exercise ourselves, perhaps quite a high proportion of readers might say, "Yes," honestly, sincerely, "yes, I do feel the sacredness of that rock." But if we do this exercise with the general population (or even with a lot of people who *talk* about sacredness), I think most would say, "Actually, no. I do not feel in my being that rock has sacredness. I don't even know what that means. A rock is a rock, right? It's matter. What does it mean to say it has sacredness? I don't get it at all."

And we ourselves—though we may *feel* sacredness when we're in a heightened situation—if we go into our everyday lives and ask ourselves, "Is that rock sacred?" we most likely will come across doubt. We might say, "I don't know, really." Or even, "I actually don't think so, and I don't even feel so." Then, asking the same question about a plant, an animal, even a person, "Are they really sacred?" sadly, we might find the same doubt.

So I would like to focus on the obstacles to really *experiencing* the sacredness of our world. The problem that I want to present to you is that we grow up, until we become teenagers, with constant, constant training in materialism. Whatever we may *think* about ourselves, we are all materialists deep in our bodymind system. You might say, "I hated science in school. I didn't believe in any of that nonsense." But it really doesn't make much difference. Most of us, with very few exceptions, grow up in this society conditioned to become materialists. Unless we examine this—unless we actually look at our conditioning, look at how we feel about the world, how we perceive, how we relate to a rock, what we feel about the rock, what we feel about space, what we actually feel about each other—then spirituality is perhaps like a nice coat that we put on to cover our gushing wound in our heart.

We grow up to perceive certain things and not to perceive other things. And what we can and cannot perceive depends to a surprisingly large extent on what we believe: on our vision of our world and what it is made of. Many of us are perhaps rather tired of metaphysics and philosophy, questions like "What is the world made of?" We say "Give me a break" or "The scientists have solved all that, leave it to the scientists." But actually, to be human, we need to have a guiding vision, even though it may be largely unconscious. There is no way of escaping that—otherwise we are not human. The guiding vision of a culture is generally given by society: by leaders, by parents, and especially by educational institutions. Now, generally speaking, the guiding vision by which we grow up in this culture gives us two choices: materialism or materialism with transcendental theism (belief in one God as creator and supreme ruler of the universe) added on. These are our two choices.

However, we *all* grow up with the materialist vision (if you can call it a vision): that this world, the real world, is made of nothing but dead stuff, which we call matter. That's what we learn at school. I would like to tell you a little story about my daughter, Vanessa, which I think illustrates this quite well. When Vanessa was in third grade, she came home one day and said excitedly, because she knew I was a scientist, "Daddy, Daddy, I learned what matter is today." I said, "Oh, yes, Vanessa, and what is matter?" She said, "Matter's the stuff the world is made of," and I was very unhappy. I contemplated calling her third-grade teacher and saying, "How dare you indoctrinate my child with your religious dogma?"

Of course I immediately realized that the poor third-grade teacher would have no idea what I was talking about. She was a third-grade teacher. She had learned science in teachers' college—and they generally teach the most pathetic, out-of-date science in teachers' colleges. So she thinks the world is made of matter, and that scientists have proved this and it has nothing to do with religion. In parenthesis,

I should tell you that in the same class a few weeks earlier, at Eastertime, Vanessa came home singing a song about Baby Jesus feeding the animals. I felt fine about this because I thought, "Well, she's learning about that kind of caring and loving so it doesn't really matter whether it is Jesus, Buddha, or whomever." So it was not religious instruction per se that bothered me.

The statement "matter's the stuff the world is made of" saddened and angered me, because I could see what was coming. I knew very soon Vanessa would learn that other than matter all there is is vast empty cold dead black lifeless space and a stream of time over which we have no control whatsoever, but into which we are born and die. And that is it! Space, time, and matter/energy—all understood to be completely devoid of feeling, awareness, or life. Likewise, that the entire cosmos itself has no inherent awareness, feeling, or life. That is the dreary belief about the "real world" that Vanessa was going to learn, to receive into her system.

Now, I want to make it really clear that my remarks are not anti *science*. They are criticisms of a completely erroneous perception of science that has gotten deep into every aspect of our society. Even if by sixth grade you say, "I don't want to have anything else to do with science," it doesn't make any difference. You already see the world in this way. For example, when we look around, we don't see or feel space because we regard space as nothing but a container for things. Sometimes I do an experiment of asking people to make a list of whatever they are experiencing in a room. And very rarely does anyone write "space." People just don't think of space as being a vital part of our experience. It's merely the dead, empty container of things.

So that is the primary version of reality that we all grow up with. Then—if you are so inclined, or if your family is religious—you might believe in some kind of otherworldly deity. In other words, a transcendent God. And this God *has* to be beyond this world, in an altogether separate realm, because *this* world is made of nothing but dead matter and lifeless empty space. These are the two alternatives we have: deep in our system, we are fundamentally science people, and then, if we like, we might say, "Well, there is also some kind of other world and otherworldly God, and we all have a soul that comes from that other world."

Now, it is true that when we come to our teenage years we almost always start to question the beliefs we grew up with. Teenagers love to question authority. I am sure those of you who are no longer teenagers still remember that time. To me that was perhaps the most brilliant time of my life: when we were always debating and questioning, questioning, questioning. But the funny thing is, I rarely find a teenager who questions the dogma that matter is what the world is made of, or even realizes that there is something there to question. Do teenagers actually question whether matter, space, and time are what the world is made of? Not too many. Mostly it is questioning of religious principles, political situations, and so on. But they don't question materialism, because everybody knows the scientists have proved that.

Nowadays even most neurophysiologists believe that even consciousness is nothing but the behavior of the matter of the brain. For example, Francis Crick, the Nobel Prize winner who discovered the helical nature of DNA, recently wrote a book for the general public called *The Astonishing Hypothesis*. According to Crick's astonishing hypothesis, "You, your joys and sorrows, your memories and ambitions, your sense of personal identity and free will are no more than the behavior of a vast assembly of neurons." And he is one of the leading mainstream neurophysiologists! This matter-based religion has now taken over consciousness, so that consciousness is the exciting forefront of current science, and the leading edge of science conferences around the world. I must say that there is a school of brain scientists who say, "No, sorry, it doesn't work. Consciousness cannot be reduced to brain function." But they are very much in the minority. And the mainstream media, as well as academics and teacher training colleges, strongly cling to the materialist view. This narrow-mindedness in the cultural authorities of our time is frightening!

So what is the problem here? The problem is that this materialist worldview, even with the addition of a transcendental Deity, constitutes a denial of a vast realm of real human experience. That realm of experience is what I want to focus on here. It is what gives meaning, quality, and value to our life and experience. I strongly recommend a very insightful book by Huston Smith, who is probably the most well-known American scholar of comparative religion. Now, Huston didn't just sit in his ivory tower writing about the different religions, he actually studied with a Zen teacher and with a Hindu teacher. He is famous for his book called *The World's Religions,* but has another book which is, I think, more interesting. It is called *Forgotten Truth: The Common Vision of the World's Religions.* You could say this book is about the inner teachings common to all the world's religions. While Huston specifically addresses the common inner teachings of Judaism, Christianity, Islam, and Buddhism, this inner vision is shared by just about every society that has ever existed on this earth before this one. Practically every society has seen a spectrum of experience, or a three-leveled reality of experience. In the Middle Ages, this spectrum of reality and experience was called the Great Chain of Being. I want to briefly describe the three levels, which are actually the two ends of the spectrum and everything in between.

At one end, there is the experience of the so-called outer world—the ordinary physical level, the earth level. This is the same level as our experience of body. Then at the other extreme is the level of transcendent being or nonbeing. Some people call it God, but every great theistic tradition—Judaism, Eastern Orthodox Christianity, and Islam—has also had schools of teaching that say "to even say 'God' is putting a kind of human concept on it, so what we really have to say about that vast transcendent level is 'beyond God.' But even that is too positive, so what we should really say to try to capture the ultimate is 'nothing.'"

Every theistic tradition (excepting Western Christianity) realized that the idea of a creator God is a stage of human understanding, and that to point beyond *that* we have to say "nothing." There was a thread of this realization in Western Christianity as well, but it was always condemned as heretical, whereas in the other traditions such teachings were accepted views of particular schools. I recommend to you another excellent book that deals with this: *A History of God,* by Karen Armstrong.

The point I want to make here, however, is that in between the matter level, the physical level, and the ultimate level of openness, of emptiness, of "beyond God," of whatever we call it, between those levels there is a complete spectrum. Spectrum of what? we might ask. We could say, a spectrum of finer and finer "energy," but it is not just physical energy. There is an inner aspect to this spectrum as well. Energy is very closely related to awareness in direct experience. So I wouldn't just call the intermediate level "energy," I would call it "awareness-energy" or "psycho/spiritual/material energy." Something to show the unity of material with mental/spiritual, outer with inner. So there is a continuous spectrum of finer and finer, subtler and subtler, levels of energy and awareness, or energy-awareness, two sides of the same stuff. Even at the level of rocks and trees, then, there is an element of some kind of awareness.

Now, this intermediate level between the earth level and the ultimate level is a vital aspect of human experience. This is very important to understand. We should not imagine that human life and being takes place purely on the physical earth level, and that all else is above or beyond us. This is a quite wrong idea that has, again, arisen because of the separation between our physical world and the transcendent God. Human life and being spans the entire spectrum from the physical, all the way through the subtle, to the unconditioned.

To imagine how this is so, we should think of this whole spectrum as interwoven levels of being, rather than levels stacked one upon another. As an analogy, consider a patch of skin on the palm of your hand. If you simply look with your naked eyes, you will see a patch of skin recognizable as a piece of your palm. If then you look at it under a microscope, you will see an entirely different world—a world of single cells and microbes that could have come from almost anywhere on your body. Then, if you look at that same patch of skin in an electron microscope, you will see an entirely different world again—a world of atoms and molecules. And this world could have come from many places in the universe other than a patch of skin. So these three worlds are very different, yet they are all included in your skin. Likewise the three levels, or spectrum, of being are all included in your own being.

Experience of the intermediate level of being was denied and finally lost in our society through a kind of collusion between the original scientists and the Church (a story that we don't, unfortunately, have space to go into here). So the ultimate level and the earth level became fundamentally separated, instead of being just the ends of a spectrum connected through what is sometimes called the Great Chain of Being: finer and finer levels of energy-awareness going from the concrete to unconditioned openness, beyond God. The Great Chain of Being became reduced to two separate extremes: a distant "other world," abode of the "Creator God," and this physical world, with no connection between them.

Genuine connection with this intermediate level of our own being is desperately needed in our society now. I would like to quote here from an interview with Kees Zoeteman, the deputy secretary-general for the environment in Holland. He, of course, is a bureaucrat, and bureaucrats are supposed to be pretty rational people. Anyway, you would think he is pretty serious. So he went on public television and proclaimed his belief in elves and gnomes. Following the TV program, Zoeteman was interviewed by a Dutch magazine. He said:

> *I have been trying to tell people that it is not just about gnomes, it is about the world of the unseen. . . . There are countless beings around that we cannot see but we can feel them. I can feel their warmth in my heart. You can connect with them and feel their energy. Basically you can communicate. . . . A landscape angel is meters tall. It is a glowing being of various colors. And it uses energy to maintain nature's growth processes. [Knowing this] helps us to have a feeling of respect and thanks to nature. . . . It is good to call attention to this side of reality. If you open yourself up to this world it is not crazy, it's enriching. We*

live in this technical world of concrete buildings where you have to fo-
cus your energy inward in order to endure. The domain of the [subtle
realm] has been lost.

This is the deputy secretary-general for the environment! Wouldn't it be nice if our deputy secretary of the environment would talk like that. The point is, there are countless such accounts. A couple of years ago, on the Discovery Channel, there was a program about a psychology professor at the University of London who had offered an extension course for people who saw fairies. This psychologist was interviewed and said that he was really amazed that thirty people signed up, all sane and intelligent people. They were so relieved, because every single one of them had been afraid to tell anyone—even their spouse—because they thought they would be considered crazy. It was an incredible relief for them to be able to talk about their real experiences of these beings.

Perhaps some of you who are interested in Buddhism know of a gentleman called Evans-Wentz. He translated a lot of Tibetan Buddhist texts. But before he became interested in Buddhism, he studied the Celtic myths and stories. Evans-Wentz went to the Isle of Skye, an island off Scotland, and interviewed all the old people there, and they said, "Oh, yes, we see fairies, no big deal. But when the education came the children were told fairies don't exist so they don't see them anymore." And there are several reports where you can see this transition: the older generation sees or feels the presence of these things, and the younger generation doesn't.

What all this points to is not so much about fairies and such but to the universal human experience that there *is* such a realm. There *is* something going on. My point here is not to encourage people to try to start hearing voices or seeing strange things; but we could compare our situation to the time when people believed the earth was flat and then someone would say, "Well, I sailed all around the world, so it can't be flat." Most people would say, "Oh, he's crazy," but then someone else would say, "Well, I've sailed around the world too." After a while you have to start paying attention, and say, "Well, they can't *all* be crazy." So it is like that for us now in relation to the flat world we live in, the one-dimensional world in which all that exists is lifeless matter. We should pay attention to these stories. Not only to these stories but to our own feelings, our own sense of wonder and magic. Because as soon as you open your mind to the fact that, "yes, there is obviously something going on and I should pay attention to it," then you start to realize that you can *feel* it going on. There are many ways that we can feel it going on in our own lives, and we can begin to connect with that realm of nature spirits, gods, and muses. But we deny or have lost touch with that experience. We have lost the means to perceive the intermediate level because our entire culture has denied its existence for so long.

Now I must warn here that there is a whole spectrum within the intermediate realm, including some very negative forces. If we just try to play around, and say, "Oh, I think I'll try to play with my Ouija board," we might actually connect with something quite negative. We have to be careful, because that spectrum itself goes all the way from some negative forces—by which I mean forces that would like to destroy the heart of a human being, anticontemplative forces—through neutral energies, landscape angels, and so on, to the benevolent dralas of the Shambhala tradition, the yidams of the Buddhist tradition, and the gods of many other traditions. If we want to connect with this realm of being we need to be very careful and disciplined.

At this point, you might be thinking, "Well, I'm perfectly rich and famous, why should I connect with this intermediate realm of gods or nature spirits?" It has to do with harmony, wholeness, and power. All traditions that recognize the intermediate realm also recognize the importance of connecting this realm with our life, because it is a part of our world. Just as, if we ignore our parents it brings disharmony in our hearts, so too if we ignore our helpers and partners in the other levels of reality, it brings disharmony and pain.

Very often in native traditions around the world, when there is disharmony in a village, or between two villages, the solution to the disharmony is to dance for the gods, and that brings harmony. Because the cause of the disharmony is the disruption of the relationship with the gods.

There is a very delightful story told by Richard Wilhelm, the first translator of the I Ching. Carl Jung liked this story a lot.

> *In Kiaochou came a great drought so that men and animals died in the hundreds. In despair, the citizens called for an old rainmaker who lived in the mountains nearby. Richard Wilhelm saw how the rainmaker was brought into town in a sedan chair, a tiny little gray-bearded man. He asked to be left alone outside the town in a little hut, and after three days it rained, and even snowed! Richard Wilhelm succeeded in being allowed to interview the old man and asked him how he made the rain. But he answered, "I haven't made the rain, of course not." And then, after a pause, he added, "You see it was like this—throughout the drought the whole of nature and all the men and women here were deeply disturbed. They were no longer in Tao. When I arrived here I became also disturbed. It was so bad that it took me three days to bring myself again into order." And then he added, with a smile, "Then naturally it rained."*

So this is the approach of bringing harmony to our society, amongst us, and between us, the earth, and the natural world. But connecting with the intermediate realm also brings power. If we really succeed in diminishing ourselves into the merely physical level of being—which apparently the modern world would like us to do—we will lose any power to build a good society, a good world. Human power comes from the fact that our own being *includes* the entire spectrum of the Great Chain of Being. Power comes, in other words, from our relation with the gods or goddesses.

Now, this is not necessarily a theistic statement. "Theistic" meaning a belief in a supreme all-powerful, transcendent creator God and Savior—so that the only way we can be saved is by believing in that thing. What I am saying is not theistic in that sense at all. What I am saying is that within this wonderful universe, of which we are a part, there is so much more than we normally perceive and feel. There is tremendous vitality and energy circulating around us all the time. We can bring that energy into our world, revitalize it, activate it.

So harmony and power are *why* we might want to make this connection. And basically *how* we do this is to appreciate the sacredness of the world. As you see from the discussion with Zoeteman, the intermediate level is the level of feeling, perception of the heart, passion. So we need to appreciate sacredness not merely as a nice idea but as *feeling,* in body, mind, heart. Appreciate that the world that we live in, every aspect of the world—the trees, the animals, the sky, the clouds, the mountains, the earth, the rocks—is alive, is living. Recognize that our world is imbued with living vital energy, through and through.

Appreciate this, join in this, be part of this living world—and then you will begin to attract the dralas. Appreciate time, the sacredness of time, moments in time. Appreciate place, or space—place is the reality of space. Appreciate passion—whatever your passion, whatever you love. First find what you love; and then do it, whatever it is. You won't harm anyone or anything if you actually love. Find your passion, express it, and that way you will attract the muses, the gods and goddesses of creativity.

A muse arrives when someone has been so wholehearted about their creative activity that they attract interest from the intermediate realm. When we are wholehearted, mind and body become one, heart becomes one, energy becomes unified and harmonized, and that is passion. When I say passion I don't mean purely sexual passion. If we think passion is purely sexual, then we are reducing ourselves to that materialist view. Passion is much more vast than that: passion comes when mind and body are one. And then, whatever it is we do—be it music or poetry or cooking or writing, or caring for dogs, or loving another person, or sitting looking out of the window at the weather—if we do this with love, then we may begin to feel the presence of the muse.

There are many examples of poets, composers, and ordinary

people experiencing their activities being empowered by muses. For example, Richard Strauss described how, "while the ideas were flowing in upon me, the entire musical, measure by measure, it seemed to me that I was dictated to by two wholly different Omnipotent Entities. . . . I was definitely conscious of being aided by more than an earthly Power, and it was responsive to my determined suggestions."

Giacomo Puccini said that the music of his opera *Madama Butterfly* "was dictated to me by God; I was merely instrumental in putting it on paper and communicating it to the public."

Poet Amy Lowell said, "Let us admit at once that a poet is something like a radio aerial—he is capable of receiving messages on waves of some sort; but he is more than an aerial, for he possesses the capacity of transmuting these messages into those patterns of words we call poems. . . . I do not hear a voice, but I do hear words pronounced, only the pronouncing is toneless. The words seem to be pronounced in my head, but with nobody speaking them."

Novelist Thomas Wolfe wrote, "I cannot really say the book was written. It was something that took hold of me and possessed me. . . . It was exactly as if this great black storm cloud had opened up and, amid flashes of lightning, was pouring from its depth a torrential and ungovernable flood. And I was borne along with it."

The English poet William Blake wrote that the poem *Milton* was written "from immediate dictation, twelve or twenty or thirty lines at a time, without premeditation, and even against my will."

There is a beautiful series of books that I strongly recommend by Tom Brown, Jr. The first one was called *Tracker*. When he was eight, he met an old Apache grandfather and his grandson. And he describes how the two boys would go out into the New Jersey Pine Barrens for days, just looking, watching the snow, and how the snow changed its quality as the day went by, and then the night. That's passion. It doesn't have to be dramatic, to watch the changing snow for hours and how the footprints of the birds in the snow changed as the day went by. Brown also describes meeting the nature spirits of the Pine Barrens in a very simple way.

Now, to return to the issue of sacredness and science education. First, I want to say that if we look back at the history of science, there is nothing whatsoever that actually shows that the intermediate realm does not exist. The destruction of our possibility of perceiving this intermediate realm in Western society came about for economic, religious, and political motives and forces. Beyond this, and more important, if you look at the totality of scientific understanding that has unfolded over the past half century, you will see that science could be just as compatible—if not more compatible—with a view that included sacredness and the all-pervasiveness of awareness. I will just mention here quantum theory, chaos and complexity theory, the biology of cooperation and large ecosystems, and the search for a theory of consciousness. All these areas of modern science have insights that clearly point to a view of mind and consciousness as not merely a product of the brain but in some way spread out through all of space.

Beyond this, there are actual experiments, conducted with all the controls and precision of excellent science, that suggest that in some sense mind, or awareness, or consciousness has a wavelike, space-pervading aspect. I want to mention a series of experiments taking place at Princeton University, in the aeronautical engineering department. There, for nearly twenty years, in a small laboratory called the Princeton Engineering Anomalies Research, or PEAR, laboratory, experiments have been conducted on psychokinesis and remote viewing, or clairvoyance. Psychokinesis is the ability of a human to affect the behavior of a machine simply through his or her intention—that is, without physical interaction with the machine. Remote viewing is the ability of someone in the laboratory to describe a scene that someone else is viewing many miles away.

The scientists deliberately did not choose subjects who claimed to have special "psychic" powers. They were looking for indications of an interconnection between consciousness and the physical world, not for any special human talents. Over the course of nearly twenty years, hundreds of ordinary people have visited PEAR and taken part in these experiments. The experiments at PEAR are carefully controlled.

There is no possibility for the operator to cheat or for some kind of hidden bias in the machine to create these results. In fact, the laboratory directors, Robert Jahn and Brenda Dunne, have considered every challenge by the skeptics and been at great pains to take all their concerns into account.

The upshot of all the psychokinesis work is that the PEAR laboratory has established with a very high degree of certainty that *awareness can influence physical reality*. The intention of a machine operator can indeed affect the output of a machine. Taking into account all the trials over the years, the probability that the effects are merely chance is around one in a million. This would be a remarkably high degree of certainty for *any* scientific experiment. Likewise, the remote viewing work showed beyond any reasonable doubt that ordinary people, not claiming to be "psychics," are capable of perceiving a remote scene through the eyes and mind of another.

The results of the PEAR work—as well as the work of other laboratories—confirm that there is a very real effect here. The experiments have been reproduced by 68 different investigators in a total of 597 experimental studies. It has been estimated that when the results of all these studies are included, the odds against chance being the explanation for them are astronomically high. Considering these experiments, and others like them, Jahn and Dunne put forward the suggestion that some aspects of mind must have fieldlike, or nonlocal, characteristics.

Science itself, then, can be seen as tending to the view that in some sense mind pervades all of space. And, since space pervades all of material things, we could say that these experiments, as well as the theories I mentioned above, point to the fact that all things from rocks to plants to animals to humans, to the gods, have some quality of awareness or inwardness.

I want to conclude by bringing us back to the issue of "spirituality in education." I hope I have begun to show you that the greatest obstacle to bringing spirituality into our educational system, into our schools, into the lives of our young people, is the way we teach science in school. The doctrine of materialism, which is fundamentally antispiritual, has become the dogma of our time. It is taught in precisely the same dogmatic manner as "religion" used to be taught. There is in our society and in our schools now an emphasis on blind faith in the "authority" of the science professionals, which seems little different from the emphasis on blind faith in the authority of priests a generation ago. In that sense science has become the "religion" of our time, not in the best sense of religion or science, of course, but in the worst sense of dogmatic insistence on blind faith and absence of open-minded questioning and exploration.

To bring spirituality back into education we must radically alter the way science is taught to science teachers, as well as to grade-school teachers. We need to teach true science, the spirit of inquiry and openness. We need to teach that the sciences of this century are in no way incompatible with a sacred world: a world in which matter and mind or spirit were never separate in the first place. And, as part of our training of teachers, we need to rediscover our own traditions of how to connect our mundane world with that inner world of gods and nature spirits, dralas, and muses. In that way we can again teach ourselves and our children to live in a sacred world of harmony and power.

II. IDENTITY

AS HIS HOLINESS the Dalai Lama has often pointed out, we are all the same "insofar as each of us desires happiness, and doesn't want suffering." Yet we live in different places—and in an infinite variety of ways: we each have our unique perspective on and experience of the world. We are the same and yet we are different. We are, as the poet e. e. cummings so wonderfully put it, "so both and oneful."

We are a mixture of senses, a mixture of emotions, and a mixture of perspectives. We might be children, partners, parents, students, and teachers—all of these and more—and all at once. Identities can shift as well: from one to another, from enemy to friend, and back again. In one way, identity is like a mirage—appearing yet somehow elusive. In another way, however, our *sense* of identity is something extremely important, even central, to us.

Our sense of identity can be established in two different ways: either from outside in or from inside out. What comes from outside in we understand as imposition or indoctrination. What emerges from inside out—arises out of our experience—we understand as expression.

A great irony is that while spiritual indoctrination, in particular, has been banned from our classrooms, indoctrination and imposition continue unimpeded. Students aren't indoctrinated into religious liturgy but instead into dualism, scientism, and most especially consumerism. We have been indoctrinated into a severely limited, materially biased worldview.

Rather than learning to nurture and preserve spirit, we learn to manipulate the world: to earn, store, and protect wealth. Rather than learning to be sensitive—understand and attend to the needs of others—we learn to want, rationalize, and do for ourselves. With the rise of a kind of "economic individualism" as our basic sense of identity has come the centralization of wealth and power, the loss of the commons, and the ravishing of the planet. The fact is, within our schools and culture, identity *is* being imposed: not spiritual identity but material identity. This sense of mistaken identity is reinforced by the media: advertising, newspapers, magazines, and especially television and film.

Our identities *are* being created from outside in. Beliefs, desires, and judgments are placed, undigested, in our minds. Our experience is constantly being mediated. Rather than taking in and exploring our experience, in so many cases we merely receive information from subsidiary sources as concepts. Conceptual understanding—a specific kind of intelligence—is important, yet it offers us only a biased, partial picture of the world. Unfortunately, with education often reduced to the transfer of bite-sized images and information, the education of our senses, our sense of attention, and our awareness dwindle. Our sense of the community of all beings is lost as well.

We find ourselves faced with an identity crisis. We are not quite sure of who or what we are, or where we fit in a bigger picture. Many of us have no big picture at all. We have lost touch with the sustaining qualities of spirit, community, and the earth. We have no notion of inner landscape, or inner lives. We don't see or understand the impact of our actions on others, and on the planet. We have become desensitized to violence, unmoved in the face of suffering. We experience a huge gulf between ourselves and others. We experience identity at best as individuality, and at worst as isolation and loneliness.

This gulf is like a vacuum that buffers or protects our collapsed sense of identity. In this state, we still have experience, ideas, and feelings, but are contracted and withdrawn. Invisible walls—conceptual, emotional, psychic—have been erected between our sense of who we are and our sense of the outside world. Instead of looking inside to our awareness and feelings, or in between at the actual quality of our relationships and interactions, we simply look out at surfaces: across an apparent gulf between us and the things of the world.

This gulf—perversely—fulfills a need: it enables us to feel more secure in the face of change and groundlessness. It protects our collapsed identity. It gives us a sense of control—that we *know:* know what's coming, know our place, know what to expect. This insulation, however, comes with a price. In return for the illusion of safety, and the seeming solidity of identity, we trade in full contact with the world.

Education within the spiritual and contemplative traditions is very much about seeing the *permeability* of the barriers between self and other, and opening us to the point where there is real presence, interaction, and engagement with the world. Certain religions teachings use specific words or concepts, but the processes can be quite similar. The maxim of Rabbi Hillel teaches to "love thy neighbor as thyself." Buddhism teaches the practice of "exchanging self and other." The Iroquois tradition teaches the concept of "all my relations." In each of these cases, the teachings point us towards a greater sense of awareness, identification, and responsibility.

Specific practices which develop body and mind awareness—meditation, yoga, tai chi, aikido, shamanic practices, and so on—have evolved around the world, and been taught as ways to open to the world. These disciplines can assist us in moving through blocks; experiencing the flow of spirit; becoming more aware of subtle and gross blockages; and filtering preconceptions, prejudices, or habits.

Sadly, our current education system, rather than cultivating our sense of openness and engagement, instead heightens our feelings of isolation and insulation. Schooling, especially as inculturation, *builds up* preconceptions, expectations, and rigid notions of order and behavior. It *breaks down* our experience of an alive whole into an endless array of categories, taxonomies, concepts, criteria, and evaluative judgments. These categories are then studied, almost exclusively, using conceptual and material approaches.

Through approaching the world in this fashion, with each year of schooling our spirit, and the sense of aliveness and richness of the world, deflate. This should not be the case. Children and adults should continue to learn and grow throughout their lives, eventually becoming what some traditions refer to as elders or wisdom keepers.

By learning to see through the sense of separation—moving from identity as conception to identity as expression—the view of dualism, of isolation, is cut. Grounded in the actual experience of identification with wholeness, the view of the sacred begins to emerge. Viewing the world as whole, one begins to feel *a part* of something rather than *apart* from something. Feeling a part of the world creates a sense of place and relationship. Feeling in place and relationship begins to nurture the spirit. Nurtured spirit, then, begins to grow, and grow outward.

The question that remains within the practice of education is "How do we establish or support the formation of inner spiritual identity without resorting to indoctrination or imposition of ideology?" The answer is simply to ground education within experience. Examining closely our perceptions, emotions, and beliefs—our experience—awareness and insight naturally arise. We are already endowed with the qualities of seeing, recognizing, feeling, and knowing. Spiritual identity arises in and of itself from identification with experience rather than submission to a particular set of concepts or beliefs.

Schools should in no way enforce an inner life, yet by the same token they should not completely ignore it. Ignoring spirit—removing it from inquiry—banishes a very significant portion of not only human history but also human experience. Students—just as they are encouraged to think abstractly—should be encouraged to see, smell, hear, touch, and taste. We should learn not only how to experience outside with our senses but also to see with the eye of the mind, to feel with the heart, to find and learn to see with the eye of the spirit. Along our path of learning, we should consider not only *material* material but also the emotional and the spiritual. This work—understanding ourselves, others, our nature, our place in, and our effect on the world—is crucial work; it is the real challenge of education; it *needs* to be done within our schools, within our lives, and throughout our lives.

The world is rich, complex, multifaceted. Our personal experience mirrors this complexity. Our sense of who and what we are mirrors this complexity as well. A sense of identity is illusive, shimmering. Thus, each chapter in this section approaches identity from a different vantage point. His Holiness the Dalai Lama begins by focusing on the ways in which we are all the *same:* we are the same in that we are human beings; we are the same in wanting happiness and not wanting suffering; we are the same in experiencing the vicissitudes of happiness and suffering. Moving forward from this notion of commonality, His Holiness advocates a notion of identity based in the practice of mutual recognition and respect. Judith Simmer-Brown raises issues not merely about how we are different but about how we experience *difference.* She exposes the different strategies we use to lessen the discomfort of difference—the rub between identities. Judith advocates an approach which is engaged: which meets and explores difference openly and fully, without escaping into the safety of concept or judgment. bell hooks moves from the inner experience of difference to our experience of *interaction* in a shared world. She challenges us to bring our notion of identity completely on the spot—completely open and vulnerable to the direct experience of here and now. Identity, for bell, is something that arises spontaneously, in communion with others.

How we answer the question of identity is crucial for this moment, for our time. Issues around difference, gender, race, religion, and multiculturalism abound. The amount of difference that we can meet is growing and growing. With the globalization of technology and the economy, the effect that we have on each other and the planet is escalating. The hidden chains of cause and effect behind each interaction are vast. We can ill afford to hide behind distance, objectification, abstraction, and fear. We must be willing to really look, really see, really feel. Dare we?

5.

EDUCATION AND
THE HUMAN HEART

His Holiness the Dalai Lama

Tenzin Gyatso, His Holiness the fourteenth Dalai Lama, is the spiritual and temporal leader of the Tibetan people. He fled Tibet during the Chinese occupation of 1959 and, since then, has resided in Dharamsala, India, the seat of the Tibetan government in exile. Among his many publications are *Kindness, Clarity and Insight* and *A Policy of Kindness*. In 1989, His Holiness the Dalai Lama was awarded the Nobel Prize for Peace.

WHAT IS THE PURPOSE of our life? Of course, I believe that it is happiness. Our culture, our education, our economy—all human activities—should be meant for that goal. Nothing else. However, although we often assume that certain activities will enable us to achieve this goal of happiness, in reality, we are often deceived by our own ignorance or shortsightedness. Although each individual wants happiness, nobody wants suffering, and all beings are trying to achieve a state of happiness, ignorance and shortsightedness often lead us astray or cause us to apply a faulty method. Ignorance causes pain and suffering not only for ourselves but for others as well.

Therefore, in order to eliminate ignorance, education, no doubt, becomes very important. But even as knowledge can be very helpful, I think a good heart, a warm heart, can expel this shortsightedness. If one looks at a very particular or limited area, and says, "I am only responsible for this much"—and does not bother to consider the consequences of one's actions on the larger community—this is where problems begin. However, by keeping this in mind, and actually *taking care* of others—the larger community—we can eliminate the various problems that arise from narrow-mindedness, shortsightedness and extreme selfishness. Despite the apparent self-interest of these views, none of these approaches actually helps a person or a community achieve the goal of happiness.

Thinking along these lines, you will come to realize that what we call love and compassion are not necessarily a religious matter. Love and compassion are basic necessities of life—not only for the individual but also for society.

A thousand years ago on the European continent, separate distinct educational institutions first began to appear. Until that time, the churches and monasteries served as the educational institutions. Even with the founding of these new specialized institutions, the church and monastery still had great influence on society. The religious institutions maintained the responsibility to look after the development of "a good heart," for teaching compassion and other human and spiritual values. The educational institutions were left alone to concentrate on the knowledge side, on fostering intellectual development.

Consequently, during that time, the responsibility carried by each one of the two types of institutions was insufficient in itself—the two institutions together were necessary. As time went on, however, the influence of the religious side waned: more and more people took less and less interest in the religious traditions and values. As a result, the society gradually lost the realization of the importance of love and compassion, and a sense of forgiveness. These things were neglected.

Furthermore, with the advancements and development of science and technology, people began to develop an increased expectation or belief that all problems could be solved through technological means. This attitude is another factor which contributed to the negligence in general about the importance of cultivating inner values.

The society of today—this generation—despite its material development and wealth of material facilities and resources, is *still* faced with many difficulties. Clearly something is lacking. Of course, our education facilities are very good and also, generally speaking, the educational standards are fine. The economy is strong, and, generally speaking, there is a high standard of living. While of course there are some pockets of people for whom this is not the case, in large part this is true. We can imagine that if someone were to come visit from a very poor, underdeveloped country, and were thrown into a materially affluent society like the United States, they might feel puzzled. They would see a lot of material affluence—almost all the comforts one could want. But despite this outer material wealth, they would still see unhappiness, the inner longing. They would initially think, "Why are people still unhappy?" I think they would truly be puzzled.

In the 1960s, about one thousand Tibetans immigrated to Switzerland. When they first settled there, some people began to say, "Oh, this is really the land of Sukhavati," of heaven. Some thought that their prayers had been answered to be reborn in heaven. In fact, some made claims that they had been able to be reborn in the pure land without even having to die or change their lives! But eventually, as time went on, people got a clearer picture of what was underneath the initial appearances. These very same people now express to me their intention to return to India. They say, "Oh, this is a nice place for making money, but not a nice place to die." I use this as an example to say this: Material comfort alone is not sufficient. We are more than our material identity, and other values—human and spiritual values—are very important as well.

From my rough impression of the Western educational system, although it is very impressive to see the high standard of the facilities, the many material resources, and the perfection of so many different aspects of intellectual development, the thing that seems to be lacking is the dimension of enhancing and developing the heart. The questions we must ask are how to promote these other human values. How to teach the development of a good heart?

I think one point that it is necessary to make perfectly clear is this: When we talk about trying to promote a sense of caring or compassion, forgiveness and loving-kindness, these values are not particularistic: These values are important to all the major world religious traditions. It is, therefore, necessary to understand that as we promote these different human values, we are not trying to promote a specific religious faith. I believe that religious faith is a matter of individual freedom. Whether you choose to have a religion or not is an individual right, an individual choice. When one tries to promote a religious faith, it becomes complicated—very complicated. If, for example, one believes in the Buddhist teachings and tries to propagate Buddhism, this might perhaps make others feel awkward. Or someone else, trying to convert a Buddhist, might make the Buddhist feel very uncomfortable.

In Mongolia—traditionally a Buddhist country—some Christian missionaries have begun to do some mission work. The results have been a lot of discomfort. In my own experience, when I give a lecture on Buddhism in a Western country, a Christian or Judeo-Christian country, I usually feel very uncomfortable, even reluctant. I believe that it is much better to follow or keep your own religious tradition and values. It's much better. It's safer. If you change your religion due to some outside factors, or for some immediate causes or conditions, the result might be that you only find more confusion. That's not helpful. So in order to be respectful, and in order to promote these important human values to all people, the method of using a particular religious faith is not very appropriate.

So what is the other option? I think the best thing is to develop secular ethics. Simply make clear the essential human values: a warm heart, a sense of caring for one another. Make these things clear. These values can be taught without referring to a religious point of view. They can be taught using secular arguments. For example, basic to human nature is that we are social animals. We can't survive as single persons, without the company of others. Although when we find ourselves in the company of even a small group of just two or three people, we often end up quarreling or disagreeing, the fundamental fact of our existence is that we need these individuals—the objects of our complaints, quarrels and disagreements—for our very survival.

These individuals are necessary for our being; they are indispensable. Therefore, learning to care for others is a key point in our survival.

Then, from another point of view, modern medical science is beginning to recognize that peace of mind is a very crucial factor in good health. The most important sources of inner peace are an open mind and a good heart. There is no question about this. A compassionate attitude, an affectionate attitude, a sense of caring therefore is not only of benefit to society but also of benefit to oneself—to one's health. An open mind and heart generate immense benefit.

On the other hand, hatred and ill feeling not only create pain for others, they also cause suffering for oneself. If we carry in our minds and hearts ill feeling or hatred or jealousy, we feel these as real emotional and physical discomforts: we lose our appetites, lose sleep and begin to rely more and more on things like tranquilizers, sleeping pills, alcohol or drugs. If one has lost the inner ability to sustain peace of mind, happiness or joyfulness, then regardless of the external circumstances, you will find these people seeking some sort of refuge outside of themselves, in drugs or alcohol, things like that. These are very limited remedies; once one becomes stuck within a false refuge, refuge within limited circumstances, there are few options left. Therefore, I think it is a mistake to rely too much on external means of finding happiness while completely neglecting our inner life—our inner potential and our inner resources.

Negative emotions, too, can be very harmful for one's self, one's body and one's mental well-being. Negative emotions can destroy or spoil all of our opportunities for the future. On the other hand, an open heart, a warm heart, will bring more smiles, more friends, more reliable friends, and in that way more good fortune in life.

If you have devoted your life to meaningful activities—have been motivated by a sense of caring—then I think that when the last moment of your life comes, you will have no regrets. You might think, "Now I am dying. My life is ending here and now, but I have no regrets. During my lifetime, I made every activity I was a part of both purposeful and meaningful." But if your whole life has been spent under the influence of hatred, anger, jealousy, greed or discontent, with all energies being expended to acquire more—more things, more money—then at that moment, when the moment of death comes, what use is this? I think at that moment, one will feel great regret, great remorse.

If you look at a neighbor, who may be poor but who is in a home that is full of human feeling, human warmth and human affection, then you will see on the faces of the parents and children more smiles. This is good, and good education. Although they may not be rich, they have learned that true wealth is happiness. Another neighbor might own a big house and a big car and occasionally hold a big party, with many important persons in fine dress. But if inside that house the day is full of hatred—full of competition, fear, doubt and jealousy—then that family, in spite of all of the fascinating possessions and good fortune, may not be a happy family at all. That person, though rich, may not have the true wealth of happiness.

Judging from this reality, we can conclude that our inner peace is something really priceless, really precious. You cannot go and ask a doctor for a compassion pill. Nor can you buy happiness at a supermarket with a big check. No: Everything that is really precious is right here, in our hearts. Everything is already right here. Our parents, in giving us this life, also gave us this potential. We need to recognize and realize this inner potential. I think it's up to us, through education, to explain and teach this potential—inner peace.

Through education we can explain to our brothers, sisters and especially the young children that there is a secret treasure that we all have—whether educated or uneducated, rich or poor, this race or that race, of this culture or that culture: we are human beings. We have tremendous potential. The potentials for kindness, compassion and inner peace. Then, we can try to teach or promote the basic human values that I call secular ethics.

Though we cannot force others to become warmhearted, we can teach them, help them discover the value of being warmhearted for themselves. We can't enforce this, but we can explain it to everyone.

Everyone wants happiness and a successful life. There's no question about this, is there? We need to make clear to them the most basic, effective ways or means to achieve a happy and successful life. It is my belief that the most practical way to achieve happiness is to open our minds to the awareness and importance of our inner potentials.

Then, for people who have a particular religious faith, they may live according to their chosen religion. For others different approaches may be helpful. Basically, religions can be divided into two groups. One group, including Judaism, Christianity, Islam and some ancient Indian traditions, I call God religions. Their fundamental faith is in a creator. The other group of religious traditions, including Jainism and Buddhism, I call godless religions. The latter do not believe in a creator. If God is understood as a sense of infinite love then the religions are not so different. But if God is understood in the sense of the creator—something absolute—then that is difficult for a Buddhist to accept. According to some people, the godless religions are more effective; according to other people the God religions are more effective. No matter: the position is individual, it is a matter of personal choice.

However, once one accepts a particular religious faith, it is not sufficient just to claim oneself to be a Buddhist, a Christian, a Muslim or a Jew. Claiming membership like that is not sufficient. In accepting religion, one should implement the religious values sincerely— twenty-four hours a day—so that religious practice and faith are truly part of one's life. Religion is something like medicine. When pains come, when illnesses come, then we apply medicine. When there's no pain, we don't need the medicine. Similarly, during the twenty-four hours of our day, when the negative emotions come—when the mischievous thoughts and activities come around—that is the moment that our religious discipline must be there. When things are okay, when everything is pleasant, it's easy to say a mantra, to do some meditation or practice patience. However, if someone comes to us, uses harsh words, and we completely forget about meditation or tolerance and just argue back, what use is that? That is not religion.

So as we begin to implement these things seriously, we should keep our focus on the transformation of our minds. Changing our minds is not easy. It will take time. Right from the beginning, we need a long-term plan. We should not expect that we can, in a few days or weeks, complete this transformation. That is wrong. It is unrealistic. Transformation requires constant effort, without losing determination. Through mental training and constant effort, however, positive transformation will certainly take place.

QUESTION: This question has to do with our young people. They are often filled with passivity, despair or nihilism. They feel that this culture has nothing to offer them. Many of the most intelligent ones simply withdraw from school. Others are destructive to others, or self-destructive. Do you have any advice on how we can approach and work with young people who are so distressed?

HIS HOLINESS THE DALAI LAMA: Of course, each individual case will have different factors involved; and in order to be able to effectively deal with these problems, one has to be sensitive to the individual circumstances, context and so forth. But a fundamental belief that I have is to find some way of giving the individual a sense of hope: somehow helping them believe in their own inner potentials.

Another very important factor is the atmosphere in which the children grow up—particularly in the formative stage, from birth through the first year and a half. We need to carefully create the right atmosphere within the family environment for children to grow in. Also, it is my own religious belief that many of the problems we face in the present have their roots in the past. This includes our negligence of conditions created in the past. Karma is infallible: when the karmic potentials have come into fruition, at that particular point there isn't much one can do. One can learn from this kind of ripening experience, however, and develop full recognition of the fact of karma.

Being mindful of this we can become more mindful of our future actions and interactions.

QUESTION: I hear you saying that the family is very important. In our society, families are in a state of great stress: oftentimes both parents work, children are sent to child care before they've learned to walk or talk and so on. Do you have any suggestion on how we can begin to strengthen our families?

HIS HOLINESS THE DALAI LAMA: That is a very difficult question. Sometimes I have the feeling that if we look at the lifestyle of an individual living in modern industrialized society, one gets the impression that because of the overreliance on the external means of solving problems, there has arisen a kind of instrumental attitude even towards other human beings, viewing even human beings as some kind of object.

So when that way of looking at human beings becomes extended, pervasive, then, of course, it is very easy to just leave a child somewhere—like an object you leave under someone's care. Through this approach, it seems that human beings become more and more alienated from their basic human nature.

It also feels, in contemporary society, that almost every aspect of individual lives has become mechanized; it's as if we've become just a tiny part of a big clock or a machine. And so when the clock, or the machine, moves, we move too: we have no real control or choice. But the problem is, what can we do about this? The scope of this problem is so enormous that it is not something that can "just be fixed." Fixing this means overhauling our whole way of looking at the world, and being in the world.

One factor which I believe is probably very crucial here is to somehow try to restore a greater appreciation of the human touch within one's life. We mustn't forget that where we find ourselves now—modern, industrialized society—is the product of a gradual, ongoing process, and that many results of the process were not consciously planned. Originally, the plan may have been about industrialized development or economic development, but the results obtained were different, or mixed. This is not to say that science and technology are in themselves negative or destructive—but as a result of not really thinking about the wider ramifications of these changes, we find ourselves in this situation today. Given these complex forces, we have to appreciate that change is not going to be a simple task.

QUESTION: You talked about secular ethics as a way of trying to cultivate human warmth and goodness—not necessarily in a religious way. In the Buddhist tradition, there are specific practices to develop compassion, like *tonglen* (a particular kind of meditation). Within a secular context, how can people develop their warm heart?

HIS HOLINESS THE DALAI LAMA: Within the context of secular ethics, the emphasis really should be placed on the immediate benefits—not only for the society but also for the individual himself or herself. This means there is no need to invoke religious concepts like rebirth, karma and so on. If our approach is to convince someone of the value of love and compassion on the grounds that it is meritorious—that it will reap benefits in a future life—that is a religious approach. Whereas, if you say that by cultivating love, you yourself will enjoy a happy life, a contented life—that is a secular approach.

QUESTION: I find personally that if I believe that compassion is important, that's all well and good. But I also have to do practice. I have to do *tonglen* or my heart stays hard. Do you feel that with secular ethics it's enough to have the right view? Or does there need to be an actual practice to develop compassion?

HIS HOLINESS THE DALAI LAMA: Yes, there would need to be parallel practical approaches within the secular context. One could call these reflections. They might be mental exercise to convince oneself of the value of compassion and love: that love and compassion are fundamental human values; that they are expressions of our deeper nature; that they are beneficial to one's health; that they are beneficial for other fellow beings. One might also reflect upon stories of individuals whose lives either testify to the value of love and compassion, or testify to the shortcomings of hatred, anger and so forth. These could be justifiably called meditations—analytical meditations.

6.

COMMITMENT AND OPENNESS: A CONTEMPLATIVE APPROACH TO PLURALISM

Judith Simmer-Brown

Judith Simmer-Brown serves as chair of the religious studies department of The Naropa Institute. Trained in South Asian religious studies and Sanskrit at Columbia University, she is on the board of the Society for Buddhist-Christian Studies. Before coming to Naropa, Judith taught at Fordham and Western Washington Universities. She is completing a book titled *Dakini's Warm Breath: Feminine Principle in Tibetan Buddhism.*

ONE HUNDRED AND FOUR YEARS AGO, the city of Chicago hosted the World's Columbian Exposition in honor of the four hundredth anniversary of Columbus's "discovery" of America. In conjunction, the World Parliament of Religions was planned as a conversation "higher and nobler," exploring the foundations of religious unity in the world. The Protestant hosts invited presenters from all the major world religions; and those present were exposed—most for the first time—to Hinduism, Buddhism, Islam, and other Asian religions.

The purpose of the parliament was, according to reports, "to indicate the impregnable foundations of Theism,"[1] especially to prove the superiority of the Christian religion. What occurred, however, was much more significant: white American Protestants met Buddhists, African-Americans, Hindus, Muslims, and Jews, and found them powerful, worthy of respect, and remarkable. What occurred has been called the "dawn of religious pluralism" in America: the first time that mainstream America really looked at the question of difference in religion, acknowledged there were actually a variety of different religious paths, and realized that the superiority of Christianity was not obvious to everyone.

Now, at the end of the twentieth century, as we look forward to the next, we realize that we have only begun to digest the power of pluralism. A major task before us in the twenty-first century—indeed the next millennium—is to learn to fully engage diversity, plurality, and pluralism in our religious lives. For contemplatives, pondering pluralism is essential to the integrity of our spiritual journey. I would like to suggest that we cannot consider ourselves contemplatives without pluralism at the heart of our spiritual practice and lives.

When we talk about religious pluralism, we are speaking of an encounter with difference or otherness—in whatever religious form it may take. Raimundo Panikkar, who has done a great deal of work on interreligious dialogue, says that "What to do with the barbarian?" is the central question for religion in the time of pluralism.[2] We all have some notion of "barbarian" in our minds: some presence, some person, or some tradition that appears barbarian to us. In practicing religious pluralism, we ask the question "How is it that we make a relationship with that which is other or different from ourselves?"

When we encounter the "other," we often encounter the power of the hidden wound of society as well. There is in our culture an unacknowledged inwardness: a woundedness we carry around with us both individually and collectively. Our usual strategy is to project this woundedness outward, onto those who are different from us, and then become alienated and fearful of this other. This can be seen again and again in our society in discrimination based on race, sex, ethnicity, class, age. Because of this wound, however, an encounter with other can carry an additional power (and wisdom too) that we have not yet acknowledged.

In the area of religious pluralism, I have been most moved by the writing of Diana Eck, professor of religion at Harvard University and director of the Harvard Pluralism Project. She wrote an essay called "Is Our God Listening?"[3] in which she raised questions concerning the challenges of pluralism. Diana Eck is a Christian who has devoted her scholarly work to a study of Indian religions, especially Hinduism, and to religious pluralism. In her essay, she described three possible stances regarding religious diversity and spiritual community: exclusivism, inclusivism, and pluralism.

Exclusivism is the stance that "my community, my tradition and set of values, are the only correct ones, excluding all others." We are familiar with this approach in the religious right in conservative Christianity, but are unaware of how it prevails within contemplative traditions in America as well. In the climate of contemporary American spirituality this view sometimes surfaces as "My practice and my teacher have presented the true way—the rest of you are to be pitied for not having met or studied with him." In the interaction of world religions, this approach has led at best to peaceful coexistence, and at worst to violent clashes and centuries-long warfare of which we are painfully familiar. What about the peaceful coexistence of contemplatives? In our communities, how much do we maintain a surface respect while privately denigrating each other?

Inclusivism suggests that there are many religions, communities, and nations, all with important values and truths, but "my own religion's way of seeing things is superior to all others, the final truth. In fact, my own way is so profound it can *include* all other approaches as valuable but lesser elements."

As an example, a dogmatic Buddhist-inclusivist position might say "Insofar as other religions reflect the values of Buddhism, they are valid. Christ was great because he was a bodhisattva; or Christian love is a pale expression of what Buddhists call compassion. But it was the Buddha who became enlightened and who really understood how it all fit together." This approach may at first seem superior to exclusivism, but a subtle and pervasive chauvinism is always translating, and always dominating.

Pluralism suggests that spiritual truth is not exclusively (or inclusively, for that matter) possessed by any single religious lineage, community, text, or teacher. Pluralism recognizes that there are truths in the many religious traditions of the world, and the range and expression of these truths is a cause for engagement and conversation. Indeed, the varieties of religious expression can pique our interest and curiosity—rather than our dogmatism—and be the occasion for celebration of the richness of the feast the world has to offer.

This is a shift in paradigms in religious understanding. Our customary stance with regard to the spiritual path is to fall into either of two extremes. First, we may feel fervently connected to a particular path—in a style similar to exclusivism or inclusivism. Or we may conclude that, given the diversity of religious truths, it is impossible to commit to a single perspective. The pluralistic path resides in between these two stances. Pluralism acknowledges and relates to one of the most threatening aspects of human life: otherness, or difference.[4]

In a pluralistic setting, relationship is transformed: it is the genuine meeting of two people or two traditions, for whom the common ground is uncharted. On such sacred ground, customary assumptions and power plays hold no sway for a time; we open with curiosity to the realities for another person and tradition. This is a simple notion, but deeply radical in the encounter of spiritualities and religious traditions.

It is important that we understand what pluralism is not. As Eck explains, *pluralism is not diversity*. Diversity is a fact of modern life, especially in America. There are tremendous differences in our communities—ethnically, racially, religiously. Diversity suggests the *fact* of such differences. Pluralism, on the other hand, is a response to the fact of diversity. In pluralism, we commit to *engage* with the other person or the other community. Pluralism is a commitment to communicate with and relate to the larger world— with a very different neighbor, or a distant community.

Pluralism is also not relativism. When we encounter difference, or diversity, it is tempting to shrug our shoulders and proclaim, "There is no truth which can be discovered: all truths are relative. Every religion or spirituality represents a particular, limited context; and none of them have real ultimacy. It really doesn't matter which path we are on, or indeed if we are on any one of them at all."

The most serious flaw in relativism is its tendency to see commitment to specificity as incompatible with an acceptance of diversity. Unfortunately, relativism pervades religious studies departments. Professors have studied enough religion to understand diversity, and sometimes suggest that it is pointless to practice religion anymore. When this occurs, university religious studies training becomes deeply cynical about the whole endeavor of spirituality and religion. This is not the pluralism of which we speak; pluralism embraces spirituality and religious life through commitment, community, and engagement with others.

Pluralism is also not syncretism. Syncretism cannot tolerate difference, and so two traditions or truths get blended together, mixed, creating a new, unified system. Many of the spiritual teachings of the New Age fall into this category, weaving together Native American ritual, Buddhist meditation, Oriental medicine, and Hindu yoga into a new, creatively expressed movement.

This is an approach which avoids the challenges of diversity through homogenizing and blending difference into a single path. This is not pluralism. Instead, pluralism respects the differences which reside in the variety of religious traditions, without reconciling or integrating those differences into a single path. Pluralism is willing to rest in the ambiguity of religious difference. From this point of view, pluralism is a very courageous practice, an engagement with the fact of diversity in our world.

CONTEMPLATIVE PLURALISM: COMMITMENT AND OPENNESS

How might a contemplative respond to the challenges of pluralism? By contemplative, I mean one for whom ultimate reality is discovered in the heart of one's own experience. For the contemplative, spirituality is more important than religion; meditation and prayer are more central than doctrine; journey is more important than goal. I would like to suggest that pluralism provides an ideal ground for the development of the contemplative path, for it challenges us to "commitment without dogmatism and community without communalism,"[5] in the words of Diana Eck.

From a contemplative perspective, why would we engage with a pluralistic perspective? For sometimes it seems we are interested in pluralism because of guilt; we are moved by past prejudices and insensitivities which we would like to overcome or erase. We are moved by the desire for justice. But this is not a good enough reason. If we bring guilt to the pluralistic question, our encounter will be subject to merely moralistic concerns, and keep us from the depths of real transformation. Engaging with pluralism is necessary for our spiritual development—and for the further spiritual development of the world.

Our contemplative path cannot be insular. We must be open to the varieties of the world, to being touched by what we encounter, to being transformed. If we draw a rigid boundary around ourselves, our contemplative development is over: contemplative practice becomes formula, dogma, ritual, institution. When we encounter the "other"—that which we have ignored, excluded, or just not known—we have the opportunity to question our conventional minds, to expand our horizons, and go deep. The "other" is our greatest teacher. The contemplative, I would submit, needs pluralism in order to remain authentic.

A contemplative approach to pluralism begins with commitment to a particular spiritual path. By commitment, I do not mean a profession of faith. Faith professions have the problem that they are based in concept and ideology, and place doctrine above experience—a stance which is contrary to the contemplative life. Rather, for the contemplative, commitment has to do with experience: with trusting in what we learn or experience directly, what we know personally. In the Dzogchen tradition of Tibet, "deciding on this alone" is one of the key foundations of the meditation journey.[6]

"Deciding on this alone" means that when we sit down to meditate, contemplate, or pray, we are willing to commit to that situation and whatever it brings up. We are willing to be present with our doubts, distractions, and emotional attacks, and open to the process and to what unfolds. This means commitment to our practice or discipline becoming the center of our lives, the venue for discovery and transformation.

We find this out over and over again in the sitting practice of meditation. When we sit down and sit still, whatever we have been holding at bay—whatever it is that we would rather not acknowledge or deal with—comes right at us. When the Buddha, sitting under the tree of enlightenment, was attacked by Maras, these were not foreign beings but rather aspects of his own mind and the world in which he lived. He was able to remain there because of his commitment to sit still until his confusion had vanished, to sit until he completely understood the flows and patterns of his mind and life.

Several days ago, at an audience with His Holiness the Dalai Lama, I was delighted to ask the question: "How can we, at The Naropa Institute, counteract sectarianism in the world?" He answered, "The first thing we must do is practice deeply." It is true, we need to find a way to get deep. We have to get beyond concept—that's what I mean by going deep—beyond belief, beyond religious tenet or dogma, beyond ideas that we hold that we have just sort of borrowed from someone else. We need to get deep into the heart of our experience, to the things that we really know.

There is an example that has been used a great deal: if we want to go deep spiritually, we can't go around and dig lots of little holes. We need to find one place and dig a deep hole. And so as contemplatives, we need to find in our own experience what it is—what practice it is, what approach it is—that takes us deep in this way. So when I talk about commitment, I'm talking about commitment to practice, to engaging our direct experience.

The second point of pluralism is openness. For the contemplative, openness is implicit in the practice of meditation or contemplative prayer; and it is openness which draws us more deeply into our experience and our hearts. But it is important that this openness draws us out into engagement with diversity, with difficulty, and all the rough edges in the suffering world.

When His Holiness the Dalai Lama answered the question about how to counteract sectarianism in the world, he said first we must practice deeply. Then he suggested that we have contact with others, and suggested five ways we could initiate such contact. The first way was to invite the scholars from other traditions to Naropa. The second way was to talk intimately with real practitioners from another tradition. The third way was to go on pilgrimage to sacred sites with people from different traditions. The fourth was to get religious leaders from different traditions together for simple, superficial conversation—he said it's good for people just to see them getting together, it doesn't even matter what they say. And finally, to encourage people from different traditions to do socially engaged work together.

These are fabulous, creative suggestions. But the main point is this: opening up, having contact with others, engaging each other, really connecting, and cultivating intimacy which does not annihilate difference. Thomas Merton in 1968 went to Asia with great excitement. During his journey, he kept a journal of his encounters with Asian teachers, which has been published as his *Asian Journals*. In an October 1968 entry, shortly before his accidental death by electrocution in a Thai hotel room, he wrote:

> *I think we have now reached a stage of long overdue religious maturity at which it may be possible for someone to remain perfectly faithful to a Christian and Western monastic commitment and yet to learn in depth from, say, a Buddhist or Hindu discipline and experience. I believe that some of us need to do this in order to improve the quality of our own monastic life.*[7]

This is a perfect expression of the pluralistic combination of commitment and openness which Merton most enthusiastically embodied.

This is mirrored in Buddhism by another saying from the Dzogchen meditation tradition. If we think of spiritual journey in terms of climbing a mountain, the slogan says "we ascend from below with our practice." This means that with our meditation practice we begin very humbly, relating to the details, committing to our experience as we have discussed. But, simultaneously "we descend from above with a vast view."[8] This means that our guiding principle must be the infinite expanse, without limitation or bias. When we do this, there is no prejudice, sectarianism, or criticism of any kind. In the context of vastness, who can say what tradition is best or worst, who is enlightened and who is not? Our view must be open in this way.

When we ascend from below with our practice while descending from above with a vast view, we can practice pluralism with a contemplative perspective. This requires of us a willingness to embrace ambiguity. This is very different from contemporary American education. At least in my case, in my undergraduate and in particular my graduate studies, I studied and learned other people's theories in order to make up a theory of my own. I was encouraged to hold and defend a particular theory or fixed point of view. I mean, to get a Ph.D. in America, you have to have a theory no one else has had, and then spend the rest of your academic life defending it. This methodology is contrary to the kind of discipline involved in contemplative practice: the willingness to drop theory in order to experience more fully the actual flow of what one knows. And this means times of tremendous uncertainty; of simply not knowing; of experimentation; of floating. Embracing ambiguity is essential for our educational experience.

As educators, one of the best things that we can do for our students is to not force them into holding theories and solid concepts but rather to actually encourage the process, the inquiry involved, and the times of not knowing—with all of the uncertainties that go along with that. This is really what supports going deep. This is openness.

GROWING INTO PLURALISM:
THE DAKINI REVEALS THE ESSENCE

This is a grand vision, but how do we actually accomplish it? We begin at the beginning, which means that we emulate the great teachers of the past who learned the hard way. I'd like us to investigate two examples of engaging the other from the tradition of Tibetan Buddhism.

These examples are drawn from the literature concerning the *dakini,* a sky-dancing woman who appears in prophetic, instructive visions for the Tibetan Buddhist practitioner.[9] She appears in the famous biographies of Tibetan yogis of old, as a meditational deity in the practices of contemporary practitioners, and some say she appears in our everyday lives as the unexpected woman who speaks the truth to our opinionated, speedy minds. The dakini symbolizes the ancient, intuitive wisdom of the heart of the world which is missed in the merely intellectual or technical mastery. Her wisdom is necessary on the path to enlightenment—yet cannot be taught by conventional methods. For this reason, dakinis appear to great meditators at key points in their practice to point out the essence.

It is significant that dakinis are female, because in institutional life in patriarchal cultures like India and Tibet (and the West too) women are so often excluded. Because of this, dakinis hold the key to "otherness," the shadow and wound which must be included to puncture the merely conventional mind. Women play the role of holders of the forgotten wisdom in patriarchal culture; and in Tibetan Buddhism, one must always pay attention to this wisdom.

For the first dakini story, I would like to turn to the life story of the great Indian Buddhist teacher Naropa. Naropa was an erudite professor of the eleventh century, accomplished in scripture, debate, and commentary. He was a monk renowned for purity and refinement, and a scholar with many accolades. In spite of his achievements, however—or perhaps because of them—he was arrogant, aloof, and finicky.

As he labored over his texts in the dim light of his monastic cell at Nalanda University, a terrifying shadow fell over his books. He turned to find a horrible old woman standing before him, displaying thirty-seven ugly features. It is significant that this was a vision of a decrepit old woman, the emblem of all that was counter to Naropa's life. She was as "other" as any being could be for Naropa. At that time, Nalanda maintained a strict, celibate monastic code and had no place for women. Yet, in the tantric Buddhist tradition of the eleventh century, old and ugly women symbolized the ancient intuitive wisdom that no books could ever touch.

As a woman, she embodied intuitive wisdom: the sharp and penetrating quality of nondual knowing which is beyond books and logic. She was old, as Herbert Guenther wrote, because her wisdom is much "older than the cold rationality of the intellect,"[10] representing the everyday world of life and death, childbearing and weaning, and emotions from anguish to ecstasy. And she was ugly, because through excluding her and her wisdom from his world, Naropa had stunted and deformed that aspect of his own understanding.

In Tibetan Buddhist literature, there are frequent motifs of the erudite scholar or great teacher being confronted by a dakini woman: she might be old, wrathful, and horrid; she might be a vision of graceful beauty; she might be ordinary looking, with unusual moles, features, or birthmarks. Representing an alternative perspective or mode of being, the dakini has a great spiritual power.

Naropa regarded the old woman with horror and fascination, noting all thirty-seven of her decrepit features. To name a few, her deeply wrinkled and bearded face held deep, piercing, bloodshot eyes, and a crooked nose. Her gaping mouth held rotted teeth, and constantly chewed on its tongue. Her rough complexion was darkish blue and her hair was "fox-colored and disheveled." Her body was deformed and twisted, and she leaned heavily on a stick. He felt deep revulsion, and reflected that these thirty-seven horrific features reflected the certainty of impermanence, egolessness, and unsatisfactoriness of cyclic existence.

Nevertheless, when she quizzed him about his studies, he responded immediately, eager to please.

> *"What are you looking into?" "I study the books on grammar, epistemology, spiritual precepts, and logic," he replied. "Do you understand them?" "Yes." "Do you understand the words or the sense?" "The words." The old woman was delighted, rocked with laughter, and began to dance, waving her stick in the air. Thinking that she might feel still happier Naropa added: "I also understand the sense." But then the woman began to weep and tremble and she threw her stick down.*[11]

When Naropa asked about her behavior, the dakini explained that she had first been delighted that a great scholar such as Naropa had been so honest as to admit that he only understood the words of that which he studied. But when he went on to say he understood the sense of these texts, she was deeply saddened to hear him lie so boldly.

The old woman's teaching pointed out the great Naropa's superficial understanding, and it also points out our own superficial understanding. We all have a great deal to learn from her. Conventionally, when we study for achievement, we penetrate only the words, the literal or explicit meaning (*neyartha, drangdon*) of that which we examine. We learn theories, memorize facts, regurgitate bodies of knowledge without reflecting on the deeper meaning toward which this knowledge points.

This contrasts with the implicit meaning (*nitartha, ngedon*), the sense of what is studied. The sense refers to the inexpressible reverberation of meaning which undercuts our concepts and transforms our perspective. This reverberation occurs when we include ourselves in what we contemplate, and allow our questions to haunt the very basis of our identity. The great scholar Naropa was equipped only to understand the superficial meaning of his texts on logic and epistemology. When he claimed that he also understood the deeper, implicit meaning, the old woman wept that such a great master could deceive himself so profoundly. When we miss the deeper meaning of what we study and live, she weeps for us as well.

This famous tale expresses something essential about contemplative education, which does not become preoccupied with the words alone, which are merely the outward expression of the learning process. Certainly, when we learn a foreign language, a technical field, a scientific discipline, we must master the detailed lexicon of our study. But, if we do not go beyond the words to the sense, our field of study has no power to touch us or transform us in our hearts. As educators, we know that true excellence comes from penetrating the sense of our disciplines. In this encounter, the dakini instructs Naropa on the essence of contemplative education.

The second dakini story is about a great yogin who had a much greater understanding of the power of the feminine. Padmasambhava, called Guru Rinpoche by the Tibetans, was said to be enlightened at birth.[12] He was discovered and raised by a king, and was destined to take his father's place on the throne. In many ways the narratives of his life resembled those of the life of the Buddha.

Like the Buddha, it became clear to Guru Rinpoche as he grew that he could not be of much benefit as a king. He began to behave in outrageous ways, preferring the life of renunciation. He was so outrageous that his adoptive father was forced to banish him from the kingdom. When Guru Rinpoche left the kingdom, he went to meditate in the caves and mountains, and became a great yogi.

At a certain point in his practice, Guru Rinpoche sought teachings from a renowned dakini queen named Lekyi Wangmo, who lived in a dakini palace in a very special place, perhaps even a mythical place. As he approached the palace gateway, he encountered an attendant, a servant girl carrying water. She was struggling with two large water pots suspended from a yoke over her shoulder.

Hurriedly, Guru Rinpoche demanded to be brought to see the dakini queen. The servant girl ignored him, continuing to carry her water pots. Guru Rinpoche demanded a second time, saying that he was there to request important teachings from Lekyi Wangmo. Again she ignored his request. He did not recognize that she herself was a dakini.

He demanded a third time, and a third time she did not respond. Impatiently, Guru Rinpoche employed his yogic powers to get her attention. He magically nailed the pots of water to the ground so that the servant girl could neither move nor lift them. He demanded, "Take me to the queen dakini!"

Quietly she turned to him, removing the yoke from her shoulders, and said, "You think you have powers? What do you think of this?" She drew from the girdle at her waist a hooked knife, the kind of knife which dakinis carry. It had a curved blade and sharp hook at the end and was made of crystal, sparkling with light. With it, she sliced her chest open with a long diagonal sweep. And as she pulled her skin apart, opening the inside of her body, she revealed vast, unfathomable space. And inside of it were the mandalas of deities, but in a limitless expanse of space.

Awestruck, Guru Rinpoche immediately realized his mistake. He approached her, circumambulated her, and bowed in respect. While the story continues, with Rinpoche receiving the teachings he sought, this encounter is the essential one. The dakini–servant girl taught him, awakened him, reminded him, not by the words but by a kind of direct transmission—whoosh—that her body and the bodies of all dakinis are made of complete emptiness—vast, limitless space, manifesting in whatever form is helpful or useful in a particular situation. And Guru Rinpoche realized it immediately. He understood that he had been absorbed in his own agenda, his own importance. In his haste, he had denied the sacredness of the moments of his experience. And the dakini–servant girl generously introduced him to the essence.

Again, she represented the "other" to him. She appeared in the guise of a servant girl, low in caste, humble in appearance. He had been born of royalty, and was accustomed to giving commands and receiving obeisance. Even in his yogic practice, he had been the supreme meditator, full of mastery. Here he was brought to the realization that wisdom appears in unexpected ways, and that his arrogance obscured his vision. Only when he could acknowledge this was he ready to receive the teachings which he sought.

As contemplatives, we each have blind spots and areas of arrogance which keep us from awakening. Most often, it is the "other" in our experience which holds out to us the possibility of recognizing our obstacles. For this reason, pluralism offers to us a great gift. In every such encounter, we have the opportunity to open, engage, and grow in our spirituality.

In closing, I have a confession to make. As an American Buddhist convert, I'm quite certain that I began my path entirely as an exclusivist. I was truly convinced that my teacher was the one true meditation master of the universe, the only one who could bring one to enlightenment in one lifetime. Eventually I inched toward inclusivism. This is in large part because of teaching at The Naropa Institute for twenty years, and meeting remarkable people who are students of different teachers, practices, and traditions. There have been encounters with Orthodox Jews, Lakota Sioux, American Vipassana practitioners, Trappists, Carmelites, Methodists, and Benedictines which have deeply touched me. They are deeply authentic practitioners, fully engaged on a spiritual path which is transformative for them. But probably I considered their paths profound because they confirmed to me my own path. I became an inclusivist, and probably will remain an inclusivist for a long time.

Slowly, though, I have come to recognize the arrogance of inclusivism, constantly placing others under the banners and definitions of my own tradition. In the last several years, I have become inspired by pluralism and the challenges of letting go of any particular territory regarding truth. I've become intrigued by the possibility of going forth into the uncharted territory of pluralism.

When I read the story of the great yogis Naropa and Guru Rinpoche, I learn that commitment is important in the pluralistic journey. I also learn about openness. In learning the lessons of openness, the great yogis failed again and again. With each failure, however, came a lesson. They were willing to risk, willing to fail, and willing to learn. And eventually, through direct experience with "other," they became fully awakened. In these accounts, I find inspiration to awaken to the failures of my own encounters, and to risk the movement into pluralism which is daily presented to me.

I invite you to join me on the contemplative path of pluralism, the path of willingness to take risk, to fail, and to be touched and transformed by the journey. In closing, I'd like you to ask yourselves the following questions: What is the "other" for you? What is it that you have been reluctant to engage with? In yourself? In your practice? In the world? Where is it that you need to go, need to learn, need to develop, in order to go more openly and deeply into your spirituality and the world?

7

EMBRACING FREEDOM:
SPIRITUALITY AND LIBERATION

bell hooks

Distinguished Professor of English at City College in New York, bell hooks is a writer, teacher, and insurgent intellectual, and writes about a new kind of education, "education as the practice of freedom." She is the author of many books including *Outlaw Culture: Resisting Representation*, *Teaching to Transgress*, *Killing Rage: Ending Racism*, and *Bone Black: Memories of Girlhood*.

I WOULD LIKE to share with you some of how I teach as a teacher who does not do spirituality *and* education, but does spirituality *in* education.

EMBODYING THE TEACHINGS

One of the first things I do is bring my body out there with the students: to see them, to be with them.

I never met the Buddhist teacher Chogyam Trungpa Rinpoche, founder of The Naropa Institute, because I was afraid of him. Part of what I was afraid of was what he might move in my body—what he might move in my being. His teachings through his written work, however, have molded who I am as a teacher.

Many of you say to me, "bell, I feel that I know you. I feel that I have been with you as I read your texts." A favorite text of mine, for who I am, is Trungpa Rinpoche's book *Cutting Through Spiritual Materialism*. That text constantly pushes me: it gets me to think about

113

what it means to have a life in the spirit. We can't begin to talk about spirituality in education until we talk about what it means to have a life in the spirit. So that we are not just teachers when we enter our classrooms, but are teachers in every moment of our lives.

What is charming to me about the Dalai Lama is the way he uses his body as a teaching for us, the spontaneous moment. An important thing for me about Trungpa Rinpoche is the sense of unexpectedness, spontaneity and mystery that comes through his writing.

To live a life in the spirit, to be true to a life of the spirit, we have to be willing to be called on—often in ways that we may not like.

CALLING THE SPIRIT

Trungpa Rinpoche's teachings kept calling me; but I kept saying to myself, "No, I'm not ready for this. It's too much."

In recollecting how I was invited to participate in this conference, I keep teasing people that I was an afterthought. The coordinator in turn teases me that he called seventeen states searching for me.

If we want to have intimacy with otherness, sometimes we have to search for it. We may have to search for it in seventeen different states.

This is the time of year that I normally take silence. I don't go anywhere. The conference, however, kept coming to me in myriad ways—but I kept thinking, "I don't want to do this. This isn't where I am right now." But the spirit kept on calling me.

Then I started to get sick. As I was coughing up all this blood the other day, I kept calling to say, "Sorry, I can't come." But no one answered the phone or called me back. So then I thought, I'll be really slick. I'll call my sister, who was supposed to come here with me, and I'll tell her, "I'm so sick. Do you *really* want to do this?"

But she said, "Oh, yeah, I really want to go. And I've been needing a break."

So the spirit calls. But we must not pretend, make it seem like living a life in the spirit is easy. On the contrary: living the life of the spirit is difficult. It is not a life that is about how much people are going to like you.

We all act like we "like" the Dalai Lama so much, like we're so delighted by him. But often, when we meet a teacher who plunges us into deep and profound mystery, we don't like it. It's not easy; and it's not easy to be such a teacher.

OPPORTUNITY

We missed—and this is not a critique, this is a comment—a powerful teaching moment as a group today. We had such a moment when the Dalai Lama said, as we sang "Down by the Riverside," that he did not understand what we were singing about. We did not seize the opportunity to enter that moment, to share with him that connection between the oppression of African and African-American peoples. The continuum that links us to Tibet.

Often I'm asked, "Why Buddhism?" "Why would you be interested in Tibet?" Particularly by black people who say, "What about the work here?" "What about all those white Buddhists who don't give a shit about what's happening to us right here?"

I think it is very important not to give away Tibet, but to link the freedom of Tibet with our freedom. For me to understand, as an African-American woman, an afterthought, an invisible potential monster, potential other, that my being is connected to the being of all those toiling and suffering Tibetan people. To know that though I may never see or know them, we are connected in our suffering. That connection is part of our understanding of compassion: that it is expansive, that it moves in a continuum.

I said to my sister about the Dalai Lama: "Gosh, doesn't he look like our brother?" And then I said about two monks sitting there: "Gosh, if they took off those robes, they'd just look like two black people we've known all our lives."

And to what extent would people be delighted by them if they were just black people in some regular old clothing, walking around regular old Boulder? To what extent might we feel fear? Or not seize the opportunity to have some intimacy with otherness?

LIBERATION OF THE SPIRIT

I was touched by the mystical dimensions of Christian faith. When I was a girl, I felt the presence of the Beloved in my heart; the oneness of our life. At that time, when I had not yet acquired knowledge of appropriate terminology, I knew only that despite the troubles of my world, the suffering I witnessed around and within me, there was always available a spiritual force that could lift me higher: give me moments of transcendent bliss wherein I could surrender all thought of the world and know profound peace.

Early on, my heart had been touched by its delight. I knew its rapture. Early on, I made a commitment to be a seeker on the path: a seeker after truth. I was determined to live a life in the spirit.

James Comb, the black theologian, says that our survival and liberation depend upon our recognition of the truth when it is spoken and lived:

> *If we cannot recognize the truth, then it cannot liberate us from untruth. To know the truth is to prepare for it; for it is not mainly reflection and theory. Truth is divine action entering our lives and creating the human action of liberation.*

In reflecting on my youth, I emphasize the mystical dimension of the Christian faith because it was that aspect of religious experience that I found to be truly liberatory. The more fundamental religious beliefs that were taught to me urging blind obedience to authority and acceptance of oppressive hierarchies, these didn't move me.

No, it was those mystical experiences that enabled me to understand and recognize the realm of being in a spiritual experience that transcends both authority and law.

RETURNING HOME

As a student in graduate school, seeking spirituality in education, I wanted there to be a place in my life for theory and politics, as well as spiritual practice. My quest was to find for them a meeting place.

It is interesting to me that the two spiritual teachers that have been so meaningful to me, and run like threads through my work, are so different in their own beings: Trungpa Rinpoche and Thich Nhat Hanh, the Vietnamese Zen master. Their visions are different in many ways: one so committed to the magic and mystery, the courageous. The other slightly more doctrinaire, but so committed to the notion of openheartedness.

One of the first books that led me down the Thich Nhat Hanh path was a book that he did with Daniel Berrigan, called *The Raft Is Not the Shore*. In the book, Thich Nhat Hanh writes of self-recovery. In the Buddhist tradition, he says, people used to speak of enlightenment as a kind of returning home.

"The three worlds," he says, "the world of form, of nonform, of desire, are not your homes." These are places you wander off to, the many existences alienated from your own true nature. So enlightenment is the way to get back: the way home.

Thich Nhat Hanh speaks of the efforts to go back in terms of the recovery of one's self, of one's integrity. I began to use this vision of spiritual self-recovery in relationship to the political self-recovery of colonized and oppressed peoples. I did this to see the points of convergence between the effort to live in the spirit and the effort of oppressed peoples to renew their spirits—to find themselves again in suffering and in resistance.

A concern that I have is this: What is the place of love in this recovery? What is the place of love in the experience of intimate otherness?

When I come here, and feel myself to be somehow not fully present, what allows me to enter this space of otherness—that which

117

is other to me here, this particular kind of sea of Boulder whiteness is love. It is the love that I can generate within myself, as a light, and send out, beam out, that can touch people. Love can bridge the sense of otherness. But it is practice to beam that love out. It takes work.

This morning I said hello to Parker Palmer, and Sharon, his partner and life companion. She said to me later that she was surprised that I remembered her name. And I thought: Why shouldn't I remember your name? It's been told to me two or three times. I've met you. What is the sense of the practice of compassion if we are not here together practicing compassion with one another? With how we are in the spaces of our differences here?

COME WITH ME

I think that I have been a bit awed here, by all these people who teach at places where spirituality is accepted. Most of my teaching experience has been in climates that are totally, utterly and completely hostile to spirituality. Where colleagues laugh at you if they think that you have some notion of a spiritual life.

So much of my experience, my teaching practice has been honed in that particularly harsh kind of environment. Being spiritual-in-education within an environment that is utterly hostile to that. Not naming that hostility but working with it in such a way that the spirit can be present in the midst of it: that the fire burns bright without any generation, anything in the environment generating it.

Howard Thurman maintained that the experience of redemptive love was essential for individual and collective self-actualization. Such a love affirms. In *The Growing Edge,* he contends that whether we are a good person or a bad person, we are being dealt with at the point beyond all that is limiting and all that is creative within us. We are dealt with at the core of our being: and at that core, we are touched and released.

In much of his work, Thurman cautions those of us who are concerned with radical social change to not allow our visions to conform to a pattern we seek to impose but rather allow them to be "modeled and shaped in accordance to the innermost transformation that is going on in our spirits."

To be guided by love is to live in community with all life. However, a culture of domination, like ours, does not strive to teach us how to live in community. As a consequence, learning to live in community must be a core practice for all of us who desire spirituality in education.

All too often we think of community in terms of being with folks like ourselves: the same class, same race, same ethnicity, same social standing and the like. All of us evoke vague notions of community and compassion, yet how many of us compassionately went out to find an intimate other, to bring them here with us today? So that when we looked around, we wouldn't just find a similar kind of class, a similar group of people, people like ourselves: a certain kind of exclusivity.

I think we need to be wary: we need to work against the danger of evoking something that we don't challenge ourselves to actually practice. A lot of white folks can travel all the way to Tibet to experience intimate otherness, but can't imagine the idea of finding an other in their life right where they are, and saying, "Would you like to come with me?"

There was a young woman earlier who said to me: "I'd like to come tonight, but I didn't register." And I said to her: "Well, here. Just take my little ticket, and you can come on in." I did this just as I was trying to decide for myself, for my day, the answer to the question "What are the actions I will concretely do today in order to bring myself into greater community? With that which is not here?"

BEARING WITNESS

I want to read from a letter that I wrote to one of my spiritual comrades, Cornell West. Cornell and I used to have these deep, passionate arguments about the meaning of spiritual life, and about what we were called upon to do as educators. One of the things that we argued about was the notion of sacrificial love.

There is that moment of delay that allows us—in the midst of physical suffering and pain—to remember that we are more than our pain. And that there are other ways that we can speak.

One of the things that I constantly hear Thich Nhat Hanh saying in my head is this: "When we are in the midst of the teacher, the teacher does not have to necessarily talk to us." That the presence of their body, their being itself, means something to us. Returning to the concrete.

Perhaps one of the most intense political struggles we face—and the greatest spiritual struggle—in seeking to transform society is the effort to maintain integrity of being. In my letter to Cornell, I wrote:

> We bear witness not just with our intellectual work but with ourselves, our lives. Surely the crisis of these times demands that we give our all. Remember the song which asked "Is your altar of sacrifice late?" To me, this "all" includes our habits of being, the way we live. It is both political practice and spiritual sacrament, a life of resistance. How can we speak of change, of hope, and love if we court death? All of the work we do, no matter how brilliant or revolutionary in thought or action, loses power and meaning if we lack integrity of being.

I can testify to the meaningfulness of spiritual practice and that such a practice sustains and nurtures progressive teaching, progressive politics, and enhances the struggle for liberation.

LEGACY OF INTOLERANCE

QUESTION: My name is Scott. My question has to do with the invasion of the United States and subjugation of the native peoples here, as well as the history of the African-Americans here in the United States, and how a legacy of intolerance and fear manifests in our educational system today. What actions would you encourage us to undertake in order to redirect this educational legacy of ours?

BELL HOOKS: I don't think it's a question of the institutions. The institutions that we're talking about were put in place to affirm a culture of domination to begin with. So it's not like they've changed their tune or are not doing something; it's not like they were for freedom and now they're for unfreedom.

The point is that there is a growing condition of unfreedom. The kind of fascism that we see in so many parts of the world is now encroaching upon us. The question is: What are we doing as educators to instead bring a spirit of compassion, of interbeing, into our classrooms and administrations?

That, I think, is a question that begins with where people are, and very concrete circumstances. In my concrete circumstances, I teach in Harlem. I teach students who have a wide variety of skills. Some very brilliant—young Ivy League people who come to work with bell hooks—and others who have five children, are on welfare, work forty hours a week illegally and then come to school.

So what kind of teaching practice allows me to speak to that diversity, that pluralism? And I don't use those words to mean the same thing. What do I do concretely in that setting? Part of what I have to do in that setting is to teach compassion to those who know more, and those who are impatient: compassion for those who do not have as much theoretical background, or can't read as well. I teach them that there is something to be learned from listening, especially listening to someone who is not like you. For often, the students feel they can tune out when someone other than me is speaking.

COMMUNITY

QUESTION: My name is Nancy. You spoke of how students can be afraid when we introduce them to mystery. I come from a very traditional, conservative school. What can I do to help them to open up?

BELL HOOKS: I am a great believer in starting with where people are, and going with them from there.

One of the tools that Buddhism gave me was the possibility of emptying myself in such a way that it allows others to enter me, allows me to glimpse some of a student's particular mystery. Then I try to mirror the mystery in such a way that helps it unfold for the student. Does that make sense?

I believe very much in Alice Miller's perspective. The tremendous suffering that I felt as a child, and the strategies I used to cope with that suffering, have prepared me for who I am as a teacher today.

In a discussion I had with Pema Chödrön, author of *Start Where You Are,* we talked about suffering as a potential path. We agreed that if you can be with your suffering in such a way that it opens you up, that suffering itself can become a source of wisdom and compassion.

I think it's utopian for us to talk about how we can all just "be happy." It's hard to just be happy when your life is full of deep and profound pain, or physical abuse.

I'm also very concerned with all the talk about "family values," because for many people the family is a real fucked-up kind of prison. So while we can offer the prayer or wish that the family could and should be the place where we begin with love and compassion, for many, many people this is not the case.

What I know, and can testify to from my own experience, is that if you have a community of love, you can survive whatever is happening to you. So part of what we can do is become a part of a community of love. When I used to go to school with those marks on my body—from being beaten by my parents—and someone would offer to me that love we're talking about, compassion, it was just like that song Jackie Wilson used to sing: "Your love has lifted me higher." We can be lifted higher by the spirit of community.

Many of you know what I'm talking about—know what it is like to be lifted higher by a community. Not by the family, as we have traditionally and patriarchally envisioned it, but by community. A community that shelters us in the midst of whatever storms may arise.

In one of my books I write about a Catholic priest that I met at a conference. He saw how deeply suicidal I was. He sheltered me, and gave me spiritual sanctuary. He lifted me higher. This was but a day or two in my life, but he offered me the possibility of redemptive love.

THE LOVE YOU HAVE TO GIVE

QUESTION: Hi. I'm Caria. I come from a childhood where I had a great deal of love and affection. I feel really lucky, but also guilty in some way. I'm spending the summer working with inner-city, mostly minority, kids. I feel like they're so other that I don't know what to offer them. They don't say: "Well, you haven't been there. You haven't been beaten. What do you have to say to us?" But I feel something like that.

BELL HOOKS: I think precisely what you have to offer is your unmediated love. I'm always enchanted when I meet people who have had unmediated love. That is to say, they haven't had to have their love in bits and pieces, their love in the face of cruelty or pain.

So stay with your love, that love you're telling us about. Not guiltily with that love, but with that love in such a way that it empowers you to give love.

Think: What is the love that I have to give that other person, the one who is so alien? And think: What happens if they say "You don't know. You don't know what I'm talking about." You can honestly reply: "You're right. I don't know what you're talking about. All I have to give you is my love, a love that was forged in an environment so radically different from yours. How might that love express itself to you?"

I mean, how often are we asked, "How might that love express itself to you?" How often do we ask the person we're trying to help, "What expression of love might move you to the place you want to go?" How often do we really meet them where they are, with what they need, rather than bring them back to *our* places of guilt, anxiety, or neurosis?

RACE, CLASS AND GENDER

QUESTION: I'm Julie. Thank you for your conference pass. What are your thoughts on a "sea of white people" being the role models and teachers for our young children?

BELL HOOKS: I think the danger—part of why we are all concerned when we begin to talk about race, gender and class—is that the moment we spend too much time on these issues, we forget that we are more than these issues. Now, there are people who would rather we never talk about "sea of whiteness" or "sea of blackness," but the point is about how we maintain that delicate sense of balance that allows us to both name that which limits us and that which empowers us.

I am both limited by my gender and empowered by it; I am both limited by my race and empowered by it. How do I name that, and at the same time understand that I'm more than that, and understand that I can be more than that with others? Understand that love can diminish the historical signification of oppression and exploitation?

The question is: Why do we first have the experience of the sea of whiteness or blackness rather than a sea of love? Why is the fire of love not burning so hot that we have not even a moment to think about race, class or gender? This is a question that we have to ask ourselves as we light the fires of compassion within us, as we burn away our own fear.

KNOW THEM

QUESTION: I'm Nate. I'd like to hear you say something about how to teach kids who have grown up learning violence as the only way to protect themselves—specific stuff about how to teach them.

BELL HOOKS: But see, Nate, I don't think that I can tell you how to teach those kids without knowing them myself.

There is an intimacy to great teaching. There is an intimacy about it in the sense that I'm not so sure that in a face-to-face encounter we are really, truly able to transmit teaching to those who we do not love. So what I ask you to think about, before you think about teaching is: What is the practice of love that you can embody that is not violent? Remember that violence is not just physical aggression: violence can be making someone invisible; violence can be making someone other.

It can be a grown-up white male acting as if they're terrified of a four-year-old Chicano kid, who's doing something that they wouldn't do. This can be a form of violence as well.

So think first about how you can love your students. Do this even before you think about how you're going to teach them. Think: How can I love these strangers, these others that I see in the classroom? What practice of compassion can I bring to the moment that is so fine-tuned that I can accomplish in one day that which might ordinarily take weeks, months or years to do?

This kind of awareness or mental discipline is something that meditation and other kinds of awareness practices can enable in us. These disciplines can develop in us the power of awareness. But you can't develop this kind of awareness without practice, without examining again and again how you are seeing the people you are teaching.

CLAIMING OUR PAIN

QUESTION: My name is Michael, and my experience of working with the other has been in working with native people in Canada. I've found that it's been a very painful learning curve: of seeing difficult things in myself; finding myself in situations that are difficult to work with; and finding that oftentimes the difficulty that arises is difficulty that I myself created. I was wondering if there's anything you can offer from your experience about how to make the learning curve a little easier?

BELL HOOKS: But I think that's just it. Isn't it so interesting that we are always trying to move away from that pain?

What I feel so strongly is we have to enter the pain. That this pain is the place of transformation; and we should not assume that there will be some easier way out.

One of the things a culture of domination does to all of us—irrespective of our class, race or gender—is make us ashamed of our pain. In claiming our pain as a space where we can work alchemically, we begin to move against the forces of domination. We move against the forces of fear and shame. In fact, we discover that it is precisely our pain that intimately connects us with others.

QUESTION: Can I ask a follow-up?

BELL HOOKS: Sure.

QUESTION: I agree with you completely that my pain has been incredibly rich: that's not what concerns me. What concerns me is that my stupidity has caused other people a lot of pain. So that's where my question is really coming from.

BELL HOOKS: That is a different question. When your stupidity causes other people pain, then I think that's an occasion for making amends and reparations. I think reparations is a wonderful word. I think amends is wonderful, too. It is a good thing to practice making amends to those we have hurt.

Often, I find that I have devastated a student. One of the things I think you should know by now is that I'm honest. So if a student reads a paper—a bad one—and says, "Well, do you think that was stupid?" I might respond something like, "Yeah, I thought that was really stupid. I don't know why you wasted our time reading it. This is our life and we're dying." And then I see the student crumbling.

Then I have to move: I have to go to that person and make amends. I have to be willing to move into the space where I acknowledge that, despite being a great teacher, I am also sometimes a person who wounds people with careless words, with my own recklessness of heart.

FEAR

QUESTION: Hi. My name is Rebecca and my question to you is: Are you ever afraid? I ask this question as a teacher about to go into the South Central Los Angeles school system.

BELL HOOKS: You know, when I leave my little yuppie, predominantly white, neighborhood in Greenwich Village and get on the subway to go up to 137th Street, there is a little park that I walk through. And there is clearly a lot of weird drug stuff happening in this park; there's all kinds of stuff going on.

Walking through this park, I find that I'm always afraid. I am afraid that my own otherness—my book bag, my cutesy little black clothing, my Prada shoes—is sticking out, and that I will be wounded on this walk.

If you know City College, there's a trek from the subway up the hill to the school. I think of this trek as a moment of mindfulness. Mindfulness isn't something you only cultivate in the practice of sitting meditation or what have you. Mindfulness can be cultivated right in the middle of your life.

If, when I'm making this trek, I begin to feel a greater sense of fear, that's the time when I start thinking about practicing mindfulness; that's the time I begin to think about what it means for me to practice love. This is the time for me to believe that my capacity for love is so powerful that if someone pulled a gun on me right now that my love will have its transformative moment.

I never lose my fear: I don't lose my fear when I hear that a student—what's his name—had a gun in class, but he's arrested now. Because then he's writing me from jail: will I do such and such so that he can come back to class?

I don't lose my fear. I think about this: What is my accountability to the lives of the other people here? What is my accountability to giving love to this individual? What must I do now? The fear is always there, burning in the fire along with many other things.

THE TRICKSTER

QUESTION: My name is Cheryl. I'm a student at Naropa. One of the reasons I came to school here was that I was touched by the little bit I had read by the Rinpoche, and also that he liked the trickster. Would you address the role of the trickster?

BELL HOOKS: For me, one of the magical links between Trungpa Rinpoche's teachings and the African-American experience is the sense of the chameleon, the changing self, the self that is never what it appears to be. I have written in *Teaching to Transgress* about the necessity for that chameleonlike capacity for change: for teachers taking on many different forms and shapes.

If we are to truly teach, we cannot have one little model that we put onto everybody. One thing that was distressing to me about the questions put to the Dalai Lama was the feeling that there seemed to be a desire for one model, one paradigm that could be taken and put on.

In fact, one of the things that we must do as teachers is twirl around and around, and find out what works with the situation that we're in. Our models just might not work. And that twirling, changing, is part of the empowerment.

Another thing that concerns me is the fact that the truly magical teachers—the ones that are the most tricksterlike—are the teachers that we most denounce. I'm one of them. When my students decide that they need to denounce me—and they do so in such violent ways—it is precisely because that core of sameness that they would like me to have, that they find comfort in, is not there with me. The core that says: "I know how she's going to be today. I know what she's going to say. I know how she's going to act."

Those of you who had the privilege of studying directly with Trungpa Rinpoche know just how much he did not allow this kind of comfort to people. The comfort that says, "Okay, we know what's up, what's going to be done now."

One of the things that is happening in the spiritual movement right now is that so many of us are wanting to find a sense of sameness or security in the teacher; to find the absence of mystery in the teacher; and the absence of imperfection in the teacher. In fact, however, it's that imperfection in the teacher that is so crucial to the teacher's capacity to know—to know as we are knowing. How can I have compassion for you, in your imperfection, if you do not allow me my imperfection?

As Parker Palmer wrote:

The true work of the mind is to reconnect us with that
which would otherwise be out of reach.
To connect us with that which would otherwise
be out of reach.

III. RELATIONSHIP AND COMMUNITY

LEARNING HAPPENS most often without regard to schooling or institutions of education. We have many obvious examples of this: children learn to walk, to speak, to farm, to prepare meals, or to ride a bike. People learn to take care of themselves and others: animals, siblings, infants, elders. Of course learning happens within schools, too; learning, however, does not require—in any way, shape or form—the institutions of learning.

This raises important questions: In what ways are these institutions themselves helpful? In what ways are they harmful, even a hindrance? Given the fact of compulsory public schooling, how can we more effectively foster learning?

Currently, public education values the global perspective at the expense of the local; the abstract rather than the concrete; the conceptual above the experiential. Students across the country are taught essentially the same thing no matter where they are, no matter what qualities their particular locale expresses or what that specific location might require in terms of human behavior. Our current manner of public education is totally independent of the specificity of place.

Denigration of the particular happens in so many ways: through isolation and segregation—sorting by age, sorting by intelligence; by locking students indoors, in sterile and lifeless environments; by breaking the living world into meaningless pieces—grades, curricula, lesson plans, and busy work; by modeling and encouraging individualism and competition rather than community and collaboration; and by standardization and streamlining—creating structures of efficiency—that make no allowances for differences in locale, culture, or community values.

The chapters in this section argue against this growing (and frightening) national trend. They ask the question "What would an education that actually nurtured and sustained people, places, and communities look like?" The case is made for education rooted in greater attention to the specific details of the living world as it arises for particular people in particular places and moments, for curricula rooted in local and regional history, science, arts, crafts, literature, commerce, politics, agriculture, weather, wildness. The chapters call for opening education back up and out, for relocating education in this world—in the vast processes of the social and ecological community already at play, the forces in dynamic play wherever we are.

At its heart, education is a very personal thing. It begins simply with the perfect miracle of our existence, with our ability to perceive: our ability to have sensations and perceptions, our ability to formulate and express thoughts and ideas, our ability to experience and manifest change—continually modify what we feel, know, and believe. Education begins with our awareness: with the fact of this life, the fact of this breath.

Learning happens both outside and inside of us simultaneously. Simultaneous with the "outside" experience of the phenomenal world there is an "inside" experience of perception and recognition. Looking closely, we can see that even the simple act of noting our immediate physical sensations from moment to moment would take not merely a moment but an entire lifetime. The amount that we can learn simply by paying attention is endless.

Sometime in the past, within education, real life—this endless flow of phenomena—was broken down, divided, abstracted. The fleeting transitional whole was conceptualized into a vast assembly of discrete parts: subjects of learning like geography and geology, history and literature, psychology and sociology. These separate subjects, in turn, within themselves became increasingly specialized, often with little interaction even across subdisciplines.

But where does one subject or discipline actually end and another begin? Looking closely, one finds that these disciplines are all merely words—ideas, names, abstractions—aspiring to capture or freeze an idealized and idea-ized life within a particular conceptual framework. It is as if all of these subjects were not ultimately about the same thing—about life! But incredible danger, and damage too, can result from our viewing the complex depth of the world from the single, narrow perspective.

A second abstraction took place within educational culture as well. The environment of learning was divided, set apart from life itself. Education was moved away from the field, shop, or guild and into a multitude of specialized structures: the business of administration; the bureaucracy of professional teaching and education; the jurisdictions of local, state, and federal politics. The industrial architecture of modern public schooling engendered yet a further distancing of learning from living: windowless schools, surrounded by asphalt playgrounds, enclosed by chain-link fence (and sometimes even razor wire!).

Somehow, over time, we have put a thousand different filters—physical, emotional, mental, and psychological—between students and life. Somehow, we have chosen this option instead of allowing or fostering an intimacy between them. Somehow, within our institutions, the doorway for genuine learning became narrower and narrower. To a great extent, education has become steeped in abstraction and distance. And we, as a result, have become alienated from the living world.

A great irony is that while we learn, in essence, quite naturally from our awareness, observation, and direct experience, we have somehow agreed instead to ignore or shut off all these factors of input. Instead of having an education of the senses, we suddenly have merely an education of the mind. Instead of being open to a steady stream of living information, in our attempts to create focus—remove the so-called distractions to the learning process—we have created institutions in which we learn to dull our senses.

In any given schoolroom, how many students know which direction is north? Where the food in the cafeteria comes from? Where the trash goes? What problems face the community? In a very real way we have *enclosed* our children in schools and, in doing so, have dulled their senses—their openness, their sense of connection, and their sense of appreciation and respect for the world. To say nothing of their body-based wisdom, intuition, or spirit!

Our learning environments, while perhaps designed with the aspiration of creating an efficient learning enterprise, have left us with environments so withdrawn from experience that the only kind of learning that can happen is abstraction. And a generation of abstract thinkers—with no grounding in a shared world—is a dangerous thing, as writers like Wendell Berry and Susan Griffin have told us again and again. Griffin's *A Chorus of Stones,* in particular, exposes the potentially toxic nature of abstraction: the horror born of the dissociation of the life of the mind from life itself.

For a moment, let us imagine a different style of education. If we were to put students alone, in a natural setting, the potential for learning would be infinite, the walls between the individual and experience few. And yet rarely, within the practice of education, are we offered time alone or time outdoors, or for that matter observation time, experience time, introspection time, contemplation time. While of course the control of students and subject matter is much harder to maintain within this fluid living situation, we do have the added gift of new, surprising, and meaningful curricula ceaselessly becoming available.

In fact, *all phenomenon arises as our teacher:* everything we look at, everything we touch, everything we experience, is the opportunity for a particular lesson. Every moment there is learning. The lessons can be biological, chemical, geological, historical, social, political, emotional, artistic. Right now—indeed every moment—going on within us and around us are curricula in gravity, human physiology, psychology, ecology.

In spiritual education, the world comes alive. Living and education become inseparable. Self and the world become inseparable. Something is always happening that can be learned from. The only things that are required are openness and attentiveness: the allowing and examination of direct experience.

The chapters in "Relationship and Community" look at the organic structures of our society—social, cultural, ecological—to reflect upon the richness of the lessons already being offered to us, lessons that are being ignored. They also examine the hidden curriculum of buildings, classes, grades, and schools, revealing a further structure of walls and bars that discourage or even prevent access to this living education.

David Orr, John Taylor Gatto, and Joan Halifax call on us to start right where we are—in ourselves, our communities, our relationships, and our places. Spirituality in education begins with the recognition that we are living beings who are temporarily, tenuously, and mutually sharing an ever-changing situation.

A long list of recommendations are made: arguing for more student alone-time; more direct experience; more learning through mentorships and apprenticeships; for self-mastery as a goal; learning from the body; learning from emotions; learning from life's deepest mysteries. In a profound way, however, this is hardly a laundry list. All the arguments point towards regrounding both spirit and education in the living world. The chapters call for nothing less than the pulling down of the gates and fences that surround our schools. They call on us to widen doorways, windows, and minds in order that we may truly learn the lessons of the world.

8.

REASSEMBLING THE PIECES:
ARCHITECTURE AS
PEDAGOGY

David W. Orr

David W. Orr is professor and chair of the environmental studies program at Oberlin College, and the author of *Ecological Literacy*, *Earth
in Mind*, and over ninety articles. He is the co-editor of two books,
The Campus and Environmental Responsibility and *The Global Predicament*. David serves as the education editor for *Conservation Biology*, is
a member of the editorial advisory board of *Orion* magazine, and is
a trustee of the Educational Foundation of America.

*The university as now functioning prepares students for their role in extend-
ing human dominion over the natural world, not for intimate presence to the
natural world. Use of this power in a deleterious manner has devastated the
planet. We suddenly discover that we are losing some of our most exalted
human experiences that come to us through our participation in the natural
world about us. So awesome is the devastation we are bringing about that we
can only conclude that we're caught in some deep cultural pathology, the
pathology that is sustained intellectually by the university, economically by
the corporation, legally by the Constitution, religiously by the Church.*

—THOMAS BERRY

*The worst thing we can do to our children is to convince them that ugliness
is normal.*

—RENE DUBOS

As COMMONLY PRACTICED, education has little to do with its specific setting or locality. The typical campus is regarded mostly as a place where learning occurs but is, itself, not believed to be the source of useful learning. It is intended, rather, to be convenient, efficient, or aesthetically pleasing, but not instructional. It neither requires nor facilitates competence or mindfulness. By that standard, the same education could happen as well in California or in Kazakhstan, or on Mars, for that matter. The same could be said of the buildings and landscape that make up a college or public school campus. The design of buildings and landscape is thought to have little or nothing to do with the process of learning, or the quality of scholarship that occurs in a particular place. In fact, buildings and landscape reflect a hidden curriculum that powerfully influences the learning process.

The curriculum embedded in any building instructs as fully and as powerfully as any course taught in it. Most of my classes, for example, are taught in a building that I think Descartes would have liked. It is a building with lots of squareness and straight lines. There is nothing whatsoever that reflects its locality in northeast Ohio in what had once been a vast forested wetland. How it is cooled, heated, lighted and at what cost to the world is an utter mystery to its occupants. It offers no clue about the origins of the materials used to build it. It tells no story. With only minor modifications it could be converted to use as a factory or prison. When classes are over, students seldom linger for long. The building resonates with no part of our biological, evolutionary experience, or aesthetic sensibilities. It reflects no understanding of ecology or ecological processes. It is intended to be functional, efficient, minimally offensive, and little more. But what else does it do?

First, it tells users that locality, knowing where you are, is unimportant. To be sure, this is not said in so many words anywhere in this or any other building. Rather, it is said tacitly through the entire building. Second, because it uses energy wastefully, the building tells

its users that energy is cheap and abundant and can be squandered with no thought for the morrow. Third, nowhere in the building do students learn about the materials used in its construction or who was downwind or downstream from the wells, mines, forests, and manufacturing facilities where those materials originated or where they will eventually be discarded.

The lesson the building offers is mindlessness; it teaches that disconnectedness is normal. And try as one might to teach that we are implicated in the larger enterprise of life, standard architectural design mostly conveys other lessons. There is often a miscalibration between the lesson of interconnectedness when it is taught in classes and the way a building, campus, or school actually functions. Buildings are provisioned with energy, materials, and water, and dispose of their waste in ways that say to students that the world is linear and that we are not part of the larger web of life. Finally, there is no apparent connection in this or any other building on campus to the larger set of issues having to do with climatic change, biotic impoverishment, and the unraveling of the fabric of life on Earth. Students begin to suspect, I think, that those issues are unreal, or that they are unsolvable in any practical way, or that they occur somewhere else.

Is it possible to design buildings and entire campuses in ways that promote ecological competence and mindfulness? Through better design is it possible to teach our students that our problems are solvable and that we are connected to the larger community of life?

As an experiment, I organized a class of students in 1992–1993 to develop what architects call a preprogram for an environmental studies center at Oberlin College. Twenty-five students and a dozen architects met over two semesters to develop the core ideas for the project. The first order of business was to question why we ought to do anything at all. Once the need for facilities was established, the participants questioned whether we ought to build new facilities or renovate an existing building. Students and faculty examined a dozen or so possibilities to renovate and for a variety of reasons decided that the best approach was new construction. The basic program that emerged from the year-long class called for an approximately fourteen-thousand-square-foot building that

- discharged no waste water, i.e., drinking water in, drinking water out
- generated more electricity than it used
- used no materials known to be carcinogenic, mutagenic, or endocrine disrupters
- used energy and materials with great efficiency
- promoted competence with environmental technologies
- used products and materials grown or manufactured sustainably
- was landscaped to promote biological diversity
- promoted analytical skill in assessing full costs over the lifetime of the building
- promoted ecological competence and mindfulness of place
- became, in its design and operations, genuinely pedagogical
- met rigorous requirements for full-cost accounting

We intended, in other words, a building that caused no ugliness, human or ecological, somewhere else or at some later time.

Given the opposition of the college president, this project sat on the shelf for nearly two years before being endorsed by a new president in the spring of 1995. With the approval of the trustees, the project went forward in June of 1995. The terms of the approval required funding from "sources not otherwise likely to give to the college," and two years in which to do the design work and bring the project to groundbreaking. Both requirements influenced the pace and character of the project. The fact that we could not solicit funds from donors affiliated in any way with the college required that the building be designed to be as widely appealing as possible. But no other kind of building would be worth doing. The two-year timetable required that we move quickly to select an architect and design team and get on with the job at hand.

As a first step, we hired two graduates from the class of 1993 to help coordinate the design of the project and engage students, faculty, and the wider community in the design process. We also hired an architect, John Lyle, to help conduct the major design charettes (or planning sessions) that began in the fall of 1995. Some two hundred fifty students, faculty, and community members participated in the thirteen charettes in which the goals for the center were developed and refined. In that same period, we advertised the project nationally and eventually received twenty-six applications from architectural firms with interests in the emerging field of "green architecture." We selected five for interview and in January of 1996 selected William McDonough & Partners of Charlottesville, Virginia.

No architect alone, however talented, could design the building that we proposed. It was necessary, therefore, to assemble a design team that would meet throughout the process. To fulfill the requirement that the building generate more electricity than it used, we engaged Amory Lovins and Bill Browning from the Rocky Mountain Institute as well as scientists from NASA, Lewis Space Center. In order to meet the standard of zero discharge we hired John Todd and Michael Shaw, the leading figures in the field of ecological engineering. For landscaping we brought in John Lyle and the firm of Andropogon, Inc. from Philadelphia. To this team we added structural and mechanical engineers (Lev Zetlin, Inc., New York City), and the contracting firm from Akron. During the programming and schematic design phase, this team and representatives from the college met by conference call weekly and in regular working sessions.

The team approach to architectural design was a new process for the college. Typically, the architects do their work alone, passing finished blueprints along to the structural and mechanical engineers, who do their thing and hand the project off to the landscape architects. By engaging the full design team from the beginning, we intended to maximize the integration of building systems and technologies and the relationship between the building and its landscape. Early on we decided that the standard for technology in the building was to be state-of-the-shelf, but the standard for the overall design of the building and its various systems was to be state-of-the-art. In other words, we did not want the risk of untried technologies, but we did want the overall product to be at the frontier of what is now possible to do with ecologically smart design.

The building programs called for major changes, not only in the design process but also in the selection of materials, relationship to manufacturers, and in the way we counted the costs of the project. We intended to use materials that did not compromise the dignity or health of people somewhere else. We also wanted to use materials that had as little embodied fossil energy as possible, hence giving preference to those locally manufactured or grown. In the process, we discovered how little is generally known about the ecological and human effects of the materials system and how little the present tax and pricing system supports standards upholding ecological or human integrity. Unsurprisingly, we also discovered that the present system of building codes does little to encourage innovation leading to greater resource efficiency and environmental quality.

Typically, buildings are a kind of snapshot of the state of technology at a given time. In this case, however, we intended for the building to remain technologically dynamic over a long period of time. In effect, we proposed that the building adapt or learn as the state of technology changed and as our understanding of design became more sophisticated. This meant that we did not necessarily want to own particular components of the building such as the photovoltaic electric system which would be rendered obsolete as the technology advanced. We are exploring other arrangements, including leasing materials and technologies that will change markedly over the lifetime of the building.

The same strategy applied to materials. McDonough & Partners regarded the building as a union of two different metabolisms, one industrial, the other ecological. Materials that might eventually decompose into soil were considered part of an ecological metabolism. Otherwise they were part of an industrial metabolism and might be leased from the manufacturer and eventually returned as a feed stock to be remanufactured into new product.

The manner in which we appraised the total cost of the project represented another departure from standard practice of design and construction. Costs are normally considered synonymous with those of design and construction. As a consequence, institutions tend to ignore the costs that buildings incur over expected lifetimes as well as all of those other costs to environment and human health not included in the prices of energy, materials, and waste disposal. The costs of this project, accordingly, were higher because we included

- students, faculty, and community members in the design process
- research into materials and technologies to meet program goals
- higher performance standards (e.g., zero discharge and net energy export)
- more sophisticated technologies
- greater efforts to integrate technologies and systems
- a building maintenance fund in the project budget

In addition, we expect to do a materials audit of the building, including an estimate of the amount of carbon dioxide released by the construction, along with a menu of possibilities to offset these costs.

The project is on schedule for a 1998 groundbreaking with a tentative completion date of spring 1999. The basic energy, lighting, and fluid dynamics models have been completed and we now know that the goals described in the building program can be met within reasonable costs. When completed the building will generate most or all of its electricity. It will purify waste water on site. It will minimize or eliminate the use of toxic materials. It will be designed to remain technologically dynamic well into the future. It will be instrumental to display energy and significant ecological data in the atrium. The story of the building will be prominently displayed throughout the structure. It will be landscaped to include a small restored wetland and forest as well as gardens and orchards. In short, it is being designed and built to instruct its users in the arts of ecological competence and the possibilities of ecological design applied to buildings, energy systems, waste water, landscapes, and technology.

As important as the building and its landscape are, the more important effect of the project has been its impact on those who participated in the project. Some of the students who devoted time and energy to the project began to describe it as their "legacy" to the college. Because of their work on the project many of them learned about ecological design and how to solve real problems by doing it with some of the best practitioners in the world. Some of the faculty who participated in the effort and who were skeptical about the possibility of changing the institution came to see change as sometimes possible. And some of the trustees and administrators who initially saw this as a risky project perhaps came to regard risks incurred for the right goals as worthwhile.

The real test, however, lies ahead. It will be tempting for some, no doubt, to regard this as an interesting but isolated experiment having no relation to other buildings now in the planning stage or for campus landscaping or resource management. The pedagogically challenged will see no further possibilities for rethinking the process, substance, and goals of education. If so, the center will exist as an island on a campus that mirrors the larger culture. On the other hand,

the college and those that administer it have a model that might inform architectural standards for all new construction and renovation;
decisions about landscape management; financial decisions about pay-
back times and full-cost accounting; courses and projects around the
solution to real problems; and how we engage the wider community.

By some estimates, humankind is preparing to build more in the
next half century than it has built throughout all of recorded history.
If we do this inefficiently and carelessly, we will cast a long ecological
shadow on the human future. If we fail to pay the full environmental
costs of development, the resulting ecological and human damage will
be very large. To the extent that we do not aim for efficiency and the
use of renewable energy sources, the energy and maintenance costs
will unnecessarily divert capital from other and far better purposes.
The dream of sustainability, however defined, would then prove to be
only a fantasy. Ideas and ideals need to be rendered into models and
examples that make them visible, comprehensible, and compelling.
Who will do this?

More than any other institution in modern society, education
has a moral stake in the health, beauty, and integrity of the world
our students will inherit. We have an obligation to provide our students with tangible models that calibrate our values and capabilities,
models that they can see, touch, and experience. We have an obligation to create grounds for hope in our students who sometimes
define themselves as "generation X." But hope is different from wishful thinking, so we have a corollary obligation to equip our students with the analytical skills and practical competence necessary
to act on high expectations. When the pedagogical abstractions, words,
and whole courses do not fit the way the buildings and landscape
constituting the academic campus in fact work, they learn that
hope is just wishful thinking or, worse, rank hypocrisy. In short,
we have an obligation to equip our students to do the hard work
ahead of

- learning to power civilization by current sunlight
- reducing the amount of materials, water, and land use per capita
- growing their food and fiber sustainably
- disinventing the concept of waste
- preserving biological diversity
- restoring ecologies ruined in the past century
- rethinking the political basis of modern society
- developing economies that can be sustained within the limits of nature
- distributing wealth fairly within and between generations

No generation ever faced a more daunting agenda. True, but none ever faced more exciting possibilities either. Do we have or could we acquire the know-how to power civilization by current sunlight or to reduce the size of the "human footprint" or grow our food sustainably or prevent pollution or preserve biological diversity or restore degraded ecologies? In each case, I believe the answer is yes. Whether we possess the will and moral energy to do so while rethinking political and economic systems and the distribution of wealth within and between generations remains to be seen.

Finally, the potential for ecologically smarter design in all of its manifestations in architecture, landscape design, community design, the management of agricultural and forest lands, manufacturing, and technology does not amount to a fix for all that ails us. Reducing the amount of damage we do to the world per capita will only buy us a few decades, perhaps a century if we are lucky. If we squander that reprieve, we will have succeeded only in delaying the eventual collision between unfettered human desires and the limits of Earth. The default setting of our civilization needs to be reset to ensure that we build a sustainable world that is also humanly sustaining. This is not a battle between left and right or haves and have-nots as it is often described. At a deeper level the issue has to do with art, beauty, and spirit. In the largest sense, what we must do to ensure human tenure on Earth is to cultivate a new standard that defines beauty as that which causes no ugliness somewhere else or at some later time.

9.

EDUCATION AND THE WESTERN
SPIRITUAL TRADITION

John Taylor Gatto

John Taylor Gatto was a public school teacher in the New York City public school system for thirty years. He was New York State Teacher of the Year in 1991 and New York City Teacher of the Year on three occasions. He quit his job after realizing, in his words, "I teach how to fit into a world I don't want to live in." He is the author of *Dumbing Us Down: The Hidden Curriculum of Compulsory Schooling*, and *The Exhausted School*.

UNTIL ROUGHLY a hundred years ago, America was largely a Protestant Christian nation, with one significant distinction from the Christian nations of Europe: it was chiefly made up of independent and dissenting religious minds, not congregants of any official State Church. By "Western spiritual tradition," I refer to this peculiarly *American* Christian tradition, and to three particular aspects of its religious practice and doctrine: the congregational principle; the tradition of discipline and disciples; and the doctrine of original sin. Taken together, these three principles provide a muscular framework for a contemporary spirituality in education, American style.

THE CONGREGATIONAL PRINCIPLE

When the Puritans arrived in Salem in 1629, there were no Anglican officials around to approve selection of their church authorities. That would have been mandatory in the State Church of England, so the first congregation here took responsibility illegally into its own hands. That simple revolutionary act subverted power which traditionally belonged to state-certified experts and placed it into the hands of people who simply went to church. The sole yardstick of suitability for high office was that the seeker be the choice of ordinary people whose only proof of competence was joining a congregation which took religion seriously. That was it.

History dubbed this quasi-insurrection the Salem Procedure, and for the next 231 years that simple public shedding of traditional authority, which was an act of monumental localism, challenged the right of arrogant power to broadcast any centralized version of the truth without argument. America became perhaps the only nation in human history where ordinary people could argue with authorities without being beaten, jailed, or killed. That remains largely true in the world we live in today.

In the face of widespread moral and intellectual collapse in what is mistakenly called "public" education, we're being asked once again to patiently try a variety of expert solutions, whether by James Comer, Ted Sizer, Chris Whittle, the National Education Association, or any of a large number of other masks for institutional stakeholders. Some are honorable men, some dishonorable, but all clamor to manage the lives of children in various profitable mass-compulsion schooling schemes; none has any argument with secularized systematic instruction by force—only differences with the particular system in place.

Plato once told us, "Nothing of value comes from compulsion," but pass that by for a moment and concentrate on this new praetorian guard who claims the right to drain all children from the community like pied pipers. They come from a very few selective universities, from less than a dozen private foundations, from the board rooms of about thirty global corporations, from a handful of think tanks, from a few government agencies whose operations are shielded from public view, and from various other national associations remote from everyday life. This is a body like the ephors in ancient Sparta who ruled the public through fear from behind a screen of dummy legislators and chief executives.

The reforms of these reformers appear very different in their natures, representing different constituencies, but don't be fooled. Just as we haven't had a two-party political system for a long time, perhaps since the power to issue currency was stripped from the House of Representatives and placed in the hands of private bankers, all the narrow set of cronies who float national school reforms belong to the same clubs, read the same magazines, send their children to the same private schools, and address each other using first names when they meet in Chevy Chase, Cambridge, Palo Alto, or Boulder.

You could never mistake any of the comfortable experts who have appropriated the right to speak for ordinary people—for the people who thought God more important than anything, the ones who built the New England congregations—although indeed many of the modern experts are honorable men.

Congregations were never universal, but always intensely local. Particular men and women were attached to them who knew their fellow congregants by name and by family history. They were not mere networks of pious people who met whenever it was convenient. They cared about each other, not about humanity in general. If a congregation had a school problem, it would not welcome outside intervention unless it asked for help. These places insisted upon their God-given right to do things their own way, to make their own mistakes. I don't think you can grow up unless you're allowed to make your own mistakes.

Were some of these congregations bad places? Of course they were. Some of them were horrible, but think hard about this: at least the damage stopped abruptly at the boundaries of a single church. That's the difference between a congregational reality and a State Church system or, indeed, any systematic universal governance. A system won't let you walk away—while a congregation says good luck and good riddance.

We're far from a time when we trusted each other or ourselves enough to make waves in congregations without official surveillance from outside experts. Since the Civil War, a century and a half of increasingly suffocating expert interventions in our schools has left us thinking there isn't any other way to do things. To get something done, Harvard has to be called in or Stanford or Yale or the Carnegie Corporation. Official strangers decide everything important, sometimes with token local voices allowed to ventilate before the prearranged decision is published. Often, not even that bone is tossed. Nor is there any target for our children to aim for in this society but approval from official strangers. That's a major reason our families fall apart. How can children respect their own parents when those sad souls are regularly contradicted by various agents of the State, most frequently by the school hierarchy? Our parents have been made childlike by people, doubtless honorable, who have fatally trivialized the institution of parenthood.

The Salem Procedure of picking lay people, of letting them pick their own experts, and then keeping an eye on those experts because the congregational polity was small enough to allow that, has a kinship to the powerful vision of Anabaptists—a vision which lives on in the spectacularly successful, spectacularly prosperous Amish communities that have driven the governments of Pennsylvania, Ohio, Indiana, and Wisconsin livid with rage because of their successes this past century.

But it also draws from a well of common sense innate in people who actually work instead of talk for a living. Small farmers, craftspeople, teamsters, artists, fishermen, loggers, small entrepreneurs, people who maintain an intuitive understanding of the fakery lurking near any expert claim to superior wisdom. And I'm being precise here: I mean superior *wisdom*. Of course, experts are supposed to have superior knowledge, but knowledge and wisdom are far from the same things, and to conflate the two is madness. Going to college can help you be knowledgeable, but it cannot make you wise.

The particular American genius was to locate wisdom in ordinary people while every other government on earth located it in an aristocracy, a theocracy, a military class, a merchant class, or in civil service experts.

The failure of forced monopoly schooling to check our slide into despair and moral chaos allows me to demand the subordination of the expert voice once again, on the grounds it has had a century's monopoly reign and has produced a bankrupt leadership with not the slightest idea how to get us out of this mess we're in except to ask for more. More money, more power, more power over our children, more resources for a sorry elite who are currently making a desperate effort to turn the leadership of our schools over to men and women who sell soap for a living, or cigarettes, or processed food. That's what school-to-work legislation is, of course.

It's time to turn the school business back to people where the Constitution vested it in the Tenth Amendment. It's time to let any small group that wants to try to show what it can do in schooling. A million family schools over the past decade have demonstrated that uncertified parents, many of them in modest circumstances and lacking the benefit of college themselves, can pin back the ears of the best factory-model schools, public or private.

The congregational principle is a spiritual force propelling the maximum number of people to reach their full potential by vesting everyone with an identity and a voice at the policy table and doing it in voluntary associations with members who feel in harmony with one another. That's the way the Council on Foreign Relations works; that's the way the Ad Council works; that's the way the Business Roundtable works; that's the way the Sidwell Friends School that Mrs. Clinton's daughter went to works; that's the way Groton and Saint Paul's work; and that's the way public schools will work best, too.

If you think about this, you begin to wonder what purpose is being served by arranging government schools any other way. The congregationalists knew that good things happen to the human spirit when it is left alone to make its own curriculum. No two congregational churches ever got together. They had contempt for the Presbyterians because that denomination met once a year in a synod. The congregations did not officially compare notes. They didn't inquire about each other's doctrinal purity, they had no universal management. Some churches were good, some were horrible, but each was sui generis. Each was sovereign. And what was the result? The forms, the spirit, and the leadership of New England during its congregational period produced the only coherent regional culture this nation has ever seen, with the Anglican tidewater South a distant second. Indeed, New England ships were selling ice cut from local ponds to India, if you can believe that, long before you could take a train from Boston to New York. Ninety-eight percent of the Massachusetts population could read, write, and count quite well before the legislature, at the urging of the new industrial business establishment (coal mining and railroad interests like the Peabody family and real estate interests eager to exploit the empty land to the west), rammed through a compulsory schooling law. The entire Connecticut population was also literate without forced schooling. We have never reached that degree of literacy again.

DISCIPLINE AND DISCIPLES

Wherever I go in the United States these days I hear of something called the crisis of discipline, how children are unmotivated, how they resist learning. That is nonsense, of course. Children resist teaching, as they should, but nobody resists learning. However, I won't dispute that schools are in chaos. Even the ones that seem quiet and orderly are in a kind of moral chaos beyond the power of journalism, so far, to penetrate. And restless children underline the school's failure so they come to public attention, and they must be explained some way by authorities.

I don't think it's off the mark to say that all of us, whatever else we may disagree upon, want kids to have discipline in the sense of self-control. That goes for black mothers in Harlem where I taught for five years, despite the secret religion of schooling that believes those mothers are genetically challenged. But we want more than behavioral discipline. We pray for discipline in the more specialized sense of intellectual interests well enough mastered to provide joy and consolation all our lives—and maybe even a buck, too.

A discipline is what people who drink Chablis instead of Pittsburgh red whiskey call a field of learning like chemistry, history, philosophy, et cetera, and its lore. The good student is literally a disciple of a discipline. The words are from the Latin *disciplinare* and *discipulus*. (By the way, I learned all this from a schoolteacher in Utica, New York, named Orin Dominico, who writes me and I pay attention. In this discipline matter, I'm Orin's disciple.)

The most famous discipline in Western tradition is that of Jesus Christ. That's true today, and it was true fifteen hundred years ago; and the most famous disciples are his twelve apostles. What did Christ's model of educational discipline look like? Well, attendance wasn't mandatory, for one thing. Christ didn't set up the Judea Compulsory School System. He issued an invitation, "Follow me," and some did, and some didn't. And Christ didn't send the truant officer after those who didn't.

So as Orin tells me, the first characteristic of this model is a *calling*. Those who pursued Christ's discipline did so out of desire. It was their own choice. They were called to it by an inner voice, a voice we never give students enough time alone to possibly hear. And that's more true of the good schools than it is of the bad ones.

Our present system of schooling alienates us so sharply from our inner genius, most of us are barred from being able ever to hear our calling. Calling in most of us shrivels to fantasy and daydreams as a remnant of what might have been.

The second characteristic of Christ's discipline was *commitment*. Following Jesus was not easy. You had to drop everything else, and there was zero chance you could get rich doing it. You had to love what you were doing. Only love could induce you to walk across deserts, sleep in the wilderness, hang out with riffraff, and suffer scorn from all the established folks you encountered.

The third characteristic of Christ's model of discipleship was *self-*

awareness and independence. Christ's disciples were not stooges. They had to think for themselves and draw their own conclusions from the shared experience. Christ didn't give lectures or handouts. He taught by example, by his own practice, and through parables which were open to interpretation. Orin, my coach, personally doubts that Christ ever intended to start a school or an institutional religion, for institutions invariably corrupt ideas unless they are kept small. They regiment thinking, and they tend toward military forms of discipline. Christ's followers started the Church, not Christ.

And finally, Christ's model of discipline requires a *master* to follow—one who has himself or herself submitted to discipline and still practices it. Christ didn't say, "You guys stay here in the desert and fast for a month. I'll be over at the Ramada. You can find me in the bar if you need help." He did not begin his own public life until he was almost a rabbi, one fully versed in his tradition.

One way out of the fix we're in with schools would be a return to discipleship in education. During early adolescence, students without a clear sense of calling might have a series of apprenticeships and mentorships which mostly involve self-education. Our students have pressing needs to be alone on quests. To test themselves against obstacles both internal and external.

As it is, we currently drown students in low-level busywork, shove them together in forced associations which teach them to hate other people, not to love them. We subject them to the filthiest, most pornographic regimen of constant surveillance and ranking so they never experience the solitude and reflection necessary to become a whole man or woman.

DIS-SPIRITED SCHOOLING

The net effect of holding a child in confinement for twelve years and longer without any honor paid to the spirit is an extended demonstration that the State considers the Western God tradition to be dangerous. And, of course, it is. Schooling is about creating loyalty to an abstract central authority, and no serious rival can be welcome in a school—that includes mother and father, tradition, local custom, self-management, or God.

The Supreme Court *Everson* ruling of 1947 established the principle that the State would have no truck with spirits. There was no mention that one hundred fifty years of American judicial history had passed without any other court finding this fantastic hidden meaning in the Constitution.

But even if we forgo an examination of the motives of this court and grant that the ruling is a sincere expression of the rational principle behind modern leadership, we would be justified in challenging *Everson* today because of the grotesque record laid down over the past fifty years of spiritless schooling. Dis-spirited schooling has been tested and found fully wanting. I personally think that that's because it is a liar's game that denies the metaphysical reality recognized by men and women worldwide today and in every age. One of the great ironies of Chelsea Clinton's schooling at Sidwell Friends School is that she was compelled to study Quaker history and participate in Quaker meeting. For Chelsea, it was take it or leave it at Sidwell. She seems to have survived that compulsion to learn a religion not her own.

It is ironic from a contrarian viewpoint that the most prestigious scientific position in the world today is surely heading up the Human Genome Project. Corporations are lined up all the way to China to make fortunes out of genetic manipulation, and at the head of that project is a man named Dr. Francis X. Collins who, according to *The New York Times,* personally recognizes religion as the most important reality in his life.

Collins was reared in an agnostic home in western Virginia where he was home schooled all his life by his outspoken, radical mother, who broke the law, he says, in a number of ways to give him an education. While in medical school, he came to the conclusion—I'm quoting Collins—that he would become a born-again Christian because the decision was "intellectually inescapable." It blew my mind to read that. And he has maintained that faith energetically ever since, a decision that makes his professional colleagues very uncomfortable.

The difficulty with rational thought, however valuable a tool it certainly is, is that it misses the deepest properties of human nature: our feelings of loneliness and incompletion, our sense of sin, our need to love, our longing after immortality.

Let me illustrate very specifically how rational thinking preempts terrain where it has no business and makes a wretched mess of human affairs. Listen carefully and you can tell your grandchildren you actually heard someone at the end of the twentieth century challenge Galileo's heliocentric theory:

In materially evidentiary terms, the Sun is at the center of the Solar System, not the Earth, and the Solar System itself is lost in the endless immensity of space. I suppose most of you believe that, how could you not? And yet, as far as we scientifically know to date, only planet Earth looks as if it were designed with people in mind. I know that Carl Sagan says we'll find millions of populated planets eventually, but right now there's only hard evidence of one. As far as we know, you can't go anyplace else but Earth and stay alive for long. So as of 1997, Earth is clearly the center of the human universe. I want to push this a little further, however.

Planet Earth is most definitely not the center of your personal life. It's merely a background which floats in and out of conscious thought. The truth is that psychologically, you are the center of the universe and the Solar System. And don't be modest or try to hide the fact. The minute you deny what I just said, you're in full flight from the responsibility this centrality entails: to make things better for the rest of us who are on the periphery of your consciousness.

When you deny your own centrality, you necessarily lose some trust in yourself to move mountains. As your self-trust wanes—and school is there to drill you in distrusting yourself (What else do you think it means to wait for a teacher to tell you what to do?)—you lose some self-respect. Without self-respect, you could hardly love yourself because we can't really love those we don't respect or trust— except, curiously enough, by an act of faith. When you can't fully trust yourself or even like yourself very much, you're in a much worse predicament than you may realize because those things are a preamble to sustaining loving relationships with other people and with the world outside yourself. Think of it this way: You must be convinced of your own worth before you ask for the love of another or else the bargain will be unsound. You'll be trading discounted merchandise unless both of you are similarly disadvantaged, and perhaps even then your relationship will disintegrate, usually painfully.

The trouble with Galileo's way is that it is a partial truth. It's right about the relations of dead matter, and it's wrong about the geography of the spirit. But schools can only teach Galileo's victory over the Church. They cannot afford to harbor children who command personal power. So the subtlety of the analysis that you and I just went through which can confer power has to be forgone. Galileo's rightness is only a tiny part of a real education. His blindness is much more to the point. The goal of a real education is to bring us to a point where we can take full responsibility for our own lives, and in that quest, Galileo is only one more fact of little human consequence.

The ancient religious question of free will marks the real difference between schooling and education. Education is conceived in Western history as a road to knowing yourself and through that knowledge arriving at a further understanding of community, relationships, jeopardy, living nature, and inanimate matter. But none of those things has any particular meaning until you see what they lead up to finally, being in full command of the spectacular gift of free will: a force completely beyond the power of science to understand.

With the tool of free will, anyone can forge a personal purpose. Free will allows infinite numbers of human stories to be written in which a personal *you* is the main character. All of the sciences, hard or soft—although the soft are much worse in this regard—assume that

Purpose (that's with a capital P) and free will are hogwash. All of them believe that, given enough data, everything will be seen as predetermined.

Schooling is an instrument to disseminate this bleak and sterile vision of a blind-chance universe. When schooling is able to displace education, as happened in the U.S. just about a century ago, a deterministic worldview can be imposed upon society. We can entrap children into becoming organic machinery simply by ignoring the universal human awareness there is something dreadfully important beyond the rational. We can cause children to mistrust themselves so severely they come to depend on cost-benefit analyses for every important decision. We can teach them to scorn faith so comprehensively that buying things and feeling good become the whole point of their lives.

The Soviet empire did this brilliantly for a little over seventy years. Its surveillance of individual lives was total. It maintained dossiers on each human unit, logged every deviation, and assigned a mathematical value so that citizens could be ranked against each other.

Does that sound familiar? It schooled every child in a fashion prescribed by the best psychological experts. It strictly controlled the rewards of work to ensure compliance, and it developed a punishment system unheard of in its comprehensiveness. If you want to ever explore that, read Solzhenitsyn's *Gulag Archipelago*. If human science could guarantee a stable orthodoxy directed out of the centralized leadership of a political state, then the Soviet practice reached the millennium where lives can be regarded as Galileo regarded planetary bodies.

I sat no more than ten feet directly in front of Jean Kirkpatrick nine or ten years ago in a small room in the Old Senate Office Building as she informed a little group of political party chairmen assembled there that it would be at least one hundred years before we could hope to see cracks in the Soviet Union because they had mastered every detail of deviance, and they could chart opposition and prescribe its remedy far in advance. Oh, Jean! Oh, Jean! She said the

Kremlin owns all the tanks, all the jobs, all the schools, and all the food. But just the other day, I read in *The New York Times* that eight thousand criminal gangs, many of them white-collar organizations, operate freely today in what used to be the Soviet Union. An explosion of irrationality is upon them in spite of all their scientific precautions. Finally, the suffocation of leading well-schooled lives got to be more than the Soviets could bear. Nobody could be trusted, not even the army. Everybody cheated, lied, stole, sabotaged orders, felt contempt for everyone else because they felt contempt for themselves.

The bedrock principles of human nature had just been violated too long, and so the whole apparatus fell apart. It lasted one lifetime. Our softer form of spiritual suffocation has already been in place for two lifetimes. The neglected genius of the West, neglected by the forced-schooling institution as a deliberate policy, lies in its historical forging of a collection of spiritual doctrines which grant dignity and responsibility to ordinary individuals, not just to elites. I have the greatest respect for every other religious tradition in the world, but not one of them has ever done this or attempted to do this. The Western spiritual tradition correctly identified the problems that not one of us can escape, the problems you can't elude with money or intellect or charm, science, politics, or powerful connections. It also said that these problems were, paradoxically, fundamental to human happiness.

THE CHALLENGES OF ORIGINAL SIN

We first encounter a description of these problems in the Hebrew Bible arising as universal punishments for the disobedience of Adam and Eve. Even if you believe yourself too sophisticated to accept the story at face value, it matters little to my accounting because it is certain that you do share these burdens with believers, as you'll soon see. What I'm speaking of is *original sin,* a concept which comes from the Christian interpretation of the Book of Genesis, which has powerfully affected the shape of every Western institution in the past fifteen hundred years. The fallout from a millennium-long, often bloody debate about original sin was profound. Out of Genesis came four penalties which followed the expulsion from Eden. And if you'll forgive me some slight modernization of the Genesis account, I'll enumerate those burdens.

First was *labor.* There was no need to work in Eden, but now we would have to care for ourselves. Next, there was an emotional penalty of *pain.* There was no pain in Eden, but now our natures would be subject to being led astray, to overindulging, to feeling tremendous pain, even from natural acts like childbirth, whether we were good people or bad people.

Third, there was the amazingly two-edged *free will* penalty which included the right to choose evil, which would now lurk everywhere. Recall that in Eden there was exactly one wrong thing to do. Now we would bear the constant stress of having to be morally wary or surrendering to sin.

And lastly—and most importantly—we were assigned the *limitation penalty.* The term of human life would be strictly limited. Nobody escapes death. And the more you have in wealth, family, community, and friends, the more you will be tempted to curse God as you witness yourself day by day losing physical beauty and energy and eventually losing everything. If you know the Book of Job, you'll have an idea of what I mean.

So that's some doom, I know you'll agree. The question is what to do about it? Since these penalties exist in a religious universe, but also exist as matter-of-fact, everyday material realities, two different answers emerged—depending upon how intensely one group or the other felt the spiritual pull.

THE RESPONSE OF THE DIS-SPIRITED

I'll start with the group that cast its lot on the racehorse of shrewdness, calculation, and science to find a way out because that group has commanded forced schooling, our economy, our technology, and our public philosophy for over a century. Here is its response to the challenge of original sin.

On *labor*. Work is a necessary evil, but for the smart, it is a curse which can be avoided. Machines and electronic slaves are making work obsolete. Only stupid people work. Hired hands are there for those who understand this.

On *pain*. There are many scientific ways to avoid pain and enhance pleasure. Chemicals and other modern magic have made pain obsolete and with them have come most problems of overindulgence. If you get drunk, megadoses of vitamin B will handle it. If you get fat, you can be liposucked; if you get old, there's plastic surgery. Grab for the gusto. You only go around once. Good feelings are what life is about. There isn't anything else.

On the third penalty, *good and evil*. The dis-spirited response denies that they even exist. When Alger Hiss accepted the presidency of the World Health Organization in 1948, his initiatory address said that the problem of good and evil was an illusion and had caused more harm in the world than anything else and everything else put together. From that perspective, every principle is negotiable. All ethics are situational. Nothing isn't relativistic, and you cannot know too much. With enough knowledge, you can duplicate the mythical God's powers. You can walk on water, you can fly, you can even create life.

Did God destroy Sodom and Gomorrah with fire in the Hebrew Bible? Well, wake up. We turned the night sky over the Sinai just a few years ago into flame with a gasoline-air mixture which incinerated one hundred thousand retreating Iraqis in a matter of seconds. Only one out of six of those people even had a weapon. We are God, at least the most evolutionarily advanced among us are. And you know where you find them—at Harvard, Princeton, and the Yale Divinity School.

And finally, on *aging and death*. Aging and death are the ultimate evils, but magic is available in the form of pills, potions, lotions, surgery, aerobics, to stave off sickness and extend life. Young is the name of the game when it's all said and done, so aging must be concealed as long as possible through dress, speech, personal training regimens, and attitude makeovers. We only live once, and life is the highest value, so it follows that the health industry holds the ultimate wisdom around which we should center our attention. Every day science gets closer and closer to making life eternal.

You see how easy it can be to repudiate the penalties of original sin, to grant absolute absolution. Ideologically speaking, that was the main mission of forced schooling: to redirect loyalty away from God and those who lived in a godly fashion by the Western Christian tradition to belief in a corporate industry and specialized intelligence.

THE SPIRITUAL RESPONSE

What Western spirituality taught was much different. Rather than avoiding the punishments, it asked you to embrace them. It taught the marvelous paradox that willing acceptance of these burdens was the only way to a good, full life, the only way to inner peace. By bending your head in obedience, it would be raised up strong, brave, indomitable, and wise. Now let me go through the same list of penalties from the spiritual perspective.

About *labor*, the religious voice said that work was the only avenue to genuine self-respect. Work develops independence, self-reliance, resourcefulness, and a host of other valuable things. Work itself is a value elevated far above a paycheck, above praise, above accomplishment. Work produces a spiritual reward unknown to the reinforcement schedules of behavioral psychologists like B. F. Skinner, but only if you tackle it gladly, without resentment or avoidance, whether you're digging a ditch or building a skyscraper.

If the secular aversion to work is a thing to be rationalized, as schools do rationalize minimal effort, a horrifying problem is created for our entire society, one which has proven so far to be incurable: I refer to the psychological, social, and spiritual anxieties that arise when you have no useful work to do. Phony work, no matter how well paid or praised, causes such great emotional distortions to emerge that the major efforts of our civilization will soon go into solving them. But there is no hint of an answer in sight from any familiar modernist quarter.

In the economy we have allowed to evolve, the real political dilemma everywhere is keeping people occupied. Jobs have to be invented by government agencies and corporations, and both employ millions and millions of people for which they have no real use. It's an inside secret in the top echelon of CEOs that when you want to exercise your stock options, all you need to cause a sharp rise in the stock's value is to lay off forty thousand people. And that is done regularly and cynically independent of bottom lines. I learned that by reading *Fortune*.

Young men and women during their brightest, orneriest, and most energetic years are kept from working or from being a part of the general society as they would have been in Ben Franklin's day. This is done to keep them from aggravating this work situation either by working too eagerly, as kids are prone to do, or by inventing their own work which could cause a cataclysm in the economy. The violation of the injunction to work which Western spirituality imposed has backed us into a corner from which no authority has any idea how to extricate us. We cannot afford to let children learn to work as Amish children do for fear they will discover one of the great secrets of Western history: Work is not a curse, but a salvation.

About the second penalty, *pain,* Western spirituality has always regarded pain as a friend because it forces attention off the things of this world and puts it squarely back into the center of the universe, which is yourself. Pain and distress in all its forms are the ways we learn self-control (among other valuable lessons), but the siren call of feel-good lures us to court sensations and to despise pain as a spoiler of pleasure. Western spirituality teaches that pain is the road to self-knowledge, that self-knowledge is the road to trusting yourself; that without such trust, you cannot like yourself; without such self-liking, you can never dependably love another or love God.

About the third penalty, *good and evil,* Western spirituality demands you write your own script through the world. In a spiritual being, everything is morally charged, nothing is neutral, no excuses are accepted. Choosing is a daily burden, but one which makes you fully alive because literally everything then becomes a big deal.

I heard secondhand very recently about a woman who said to her mother about an affair she was conducting openly, despite the protest of her husband and in full knowledge of her six-year-old daughter, that, "It's no big deal." That's what she said to her mother. But if infidelity, divorce, and the shattering of innocence in a child isn't a big deal, then what could ever be one? By intensifying our moral sense, we feel the exhilaration of being alive in a universe where everything is a big deal.

To have a real life, you must bring as many choices as you can out of the preprogrammed mode and under the conscious command of your will. The bigger the life you seek, the less anything can be made automatic, as if you were only a piece of machinery. And because every choice has a moral dimension, it will incline toward one or the other pole of that classic dichotomy that people hate to hear about, good and evil. Despite any extenuating circumstances—and they are legion, I know—the accumulating record of our choices marks us as worthy or as unworthy people. Even if nobody else is aware how your accounts stand, deep inside the running balance will vitally affect your ability to trust, to love, to gain peace and wisdom from your relationships and your community.

And finally, *aging and death.* In the Western spiritual tradition which grew out of a belief in original sin, the focus was primarily on the lesson that nothing in this world is more than an illusion. This is only a stage on some longer journey we do not understand. To fall in love with your physical beauty or your wealth, your health, your power to experience good feelings is to kid yourself because they will be taken away. An eighty-six-year-old aunt of mine with a Ph.D. from the University of Chicago and a woman I love very, very dearly said to me tearfully after the death of her husband of sixty years who had left her millions of dollars, "They don't let you win. There is no way to win."

She had lived her life in the camp of science, honorably observing all its rules of rationality, but at this pass, science was useless to her. The Western spiritual tradition would reply, "Of course you can win. Everyone can win. And if you think you can't, then you're playing the wrong game."

The only thing that gives our time on earth any deep significance is that none of this will last. Only that temporality gives our relationships any urgency, and passion makes our choices matter. If you were indestructible, what a curse! How could it possibly matter whether you did anything today or next year or in the next hundred years, learned anything, loved anybody? There would always be time for everything and anything. What would be the big deal?

Everyone has had the experience of having too much candy or too much company or even too much money, so much that no individual purchase can involve real choices because real choices always close the door on other choices. I know that we would all like to have endless amounts of money, but the truth is too much money wipes out our ability to choose since we can now choose everything. That's what the Roman emperor Marcus Aurelius discovered for himself in his reflections on what really matters. In the Meditations, which has become one of the greatest classics in Western history, he discovered that none of it was for sale. If you don't believe any emperor would feel this way, read the Meditations.

Too much time, like too much money, can hang heavily as well. Look at millions of bored schoolchildren. They know. The corrective for this boredom is full spiritual awareness that time is finite. As you spend time on one thing, you lose forever the chance to spend it on something else. It *is* a big deal.

Science cannot help with time. In fact, living scientifically so as not to waste time, becoming one of those poor souls who never goes anywhere without a list, is the best guarantee that your life will be eaten up by errands and that none of those errands will ever become the big deal that you desperately need to finally love yourself—because the list of things still to do will go ever onward and onward. The best lives are full of contemplation, full of solitude, full of self-examination, full of private, personal attempts to engage the metaphysical mystery of existence.

There must be a reason that we are called human *beings* and not human *doings*. And I think the reason is to commemorate the way we can make the best of our limited time by alternating effort with reflection, and reflection completely free of the get-something motive. Whenever I see a kid daydreaming in school, I'm careful never to shock the reverie out of existence.

Buddha is reputed to have said, "Do nothing. Time is too precious to waste." If that advice seems impossible in the world described in the evening news, reflect on the awesome fact that in spite of the hype, you still live on a planet where 67 percent of the world's entire population has never made or received a single phone call and where the Amish of Lancaster County live prosperous lives free of crime, divorce, or children who go beyond the eighth grade in school. And yet not a single one of that 150,000-member sect has a college degree, a tractor to plow with, or a telephone.

If I seem to have stepped away from original sin with these facts, it is not so. Until you can acknowledge that the factual contents of your mind upon which you base decisions have been inserted there by others whose motives you cannot fully understand, you will never come to appreciate the neglected genius of Western spirituality, which teaches that you are the center of the universe and that the most important things worth knowing are innate in you already. They cannot be learned through schooling. They are self-taught through the burdens of having to work, having to sort out right from wrong, having to find a way to check your appetites, and having to age and die.

The effect of this formula on world history has been titanic. It brought every citizen in the West a mandate to be sovereign, which we still have not learned to use wisely, but which offers the potential of such wisdom the moment we figure out a way to put the neo-aristocracy of global business, global government, and massive institutions back into the Pandora's box where they belong.

Western spirituality granted every single individual a purpose for being alive, a purpose independent of mass behavior prescriptions, money, experts, governments. It conferred significance on every aspect of relationship and community. It carried inside its ideas the seeds of a self-activating curriculum which gives meaning to time.

In Western spirituality, everyone counts. It offers a basic, matter-of-fact set of practical guidelines, streetlamps for the village of your life. Nobody has to wander aimlessly in the universe of Western spirituality. What constitutes a meaningful life is clearly spelled out: self-knowledge, duty, responsibility, acceptance of aging and loss, preparation for death. In the neglected genius of the West, no teacher or guru does the work for you; you must do it for yourself.

LEARNING AS INITIATION: NOT-KNOWING, BEARING WITNESS, AND HEALING

Joan Halifax

Joan Halifax is an author and anthropologist who brings to her work a rich background of Buddhist practice and years of direct study with indigenous peoples. She serves on the faculties of Columbia University, the University of Miami School of Medicine, the New School for Social Research, The Naropa Institute, and the California Institute for Integral Studies. Her books include *The Human Encounter with Death* (with Stanislav Grof), *Shamanic Voices: A Survey of Visionary Narratives*, *Shaman: The Wounded Healer*, and *The Fruitful Darkness*.

IN OUR CULTURE, the word *education* means "to be led out of ignorance into knowing and knowledge." Learning is described in terms of the accumulation of facts. In looking at how learning is experienced within tribal cultures, we discover that the complement of education as we know it in the West is *initiation,* plunging inward. Initiation takes us into the unknown and is grounded in not-knowing. I propose that the initiatory dimension of learning is imperative for Western culture now.

Within indigenous cultures, there are rituals that allow for experiential learning. Certainly, learning takes place through a wide variety of forms and styles in indigenous cultures; however, the most important context of learning occurs in the ritual process of initiation, known as *rites of passage*. The Dutch scholar Arnold van Gennep wrote an important, insightful book in the 1920s that inspired thinkers like Joseph Campbell, Mircea Eliade, and Joseph Henderson. Van Gennep examined rites of passage from many different cultures, discovering that most rites of passage move through three distinct phases. The first phase he called "separation." Separation is moving away from the familiar landscape of the social territory and into the unfamiliar, the unknown: into not-knowing. The second phase he designated "the threshold experience": an experience of the liminal, a time when myth and story unfold and where love and death become amplified for the initiate. Threshold experiences, he pointed out, are chaotic, ground shaking, and transformative. They are a time when the initiate learns to bear witness, to be present for all dimensions of reality. The third phase he called "incorporation": the movement back into the everyday world, a time of healing, of making whole again. These rites can mark a phase shift for an individual or group, a change in maturation, or even a change in status—such as profession or geographical location.

These three phases parallel the Three Tenets in the Zen Peacemaker Order founded by Roshi Bernie Glassman and the late Sensei Jishu Holmes. The first tenet of the order is "not-knowing" and denotes separation from the familiar, conditioned world of knowing, the opening of the spontaneous mind of the beginner. The second tenet is "bearing witness," and emphasizes being fully present to the suffering and joy in oneself and the world. The third tenet is "healing oneself and others" through returning to the world with the aspiration of liberating oneself and others from suffering.

I want to use these Three Tenets as a means of considering the relationship between learning and initiation. Additionally, I'd like to discuss one of the key learning practices in the order: "taking a plunge." Taking a plunge is, in essence, a rite of passage where an individual enters into a wholly different world of learning, for example the death camps at Auschwitz. In "plunging," an individual works with the

Three Tenets of not-knowing, bearing witness, and healing as a means of learning and healing in and from the world.

Contemporary Americans consider rites of passage as something that *other* cultures do. There are universal significant transitions in everyone's lives which go unmarked—unrecognized by us—but are acknowledged as significant by other societies. For example, the rituals during puberty, or the phase shift from adulthood to old age—becoming a respected elder. Yet perhaps, in another way, rites of passage *are* being acted out by us—albeit in unconscious and chaotic ways—with unfortunate and significant implications for our social and environmental landscapes.

Participation in wars are rites of passage for young males into "instant" manhood (as well as an initiation for nations into the realm of power); the initiation into gangs, partaking of extreme sports, and even "doing drugs" are all state shifts that may be understood to be sublimated rites of initiation.

The need to die and be reborn, the need to be renewed, the need to encounter profoundly life's mystery, the need to engage the imagination—these arise for every living person. But where are the rituals in our culture that denote and valorize change? Where are the rituals that open us to not-knowing? The rituals that grant us the space, freedom, and encouragement to grow or change? Almost absent. Some people have to literally go crazy in order to deepen and mature; to dare falling off the edge and into the other side's perspective; to drift alone, apart from culture, before rebounding into an arena of introspection, deep questioning and, finally, action. Some resolve to enter a strong spiritual practice. Others become physically ill and, like wounded healers, learn to heal themselves and then turn outward to help others.

But what does our society do? Certainly not acknowledge these experiences as initiation or education! In fact, most often these chaotic experiences are avoided. And if by some miracle they do arise, they are controlled or suppressed. These times—when the imagination is activated, or individuals open up to a fresh state of not-knowing—are not times with which our society is comfortable. This liminal state of being betwixt and between is not understood or tolerated, or valorized by society, our families, even us.

Rites of passage are opportunities for individuals to leave behind that which is familiar, the known and knowing, and enter, by way of a committed plunge, into the unknown and experience firsthand of not-knowing. They are opportunities to bear witness to joy and suffering in oneself and others, and to heal. Yet education seems to be, in the West, a setting where we learn not to heal but instead to "deal." James Hillman speaks of education as a kind of psychopathology where we all become dealers. We learn how to use—to deal in—the world around us. Through education we learn to objectify the world; we learn to perceive the world as an object to be explained, exploited, manipulated, and marketed. For example, the marketing of fantasy at Disneyland and elsewhere, or the media exploitation of personal tragedy.

Rites of passage, on the other hand, are opportunities for us to engender extensive subjectivity and active participation in the happenings of our families, relationships, communities, environment—even our own bodies. Separating ourselves from the familiar and habitual is important. Exposing habits, recognizing social and cultural conditioning, and the habitual patterns of our minds and bodies is crucial—regardless of whether our culture is indigenous, ancient, or postmodern. Extensive subjectivity allows us to step outside of ourselves into a larger space and view of the world, a view that reveals fundamental interconnectedness.

NOT-KNOWING

The first phase of a rite of passage is "separation," a time when we embrace not-knowing by leaving the familiar behind. Before a person leaves for a vision fast, for example, he or she encounters not-knowing in a profound way. What will it feel like to not eat? Will I be cold?

Will I be afraid of being alone? What will I do with all that time? What if I get injured? Will I survive? This experience and questioning can be translated back into every single moment of our life. How can we truly know for sure what will happen in the next moment?

Each moment is a treasure box that has never been opened and experienced before. Suzuki Roshi once said, "Wisdom is a ready mind." This mind of readiness is a mind that is free of concepts. It is the "beginner's mind" where anything can happen. The beginning phase in a rite of passage, the time of separation, is where the mind of not-knowing is opened. Here confidence can arise from our learning an important lesson: the acceptance of what is, without our attempts to control, manipulate, or judge.

BEARING WITNESS

The middle phase of a rite of passage is the threshold experience, the time when the stories that have been told by the fireside are amplified into myth and ritual. Myths are oral technologies that unwrap time, moving us into the timeless. Timelessness is a critical part of learning; it is through being out of relation to time as an absolute that the past and future are realized in the present. When time is unwrapped, we are more readily able to simultaneously touch the relative and the absolute. We often experience—through strong cultural conditioning—the relative and absolute as actually opposite of what their true essence is. In bearing witness, we realize that the relative and absolute are interdependent. Samsara and nirvana are one. We also realize that intellectual or emotional reactions are not an absolute and, therefore, all-determining factor of presence and perception. When we realize this, it is liberating; we realize that this present moment will pass, as will an infinite number of others as well—and that there is nothing to attach to.

The threshold experience in a rite of passage is thoroughly experiential. While a teacher can give us information, a teacher cannot give us wisdom. Wisdom is not an object to impart. We ourselves must have a direct experience of dying to the old life and awakening to a new life freed of conditioning; bearing witness to our suffering and joy; and opening fully to change and potential. In Buddhism, we sometimes talk about "direct practice realization": that it is only through direct experience that wisdom is realized.

In bearing witness, when the experiential is fully present, myth is no longer a story that is "out there." And there are no longer such things as symbols. We become the place we travel to. We become the gods themselves; we experience the power, the frailties, and the greatness present in the gods, in the landscape, in animals and plants, in weather and sky, in the sun and moon. We become like the Huichols who travel as gods to Wirikuta, the sacred land of peyote. *We are the story* as we bear witness; we become one with the story.

HEALING

The last phase of a rite of passage van Gennep terms "incorporation": the return, the road of healing. In a rite of passage, one returns to one's community with eyes, heart, and hands which can heal the community. Paradoxically, incorporation *is* education. It is returning with a clear and open mind and heart to the ordinary world, bringing not-knowing, bearing witness, and healing back into the world. In healing, we weave our experiences of separation and not-knowing, and the experience of threshold and bearing witness into learning through their incorporation into each moment.

TAKING A PLUNGE

What does it mean in our culture to be a wise woman or a wise man? Or a mature person? What does it mean to walk on the old paths and step into the great river of not-knowing? Where is the place for wise people in our communities? And further, what does it mean to develop, from our own direct experience, an ethic of compassion based on not-knowing and bearing witness?

How might we educate our young people so that they return to their communities with vision renewed, with love and compassion present? How can we help our young people to open themselves? How can we help our young people—all people—to open up to not-knowing, to wisdom? How can our communities learn to bear witness to suffering and joy in themselves and others?

One way may be by bringing rites of passage back into education: by allowing students to learn through their own experiences; by creating specific educational settings where learners can really "take a plunge"; by helping them touch the mythic imagination; helping them to nurture wisdom and compassion through not-knowing and bearing witness.

Many of us have experienced suffering as young people. This culture can be hard on young people. Sometimes the suffering is passive, other times it is suffering of neglect or abuse. Sometimes young people are sent off to silver-spooned institutions, where they learn a lot of facts. But they do not learn about sacredness or compassion, or about not-knowing and bearing witness.

When they emerge from these educational institutions with fact-packed brains—no matter how excellent they may be—if they are lucky, they will have an accident. The accident might be an encounter with a spiritual teacher, or an illness or a moment of realization in one's ordinary life. Or it may be a loss that is so great that the heart breaks open. Finally, at last, that which cannot be spoken of will appear. One will have taken a plunge, intentionally or unintentionally.

Often it takes an accident, a chance meeting or disaster, for us to break open. There is the story of Asanga, who spent many years meditating in a cave. He meditated on the Maitreya, the future Buddha, hoping to receive a vision and teaching from him. But Maitreya never showed up. One day after twelve years of sitting in his cave waiting for Maitreya to appear, Asanga finally had enough, and said, "I'm out of here." With his staff in hand, he began to walk down the mountain path. He walked with the mind of not-knowing.

As he walked down the path, he saw a red dog lying on the path.

Looking more closely, he found that the dog's hind quarters were covered with sores and that the sores were filled with maggots. Asanga wanted to help the dog, but he also didn't want to harm the maggots. So Asanga dropped to his knees and stuck out his tongue in order to gently remove the maggots and save the life of the dog. The red dog then transformed immediately into Maitreya. Of course, Asanga was stunned that after twelve years of trying and gaining nothing, only now—when he had given up—did Maitreya appear. That is precisely the point. Maitreya told Asanga that he had, in fact, been with him in his cave the entire time. Asanga had stained Maitreya's robes with his food, he was so close to him. But, because Asanga had been trying so hard, anticipating, expecting to *get* something rather than just sitting with no gaining idea, Maitreya had not appeared.

In our acts of true selflessness—true compassion, no time or thing, no gain, nothing to attach to, not-knowing—we experience the joy of liberation from our own suffering. With this freedom and lightness, we can better serve and heal others who are afflicted with attachment to knowing everything, who are so busy trying to get somewhere they cannot live reality just as it is. Nothing heroic or profound—twelve years or twelve minutes—it's no different when just sitting, when just living.

Education in this time, in our era, needs to be primarily about redemption. Redemption is experienced when we selflessly offer ourselves for the well-being of others. This is how Asanga was redeemed: he finally saw the Buddha Maitreya when he offered himself without ego or expectation to remove the maggots from the wound of a single suffering dog.

Reviewing human history from 200,000 B.C.E. to today, we see dramatic phase shifts from the beginnings of oral communication, the development of the alphabet, of script, the printing press, the industrial revolution, and now the electronic revolution. We see that each movement between these domains effects a kind of gap. As this phase shift happens, as new orders of organization unfold, we actually move into fields where we activate all of the other, deeper orders as well.

We are in such a phase shift right now. We are entering a time when we are moving into a new and higher order of complexity. In this transitional time—also a time of tremendous suffering—it is critical that we reactivate and recommit to rites of passage, and open ourselves to not-knowing and bearing witness, so that we may learn how to proceed, as individuals and as a culture, to heal ourselves and heal others. We need to learn how to invite imagination and mystery back into education. We must learn how to cleanse our vision so that, in the twenty-first century, we are not merely educating technicians and pragmatic *thinkers* but are calling forth new vocations: vocations based on the profound aspiration to help all beings not-know, bear witness, and heal.

To return to our starting point, we are called to realize that education in the West has left out its complement: initiation. What is required today, and for the next century, is an education that is willing to plunge into the unknown, into the unknowable; an education of redemption; an education that prepares us to return and to serve.

IV. TRADITION
AND
INNOVATION

BENEATH US, supporting us, and surrounding us is the legacy of the past. The legacy has a vast number of forms: cities and towns; businesses, churches, schools; forests, parks, gardens; neighborhoods, clubs, extended families. There are old records: books shelved in libraries; paintings on museum walls; dusty legal archives; yellowed newspapers and bank ledgers. Scattered about, too, are shards of the past: arrowheads, stone walls, battlefields, cemeteries, and dumps. There is so much to see, so much to study, and so much to learn by exploring this legacy: in seeing the traces of the past in the present; in seeing how much the past makes the present; and how it molds our future as well.

Then, out there—somewhere just beyond us—is the future. We're not there yet, but we sense that it's coming. It's coming soon. We don't know what the future will bring. What happens in the next moment—tomorrow, next month, or next year—always comes as a bit of a surprise. The future, however, is not a complete unknown. We see and know that the actions we undertake today—this moment—leave marks and traces not only in the present but also in the future. Present actions in a very real way lay the track of the future.

So here we are, right now, in the present. *This* is the present. Oddly enough, we are *always* in the present. In terms of our experience, this moment is always what we have. Whether we are deep in a thought, reflecting on the past, dreaming of the future, or simply staring out into space—we are right here. Whether we are in attention, emotion, or conception, right now is what we have. It is what we share.

Tradition and innovation, therefore, are simply about opening the present. In the face of this present—right now—and knowing what we know (and also not knowing what will come next), what will we do? How will we greet the coming unknown? This is perhaps the great question behind all culture and religion. Not merely "How do we make meaning?" but "How shall we act and respond?" Or better still "How shall we live?"

This question can appear an abstract one: a question for religion, a question of theology. Ultimately, however, this is a very practical question. With each new moment we again come face-to-face with an opportunity: What to do next? In facing this question, and in facing our future, what will be our strategy?

This final section, "Tradition and Innovation," focuses on how to educate for this moment—for full engagement with the past, present, and future. The chapters look to history, to the wisdom traditions of the world, and to contemporary insight for guidance. The question for the section is how might we really become present, right here, and ground education in presence as well. Ground education not only in our *experience* of the present but also in the *requirements* of the present.

For spirituality in education requires us to continually approach the present from three perspectives: experiencing the specific qualities of the moment, seeing the past in the present, and seeing the future in the present. Rather than relying solely on our intellect, we must spaciously blend intellect with awareness and intuition, and balance preparation with openness and a sense of timeless responsibility.

This approach requires a kind of nimble gentleness. It requires openness. It asks us to be on the spot. It depends on our awareness, sense of presence, and sensitivity. It requires us to have the commitment to facing fear, indeed facing whatever arises. Ultimately, the approach asks a single, simple thing of us: to be present and responsible—right here, right now, right in the middle of our lives—in the face of tremendous ambiguity.

The chapters in "Tradition and Innovation" offer encouragement and advice towards making this leap: right now, in our schools, beginning to care, to take care, and to teach care. These chapters articulate the steps from here to there: the steps towards spirituality in education.

Ron Miller begins by introducing a number of historical and contemporary approaches to the practice of holistic education and spirituality in education. He leads us to sources and resources that can help us on our personal or professional journey. Ron challenges us to a style of education based in awareness, engagement, and relationship.

In "Spirituality and Leadership," Diana Chapman Walsh takes the idea of engagement one step further. Moving beyond the classroom and into the realm of administrative and institutional life, she argues for a dynamic community style grounded in awareness, intimacy, directness, and collaboration. Diana points out that this style is not an option but is in fact *required* as the challenges we face, individually and institutionally, have become challenges that force us to grow or die.

Rabbi Zalman Schachter-Shalomi and Huston Smith, two elder statesman of American spirituality, follow with a dialogue that touches on three key questions for those of us who want to teach and embody spirituality in education. The first question is about the sacred: Is the sacred *apart from* this world, or *of* it? The way in which we answer this question leads to remarkably different choices, which lead in turn to different futures.

The second question explores how we understand spiritual growth: Do we believe, experience, and embrace the paradigm of progress or the paradigm of transformation? Here again, different views lead to different worlds. The final point of the dialogue is about science: How can scientific ways of knowing and spiritual ways of knowing be reconciled?

Vincent Harding then brings us back home, back from the realm of outer transformation to the inner work of our lives. He asks the hard questions: What are we going to? How are we going to change? What steps will we take to change the world? How are we going to go forth from here—from this day, this moment? Vincent offers reflections, inspiration, and challenges in encouraging us to take the next step.

In the face of difficulty or the unknown we have a tendency to run for cover. We want the safety net of prescriptions, blanket measures, action items, and bulleted lists. Unfortunately, there is no generic prescription for the present moment. Fortunately, however, the only thing that is really required is our willingness to show up—and give our all.

HOLISTIC EDUCATION FOR
AN EMERGING CULTURE

Ron Miller

Ron Miller is an historian of alternative education and was the founding publisher and editor of *Holistic Education Review*, founder of Holistic Education Press, and cofounder of the Bellwether School and Family Resource Center in Vermont. His books include *Educational Freedom for a Democratic Society*; *What Are Schools For? Holistic Education in American Culture*; *New Directions in Education: Selections from Holistic Education Review*; and *The Renewal of Meaning in Education*.

I WOULD LIKE to acquaint you with the kinds of spiritually influenced education that have emerged over the last couple of centuries, and in particular over the last few decades. My purposes are twofold. First, I want to acknowledge that your work as an educator will be difficult; there's no question about it. Our culture, as it now stands, is fundamentally hostile to the meanings of spirituality that we have discussed here. There's no way around that. On the other hand, I don't want to discourage you. We are entering a historic period of transition from one dominant worldview to another and it is my belief that the new, emerging culture is going to be radically different. Therefore, those of you who are working in this fledgling holistic education movement are pioneers on a rough and uncharted frontier. There are no reliable techniques or simple solutions to make the task easier. On the contrary, we will need many different tools, many different approaches in order to help make this transformation of culture happen.

On one hand, we need the kind of spirituality—the gentleness and humility and compassion—that was embodied by the Dalai Lama. At the same time, if we are to clear away the rubble of a declining and obsolete civilization that stands in our way, and in the way of compassion, we also need the prophetic outrage that is so well expressed by John Gatto.

Now, I've never agreed with all the details of John's historical analysis. I'm certainly not persuaded by his argument that reviving original sin is the most constructive contribution that we can make to a postmodern culture. But John is passionate; he is a true prophet, and his passion is so powerful and so necessary because he sees very clearly the terrible damage that modernist education has inflicted on the human spirit.

His critique, much of which I share, is not meant to blame any of you who work in public schools or who hope to save public education somehow. That's not the point—the point is that there are forces in this culture that are beyond your control, beyond any of our control: the colossal military-industrial-global-corporate system and a four-hundred-year legacy of reductionism. These kinds of forces will work against your efforts—however well and faithfully you work—until the emerging culture, this postmodern culture, can gain a more secure foothold.

The work that we are doing is vitally important work in preparing the foundation for this new culture. We should never be discouraged. We should never stop doing this important work. But until our culture catches up to what we're doing—as individuals, small communities, and organizations—it's going to be a rough road. We've got to be in this for the long haul. We may be defeated in many ways, large and small, in our daily work, but ultimately a postmodern civilization is going to be born.

THE CONTRAST BETWEEN MODERN SCHOOLING AND HOLISTIC EDUCATION

Modern schooling does not serve the spiritual unfoldment of the child. It serves capitalism, nationalism, and a reductionist worldview. It serves a society that is completely committed to meritocracy, where there's fierce competition between individuals to reach the top of a social hierarchy.

The procedures that are built into our system of schooling—grading, standardizing, the herding of children from room to room at the sound of a bell, teachers who answer to a hierarchy of authority, the extraordinary influence of business leaders in what goes on in our classrooms—none of these things serves the spiritual unfolding of children or the building of community.

In my historical research I found a quotation from 1908 that captures the essence of this system. A man named Colin Scott wrote a book called *Social Education,* in which he promoted the concept of "social efficiency" in public education:

> *It is not primarily for his own individual good that the child is taken from his free and wandering life of play. It is for what society can get out of him, whether of a material or spiritual kind, that he is sent to school.*

Now, the individual does have responsibilities to society. I am not advocating a kind of atomistic individualism here; but Scott is not talking about an organic kind of society where education creates connections between the person and the community. He's talking about the imposition of social discipline and social efficiency, and this is mechanistic and reductive.

In recent years another term has come to be used by the leaders of our educational system, the term *intellectual capital.* This term suggests that the minds of our children are raw material for the economy. This, unfortunately, is what schools are primarily about in this present age.

But I speak of an emerging culture, a culture that arises out of a critique of the reductionism, hierarchy, and materialism of our modern age. We see this culture emerging in the nineteenth century; in the Romantic movement and the American Transcendentalist movement. Around the turn of the century, there were a handful of thinkers who looked very deeply at the epistemological roots of the modern way of being, people like Rudolf Steiner, Alfred North Whitehead, and William James.

In the 1960s, of course, this way of thinking blossomed. It emerged in the streets, the universities, and in many other places across the continent. We also see its roots in the environmental movement, which has matured into branches such as deep ecology and social ecology; the human potential movement; the development of humanistic psychology and transpersonal psychology. The work of Ken Wilber, for example, offers a fantastic explanation of this transition to a whole different way of thinking about who we are as human beings.

We are seeing the infusion of new spiritual perspectives in our culture—The Naropa Institute is a perfect illustration of this—as Asian ways of thinking have been brought into our culture. And the work of Matthew Fox, the former Catholic priest who speaks of "creation spirituality" comes to mind—a holistic alternative to original sin.

Within science, too, new ways of thinking are challenging the stale reductionism of the last four centuries. The work of people like Gregory Bateson, David Bohm, Rupert Sheldrake, and Barbara McClintock, to name only a few. These are not romantics; they are not flaky people; these are very, very competent scientists who understand that the modernist cultural viewpoint is obsolete.

We have thinkers like David Ray Griffin who speak of a "constructive postmodernism"; we have green politics and green thinkers. People who have particularly influenced my work are Theodore Roszak, Jeremy Rifkin, Fritjof Capra, and Charlene Spretnak. And the list goes on and on. All of this literature tells us that this new culture is not just a fantasy, not just a passing fad, but is something that is truly emerging. However, it may take a long time to come; cultural transformation is not easy, but it's coming.

In the late 1970s, a group of transpersonal psychologists and people involved in transpersonal education started to talk about "holistic" education. The ideas that they expressed go back more than two hundred years. They go back to Rousseau in the late 1700s; Pestalozzi, the great educator in Switzerland in the early 1800s; Froebel, who was a student of Pestalozzi and was the founder of the kindergarten; the American Transcendentalists, in particular Bronson Alcott, who ran a school in Boston. There were also other progressive educators and other pioneers, including Rudolf Steiner and Maria Montessori. The holistic education movement, which is beginning to really take shape only now, has its roots in all of these pioneers.

What I have said all along, from the very beginning, since I first became involved in this movement, is that holistic education is not going to save our society. We cannot educate a new generation and then hope that *they* will change the world. Holistic education will only become established, it will only become accepted and widespread, to the extent that our culture itself changes. It's a give-and-take relationship. Our individual efforts as educators can help in that process, but we need that process itself to go further before we can expect to experience many changes, or very much success.

BASIC PRINCIPLES OF HOLISTIC EDUCATION

Of the myriad of possibilities, there are four basic principles of holistic education that I would like to focus on. First, holistic educators believe that the human being is a complex existential entity made up of many, many different layers of meaning. We are biological creatures. We are ecological creatures. We have a psychological dimension, an emotional dimension. We live in an ideological environment, a social and cultural environment, and have a spiritual core. We are very complex creatures because of the interplay and interactions of all of these different meanings. You cannot just take any single one of them and say, "Oh, that's who we are."

Holism is a point of view which recognizes this complexity.

There's a wonderful book out of Australia called *Educating Psyche,* written by Bernie Neville a few years back. He points to the diverse archetypal energies that flow through human consciousness. He argues that any educational method is a "partial vision" if it honors only one or even a few of these different energies to the exclusion of others.

√Certainly an excessively rational or academic education denies spontaneity and spirit. But a completely romantic or child-centered vision denies the shadow and denies the need for order and discipline. So education must address or at least respect the multifaceted mystery of human existence, or else it damages the delicate process of human development.

My second point is related to this. Human development occurs in at least two spheres. One is personal. Good holistic educators recognize the stages of a child's development—how the child's thinking and feeling and way of relating to the world change over time. They also recognize that each child develops at a different rate. But what we need to keep in mind is that development also has a universal or spiritual dimension. Rudolf Steiner, Ken Wilber, and others have told us that human consciousness appears to be engaged in a long, long historic process of unfolding. Somehow we started in an instinctive organismic existence and are moving toward spiritual realization, or transcendence. This process might take many, many, many centuries, but it's moving forward. What this means for education is that we should not be training children merely to obey the dictates of this culture. We should be enabling them to go beyond it as far as they are able.

✗The Canadian education theorist, John P. Miller, who has written wonderful books on holistic education, has said that education should be about transformation. Education should be supporting this process of evolution. It should not be exclusively concerned with the transmission of what has already been established in our culture. Johann Pestalozzi in Switzerland beautifully expressed this in 1809:

God's nature which is in you is held sacred in this house. We do not hem it in. We try to develop it. It is far from our intention to make of you men and women such as we are. Under our guidance you should become men and women such as your natures, the divine and sacred in your nature, require you to be.

A third principle of holistic education is that this spirituality should not be taken as an utterly mystical or otherworldly spirituality. The human being is composed of many, many layers of wholeness, layers of meaning. Holism speaks of wholes within wholes. It makes no sense then to have spirituality without democracy; without social justice; without the healing of hatred and racial and class oppression; without a sustainable and nourishing relationship to the biosphere. Alongside our spiritual nature, the social and cultural reality that we inhabit is a tremendously important part of our identity, and we have to address it directly.

Holistic education is not trying to train children for monastic practice. It is a way of engaging them with the world, in all its complexity. Holistic education has cultural, historical, and, yes, political implications. We, as holistic educators, should all be out campaigning strenuously to overturn Goals 2000 and all the national standards that are being crammed down our throats. Now, we should come to this position not from aggression but from a spiritual understanding, from a compassionate understanding. We, as parents and educators, seek to honor the individual spirits of our children. In order to do this, within the political arena we need to confront the mechanization and standardization of children's souls in a very fierce way.

I have my own fantasy that one day thousands of Rosa Parkses will emerge in our schools—and that they will simply refuse to administer another standardized test. That one day teachers will simply refuse to trim down their curriculum and make it conform to the mechanical and standardized curriculum that comes down from IBM and the State Department of Education. But this civil disobedience will have to be performed on a massive scale. If any one teacher tries to do this on their own, they are sure to be out of a job; and we need you in there.

My fourth principle is that holistic education cannot be reduced to any single technique. So how do we take this vision and put it into practice? There really is no particular technique. Holistic education is the art of cultivating meaningful human relationships. It is a dialogue between teacher and student within a community of learners. Parker Palmer in his writings and talks has expressed this beautifully. John Miller, Rachael Kessler, and religious thinkers such as Thomas Merton and Martin Buber have also spoken very eloquently about dialogue, connection, and the mutual creation of meaning. This is the heart of education. There's no technique for doing this. It comes out of being authentic, being who you are. Standardization, quantitative assessment, competition, hierarchical authority, and the political control of curriculum and textbooks all contribute towards diminishing or destroying the possibility of this kind of learning.

PRACTICES IN HOLISTIC EDUCATION

I can, however, point to some practices in holistic education. I will start with early childhood education. As I mentioned before, a holistic approach to early childhood education is one that starts with the developmental process. It understands that a three-year-old experiences the world very differently from a five-year-old or a seven-year-old. Maria Montessori and Rudolf Steiner were two of the brilliant pioneers who have identified these development stages and designed educational methods to specifically respond to them.

Montessori pointed to what she called "sensitive periods" in a child's life—times when particular aspects of the environment have a stronger than average meaning for the child. She taught that you needed to observe each child to know just when to connect them with these elements of their environment. Montessori also told us that "the hands are the instruments of man's intelligence." She insisted that children, especially young children, need to grasp the world literally before they can grasp it intellectually, and that education flows from experience. This is a basic point of holistic education.

Fifty years after Montessori, another Italian educator, Loris Malaguzzi, and his colleagues in the city of Reggio Emilia, developed a system of early childhood programs in which children explore and interpret their world through creative arts, stories, and elaborate cooperative projects. This model is now influencing thousands of preschool teachers around the world, including those in the United States. The difference, however, is that Reggio Emilia is a community—a city—that is completely dedicated to the welfare of its children. The schools that they've set up for their young children are beautiful places. I don't know that we have the equivalent of that kind of commitment in this country. But that's what we're working towards.

American progressive educators, primarily influenced by Jean Piaget, have spoken about "constructivism" in early childhood education, where the child does not take in information and knowledge but interprets and makes sense of the world. Teachers need to give children more opportunities—and more time—to construct their understanding.

For somewhat older children, there is Waldorf education, a very important model of holistic education. It was founded in 1919 by Rudolf Steiner. In the U.S. right now there are approximately one hundred forty Waldorf schools. I do not have the space to fully explain this complex approach, but I want to try to give you at least a bit of their flavor.

In Waldorf education, the teacher is trained very carefully to be deeply sensitive to the ways in which the soul or life force unfolds within each child. It is an explicitly spiritual approach to education. The teacher nourishes the soul directly through story, myth, art, music, and movement. The teacher remains with his or her class from first grade all the way through eighth grade. Through this process strong relationships and a sense of community are nourished.

My oldest son will be starting in a Waldorf school next year. Recently, he went to visit the first-grade class he will be joining. He came to the class actually quite fearful to be in this new environment, but the children just welcomed him in, and said, "Oh, we're so happy you're here. We look forward to seeing you next year." The teacher was just beaming in the background, saying, "Oh, I'm so proud of my kids." That's the kind of community that can be formed when your goal in education is to nurture the spirit.

The curriculum in a Waldorf school takes children on a journey through humanity's history. Each phase of civilization is seen as analogous to stages in the soul's development. There is a high degree of structure in Waldorf education, but Waldorf educators have a very good rationale for this. They believe that a person achieves true autonomy and freedom only through the careful disciplining of life energy during childhood. The teacher stands in front of the children as a moral being—as an integrated, mature human being. It was Steiner's belief that the child would really take in the teacher's example. And it does seem to work.

Another aspect of Waldorf education I want to mention is that each Waldorf school is an island of sanity—an island of this emerging culture—where organic and ecological values are honored and the gross influences of modern materialism, such as television, plastic toys, processed food, and all that, are effectively banished. Waldorf schools are little oases for children. That's a good place to start.

There are also some important developments within public education that point toward holistic directions. The whole-language movement is one of them. Whole language is an effort to bring meaning, relationship, and critical inquiry into the process of learning literacy. Although it's not explicitly "spiritual," whole language is the closest thing that we're likely to get to genuine holism in public education within most communities in the foreseeable future. This movement, of course, is under severe attack from reactionaries and fundamentalists, who do not appreciate teachers encouraging critical inquiry among young people.

There's another progressive movement taking place in public

schools today calling for more open, dynamic, multiaged learning communities. I find this movement very promising, because these teachers are really concerned about the quality and not just the quantity of their students' learning. This is a heroic stance.

We need to encourage people in these movements, even though they're not speaking our language, not speaking of spirituality in education, per se. People come to holism through various different points of entry. Not all of us start with Ken Wilber's books, or with a meditation practice.

The teachers who are on the front lines, who see how children are being damaged, are looking for answers. It matters little whether they first come to whole language or multiaged classrooms or multiple intelligences. They keep studying and looking, and eventually they discover the bigger picture—where and how all of these approaches are interconnected.

I also want to talk about a very exciting development that's quite recent, just in the last couple of years. You may be familiar with Daniel Goleman's book *Emotional Intelligence*. Back in the 1970s, there were small groups of affective, humanistic, and "confluent" educators who talked about self-esteem, values clarification, and other romantic notions. This talk also stirred up the wrath of reactionaries, and of course the reactionaries prevailed. But emotional literacy literally has come back. We realize more and more that we are damaging the children in our schools. And a great deal of recent research has shown that young people can make more sensible and, if you like, more moral choices when they are more in touch with their own internal emotional processes.

There are also educators such as Rachael Kessler, who developed the Mysteries program in California. This program helps teens work through the problems of growing up in this culture; and Chip Wood and his associates at the Northeast Foundation for Children in Massachusetts, who have developed what they call the "responsive classroom," do workshops with thousands of teachers on the East Coast. They work with a lot of inner-city teachers, to make classroom communities places where everyone feels at home. These are significant breakthroughs, and we need to encourage them.

For older children—high school age—we have rites of passage. One example is the Walkabout program developed by Maurice Gibbons, which has been practiced for several years at the Mountain Open High School in Jefferson County, Colorado. A Walkabout program sends teenagers out into the world. They can do volunteer work, or have a wilderness adventure, or intensive study of some topic, and then they come back to their community to report on what they've learned, on how they've grown. Their community supports them and welcomes them back.

I want to make a last point about this search for techniques and for methods we can apply. It is ironic that the two greatest and most influential holistic educators, Steiner and Montessori, deliberately emphasized that the teacher's openhearted responsiveness is the very core of their pedagogy, but then they went ahead and gave very specific prescriptions for educational practice, which generations of their followers have interpreted quite literally—and if I might say so, quite slavishly sometimes.

Listen to these words of Rudolf Steiner himself. This is from a lecture in 1919, right at the time he was founding the first Waldorf school. Steiner said,

> For the true teacher, pedagogy must be something living, something new at each moment. We could even say that the best pedagogy is one that the teacher continually forgets and that is continually reignited each time the teacher is in the presence of the children and sees in them the living powers of developing human nature.

I cannot end without mentioning Dee Coulter, who teaches at The Naropa Institute. Several years ago she contributed an article to *Holistic Education Review*, which I think nicely expresses what I'm trying to say here. Coulter compared Montessori and Steiner and asked why they are so different. Why do they look like symmetrical opposites? She observed that each one was responding to a specific cultural and historical situation. Each was addressing specific facets of the complex wholeness of human beings.

Coulter argued that holistic educators today would be truer to the spirit of Montessori and Steiner by reclaiming their "seed" qualities rather than by adopting their methods in every specific detail. And that's what we need to do. We can learn from these methods: we can see why they were developed, what contexts they work in—but ultimately it is up to each of us to come to our students, come to our learning communities with an openhearted responsiveness, a "teaching presence," as Rachael Kessler calls it. This is the heart of holistic education.

12

SPIRITUALITY AND LEADERSHIP

Diana Chapman Walsh

Diana Chapman Walsh is the twelfth president of Wellesley College. A leading expert in public health policy and the prevention of illness, Dr. Walsh has published on topics related to the organization and financing of health care services, the conservation of health, the prevention and treatment of substance abuse, and the health effects of work. She has written, edited, and coedited several books, including *Corporate Physicians: Between Medicine and Management.*

SOME YEARS AGO, when my daughter was in fifth grade, she was struggling with a decision. Finally, in utter frustration, she said, "My mind keeps rearranging itself." Those words stuck in my mind and came back to me as the beginning of this talk kept rearranging itself. It struck me, however, in the course of trying to "corral it," that there might be a few lessons in reviewing the directions from which this talk might have begun. So let me begin with some of the beginnings that I considered and rejected! Then I'll begin again in the middle—with the beginning that seemed apposite.

One renegade rendition of this talk started with a disclaimer, violating all of the rules of persuasive public speaking. We women especially are enjoined not to undermine our credibility by beginning with an apology. The disclaimer I am not going to make would have gone something like this: please do not hear in what I say extravagant claims for myself or for my institution, or unreasonable claims on you. What I have to offer here is one perspective of one leader of one institution, and all three of those offerings—perspective, person, and place—are inchoate, in process, and idiosyncratic.

In thinking about the impulse to offer disclaimers, it seems to me that this impulse came from without, from the environment here. I did not bring this impulse with me. It was not in the original text I wrote over Memorial Day weekend. I want to reflect on this, because if I am picking this up, other people may be feeling it too: a dispiriting, de-mobilizing, and disempowering subtext to all the "empowering talk" here. We might do well to ask ourselves why and how we can send un-dermining messages to one another at a gathering intended to mobi-lize participants to undertake the difficult work of catalyzing social change.

I want to describe three minor interactions that pushed me into this defensive stance; and I invite you to reflect on whether you have been having similar experiences. They will not be the same as mine, but perhaps analogous. As I describe them, I hope that the people in-volved, if they are here today, will not take this as criticism, because it's not. They have given me the gift of feedback from which to learn.

The first two incidents occurred on Monday, after I first spoke. A number of people came up afterwards to continue the dialogue. Two others were holding back on the side, waiting patiently, politely. When all the others had left, the first one came up to me hesitantly. "I wanted to speak to you about Wellesley," she said. "Good," I said, and smiled. She said, "No, it's not good. It's sad."

She told me about a first-year student who wants to transfer out of Wellesley College. This young woman is finding the culture compet-itive, cutthroat, and careerist. This is a wonderful, idealistic young woman, who came to Wellesley full of dreams and hopes. We chatted a bit, and I suggested that she tell the student to send me an E-mail message, and I would see if I could hook her up with some like-minded people on our campus. I hope she will do that; I do not know if she will—but it is sad.

The second interaction, right after that, was with a man who said, "I didn't want to ask you this question during the formal session because it was too confrontational." This was one of those moments as a leader when you want to say, "Thank you, I think."

"About this 'highly selective' college," he said. "The term?" I said, "You don't like the term?" "No," he said, "not the term—whether you should exist at all."

Then he talked to me about Horace Mann, and Horace Mann's dream, and questioned whether our graduates are really realizing that dream. It went something along the lines of John Gatto's very powerful critique. The underlying message, however, was "You need to just fold up your tent and go home."

The third interaction took place walking back to the hotel after all of this. I fell in step with a lovely woman who said, "Aren't you the one from Wesleyan?" And I said, "No, actually it's Wellesley. But that's close enough; people are having trouble here getting it right."

She said, "I don't know much about those Eastern schools." And I said, "Yes, I should probably say a bit about Wellesley College when I speak tomorrow." Then she told me about a young couple sitting next to her during Monday's session. She said that when I mentioned that Wellesley College was the alma mater of Hillary Clinton, one of them snarled, "Who cares?"

So there it is in a nutshell, the disarming, defeating voices that we all carry around in our heads at least some of the time. Are you really what you profess to be or are you a fraud? Have you earned the right to exist? And who cares anyway? These are the voices that push us into defensiveness, disclaimers, and apologies.

I tell you these stories because keeping these disarming voices at bay is one of the critical challenges of leadership today. I believe there is much at stake, in a very complicated way, because the way some leaders keep those harsh voices at bay is to harden their hearts—to flex them, metaphorically, like the muscle that the heart is, in order to deflect the repeated blows that come at you when you're a leader.

We can recognize in that brand of leadership—with the leader's heart closed down—one that is ubiquitous and that creates all manner of mischief. Parker Palmer wrote a wonderful analysis of this in an essay called "Leading from Within." If you have not read it, you should. I wrote a response to it that is published in a book on leadership put out by the Drucker Foundation. So this is one direction I could have started out in, off in the direction of disclaimers. I will not ride on that horse, but I think we have learned something useful about leadership from just pausing for a moment to ask what it was that was calling me to begin in such a way.

Now, another beginning I might have made would have enumerated some of the powerful challenges, some of the exciting possibilities, that have been washing over me in tidal waves during these three days we have been together. Asking myself, and orienting to Parker Palmer's vocational question: Where does my deep gladness meet the world's deep needs? Or picking up on Rachel Remen's idea, and talking about where the shadow is in my institution, and coming up with different ways to take people out of toxic environments and into situations where they can reconnect to their human wholeness. Or building on Judith Simmer-Brown's insight that we can encounter otherness as our greatest teacher if we allow ourselves to acknowledge and raise up the differences. Or taking to heart the implications of bell hooks's observation that being a great teacher and being liked or loved do not go hand in hand, indeed may at times be antithetical. That's so hard for those of us who teach. And so on. It is a long list. The lesson here, though, in the laundry list, seems to me to be about the powerful pull of the impulse to want to do and be all.

These two beginnings—two versions of my introduction—are related. The larger, freer, more daring vision of possibilities—sitting in this tent with an open heart—sits in dynamic tension with the voices of despair: It cannot be done. It is too hard. I do not have the leverage I need, or the resources.

So that is more than enough prologue. Let me begin, now, at the beginning, let me begin with a poem that I wrote in 1990, at a retreat with my dear friend Parker Palmer. Later on, when he spoke at my inauguration, one of the things that he said was, "The world needs presidents who are poets; keep your poetry alive." The "He" in this poem is Parker Palmer. The poem is called "Potbound."

He asks me a question I've never considered before.
When is it that you know you have to go someplace else?
At first I think I don't know, don't go, never have, just try to please,
do what's expected, bloom where I'm planted.
But then the answer germinates in the soil of my mind.
I see a potted plant, roots protruding from the drainage hole
in the bottom, ready to go, bursting to grow.
After weeks or months or years of putting its root system down,
of consolidating its power, husbanding its resources, it has reached
a crisis point, lost its equilibrium, has to go, has to grow.
I run down to the cellar and root around for a larger pot,
a little larger only, so my vulnerable plant won't wilt in the
unstructured vastness of a new world without apparent walls.
I have to smash the old pot to rescue my restless plant,
impacted root system now naked in my hand. A small sacrifice,
but a radical operation to deliver the plant from death.
Without the space to grow, it will shrivel and die.
When is it that I know I have to go someplace else?
When I have to grow or die.

So I want us, as we think about tradition and innovation, to think about growth and death as well. Think about what it means to enter the exciting phase of breaking that pot and holding the plant in the palm of your hand; think about the question of how not to confuse the plant with the pot; think about how not to confuse the living, life-giving tradition with the container. I want us to be thinking, as well, about the intersections between power and poetry, to think about what it might mean to be a president or teacher or administrator who is also a poet, and think about what we all can do to keep our poetry alive.

I see it as my challenge, as the leader of an educational institution, to do all that I can to hold open a space in which a community of growth and self-discovery can flourish for everyone. The president of a college or a university is constantly beset and besieged by a cacophony of competing claims for resources, for attention, for validation. I saw this in a moment on the stage when poet Anne Waldman got to talking about how excited she was about doing poetry in the inner city. She looked at Naropa president John Cobb, and said, "If you'd only give us the money, John, we could do it." That's what it's like to be a college president.

The criteria for adjudicating those varied and competing claims are much more fluid and debatable in the academy than is the efficiency test many organizations apply almost by rote. In education, the process is inextricably bound up with the product. Learning is nothing if not a messy process of discovery and unfolding. That means that how we as educators and educational administrators do our work—where we put our emphasis, what values we embody and express day in and day out, how we respond to the relentless pressures of time, of projections, of expectations, of conflicts, all of that—is fully as important as the outcomes we actually seek to produce.

In fact, the process is the outcome in a very real sense. We teach as much by the example of what we do and how we do it as by what our professors actually profess in the classroom. We create an environment through our leadership much like the one we create, and heard about yesterday, through the design of our buildings. Leadership, too, is part of the silent curriculum we teach that is not described in the college catalog.

When, as leaders, we do our work well, our students coalesce into a community of strong, self-sufficient, intellectually honest, and curious individuals. In our case—we are a women's college still—the students coalesce into women who are actualized and mobilized and excited about the contributions they can make in the world, women who are mentally, emotionally, and spiritually resilient and resourceful.

Above all else, we hope to provide an education that liberates the mind and the spirit from parochialism, and from ideology; an education that opens doors for a lifelong journey of learning, a lifelong journey of questioning assumptions and shaking loose of prejudice in an expanding world and in an expanding worldview.

That is what we aspire to do, as best we can, swimming against the mighty crosscurrents that come at us from the larger culture. As leaders, we have an ecosystem we need to protect, if we are going to foster in our students this kind of transformational growth, intellectual mastery, social consciousness, and spiritual depth. The ecosystem we need to create and protect must integrate into the educational process the totality of students' experiences. It is Ron Miller's vision of holistic education at the level of the college: and that includes curricular and extracurricular experiences—residential life, social life, inter- and intrapersonal exploration and growth.

Like all ecosystems, it will depend for its sustenance on an intricate and vulnerable web of interdependence. If we ask ourselves, as we need to do, what kind of leadership we need to nourish a fragile ecosystem like that, the obvious answer is humanistic leadership, collaborative leadership, leadership that is respectful, that values and rewards individual autonomy, that values initiative, that supports the dignity of every person, that authorizes, inspires, and frees everyone in the organization to do their very best and most creative work.

Now, much has been written and spoken about this kind of leadership for many years. There is a whole literature around this; I will not burden you with a list of names. What I can add are a few reflections on my own ongoing efforts to implement at least some of those ideals in the institution that I lead.

I assumed the presidency of Wellesley College almost four years ago, on October 1, 1993. And in these first four years, we instituted a number of initiatives that I will not take time to enumerate here. We saw some movement and change. But the more I have come to understand the institution, the more clearly I see patterns that stand in the way of the deeper change that we have been talking about at this conference: patterns that block us from being the flourishing community of growth and self-discovery that I want us to be for everyone, most especially for our students.

Various problems related to accountability, to collaboration (or its absence), and to difficulties with communication often stand in the way of ingenuity, creativity, and energy. These problems often undermine people's willingness to experiment and to take risks, and limit openness to new ideas and to new opportunities. They often prevent the development of mutual support and of the partnerships that we absolutely need if we are going to venture off into the unknown—if we are going to break the pot so that the plant can grow.

Now, spirituality, it seems to me, is about openness, about receptivity, about empathy, about the courage and faith to venture out into the unknown. So in a real sense, the managerial challenges that were serving themselves up to me are at their core spiritual challenges. In fact, as I continue to understand more clearly the role that I need to play in leading this process of cultural change, I increasingly become aware that my primary task has a spiritual dimension to it.

Fortuitously, one of the great opportunities that I found at Wellesley was the Religious and Spiritual Life program. It was established in 1993. The dean of Religious and Spiritual Life, its chief architect, is Victor Kazanjian, who leads a team of chaplains, advisers, and student leaders who are available to support the spiritual, educational, and worship needs of thirteen different faith traditions. The team offers programs on moral, ethical, and spiritual issues; they offer pastoral counseling services, and college-wide multifaith educational and community worship ceremonies throughout the year.

These ceremonies are quite extraordinary, quite beautiful, and a crucial part of our work to sustain the bonds of community and connection at a time when outside forces make them ever more fragile and rare. The ceremonies are part of our ongoing commitment to doing all that we can to affirm the necessity of relationship, and to hold friendship and service to others as an ultimate goal. We see this work as fundamental to our core educational mission, not as a nice frill on the side.

I want to return for a minute to the question of presidential leadership: I do not pretend to have this work completely figured out; it's an ongoing process. We are inventing it as we go along. But some of the key elements are emerging out of the shadow. I offer them to you in the form of four observations and four associated tasks.

The first observation: It is clear that at Wellesley—and I suspect throughout higher education—we are confronted with issues that Ronald Heifitz refers to as "adaptive challenges." These challenges do not lend themselves to the application of existing technologies. There are not technological solutions because they involve the unknown. This means we need multiple vantage points from which to see and to assess reality.

These challenges, therefore, cannot be solved without the conflict of multiple viewpoints as a resource for learning. So, in fact, conflict is a resource. We cannot do this adaptive work without it. People will be challenged to grow and to meet these challenges, and in order to do this they are going to have to confront the ambiguity, uncertainty, discomfort, and conflict that are the crucibles of learning.

In the old style of patriarchal management, the leader patrolled the borders of the organization, absorbing and managing all the uncertainty that was coming in from the outside, buffering the people inside from those sources of turbulence, so that they could go on producing the technical work undisturbed by those perturbances. In the new style of creative management, the work is not just technical, so the leader has to build partnerships that are based on honesty and trust. There cannot be secrets and lies about the realities that the organization faces. Ambiguity, uncertainty, and contradiction will be facts of life. The leader's responsibility will be to guide the organization toward an understanding of its opportunities, to guide people into awareness of their resourcefulness in the face of ambiguity.

So the first task is to clarify the values and the vision, holding the light of the organization's positive future—the possibilities for cooperation, for responsibility, for self-sufficiency, for creativity, for, in our case, concern for the whole student—holding a vision of true health for individuals in the organization.

The second observation: When faced with the uncertainty and the contradiction that stimulate this growth and change, people have different levels of tolerance. Some are ready for it and some people are not. People respond differently. If the circumstances are right, they meet the challenge and they grow. If not, they find all sorts of tactics to avoid the work. These tactics have been described in various ways in the literature, but they almost always involve conscious or unconscious efforts to seduce the leader out of role, and to subvert the difficult work.

If you can get the leader away from pushing the organization forward, then you do not have to do this hard work of personal and organizational change. So people do this in many ways: they fight among themselves; or they withdraw their effort; or they seize on an apparent technical solution; or they turn their attention to just alleviating the symptoms; or they make the leader the problem. And the latter they especially do if the leader is onto the task of doing the work she needs to be doing to address the issue of work avoidance. So leaders in circumstances of cultural change absolutely must be grounded and clear. They can easily be drawn out of role and off task—drawn into collusion—if they're not focused and clear.

The second task, then, is to look for the creative edge, the possibility of engaging the problems that people bring in, calling people into partnerships, holding them accountable for doing their jobs, getting them to think about what it is that they are accountable for doing, gently confronting avoidance of the difficult work of change—gently, lovingly confronting it; helping the community integrate and digest the ways in which the work that they are doing is enabling them and enabling the organization to learn and to grow. Someone once said that we are better served in times of change in organizations by the learners than the learned.

A third observation: Conflict is necessary. It is a creative force, because differences and polarities are a critical part of this learning process. All learning, I would submit, involves first mastering new categories, learning them, and then integrating them into a larger, more organic whole. It is an iterative process of differentiation and integration. To do this well, you need to heighten, sharpen, amplify, and augment the differences, both factually and emotionally, and widen the gap between the two opposing poles in order to open up a space for a third position that can incorporate both of those poles in a more complex, more comprehensive whole. I think we saw this beautifully enacted last night between Huston Smith and Zalman Schachter-Shalomi. Huston said at one point, "We'll agree if we talk long enough." It wasn't that either one was collapsing into the other's worldview, it was that they were finding this third space that they held with their differences.

There is a fine line to be drawn between this creative, constructive conflict and the immature conflict that can become endless, shrill, and exhausting. We have all been there. Walking this line requires a constant assessment of the capacity of the system to cope, and the capacity of the people within the system. If the capacity is inadequate (or it is being overwhelmed), it may be that you need to bring new resources into the situation. Because conflict is uncomfortable, the natural tendency is to water down or to minimize the differences: move the two chairs closer together, not farther apart, to try to find a compromise so that you can end this exhausting conflict. But this may cut short the learning at just that critical breakthrough point, and that is leaving the plant potbound. So task three is to gauge whether there is too much or too little pressure on the system, on individuals, and the organization, to gauge whether differences are being heightened in a way that opens up the field for a new, larger, more encompassing, more integrative vision of the future, trying always to move, as we keep hearing at this conference, towards both/and formulations and away from either/or.

When faced with conflict, it helps to pay special attention to maintaining bonds: bonds within oneself, bonds with others, bonds with the larger culture. It helps if people can see the value and the beauty of the greater complexity, can understand the polarities, the warring factions within and without, and be reminded of their explicit value as a tool and stimulus for growth.

The fourth observation is that a crucial part of the work in this mode of leadership (and much of its reward) is in that it forces one to focus energy specifically on increasing one's own internal capacity for learning and for growth. This makes it essential to develop working partnerships and systems of mutual support. Because the work inevitably engages so many of one's own personal resources, one is forced to make conscious efforts to replenish those resources, in order to avoid a collapse of spirit.

So task four, finally, is to cultivate inner resources for leadership; cultivate the ability to return reliably to a deeper place of knowing, cultivate access to regular nourishment from one's own spiritual roots, whatever they may be. This final task is of the utmost importance.

In conclusion, let me just say this: Of course I come to you wearing the blinders of my own position and my own perspective. We all carry our baggage, as hard as we might try to set it down. My favorite lighthearted reminder of the impact of personal perspective is the old *New Yorker* cartoon—you may have seen it—where the dog is sitting at the typewriter, typing "The quick brown dog jumped over the lazy fox." Perspective matters.

So I have my baggage, I have my resistances, and I just do not believe that writing off or abandoning the educational establishment is the answer. First of all, it will not allow itself to be written off. It has concentrated too much power. Secondly—and much more importantly—there is something quite life-affirming, quite exquisite in at least some of this establishment's history and tradition. There is something there that connects with our deepest human yearnings.

For me the question runs along the lines of bell hooks's book *Teaching to Transgress,* which I picked up over in the bookstore, and will be reading on the plane home. She writes of classroom work as "teaching to transgress; teaching students to transgress against the harmful boundaries and the stereotypes; teaching them to practice freedom."

Can we who administer our institutions of teaching and learning—including the elite ones—imagine ourselves as leading to transgress? Leading in a way that supports and enhances the practice of freedom? I think we can imagine that style of leadership. I believe we can find in our educational institutions lovely pockets of promise and hope. I believe we can gently tend and feed those pockets, tending them with all the patience, skill, and discipline we can muster. Tending them mindfully, gladly, with loving-kindness. When I look into the faces of those graduating Wellesley seniors, one by one, 526 of them, marching across the stage—each alive with excitement and hope that she can make a difference, each inspired by the legacy she picks up with that diploma, each ready to go, bursting to grow— when I look into those faces and shake those hands and feel the amazing grace of that communication, from smile to smile, I know with all my heart that we must try.

13.

SPIRITUALITY IN EDUCATION:
A DIALOGUE

Rabbi Zalman Schachter-Shalomi and Huston Smith

Rabbi Zalman Schachter-Shalomi was born in Poland in 1924 and came to the U.S. in 1941. He was ordained in 1947 and later received a Ph.D. from Hebrew Union College. Holder of the World Wisdom Traditions Chair at The Naropa Institute, Reb Zalman has published countless articles on Jewish spiritual life and translated many Hassidic and Kabbalistic texts. The founder of the Spiritual Eldering Institute, his most recent books are *Spiritual Intimacy, Paradigm Shift,* and *Spiritual Eldering: From Age-ing to Sage-ing.*

Huston Smith, noted scholar and historian of philosophy and religion, is currently visiting professor at the University of California, Berkeley. In 1996, Bill Moyers devoted a five-part PBS special, *The Wisdom of Faith with Huston Smith,* to his life and work. Huston, the holder of seven honorary degrees, is the author of over sixty articles and eight books, including *The World's Religions* (formerly *The Religions of Man*), *Forgotten Truth: The Primordial Tradition,* and *The Purposes of Higher Education.*

RABBI ZALMAN SCHACHTER-SHALOMI: It's a joy to have the chance to have some dialogue with a friend of many years. I'm thinking of two old fishermen who, after a long day of fishing, meet near the river. Each wants to show the other guy what he's got in his bucket. So it's your turn, friend. I haven't heard what's in your bucket. Tease me and tantalize me. I want to know what you've caught.

HUSTON SMITH: Spirituality in education must begin with knowing who we are. How can we know anything about the human spirit without knowing who we are? And short of understanding who we are, all of this talk about education and spirituality is like palliatives and Band-Aids—things like that.

As I say this, I do not mean to put down the work that people gathered here are doing, each in his or her own way. All of this work adds up to something significant; but for our culture as a whole, nothing major is going to happen until we figure out who we are. The truth of the matter is, that today we haven't a clue as to who we are. There is no consistent view of human nature in the West today.

What we have are a heap of notions about who we are, but no coherent theory. We have the view of the experimental psychologists, the view of the clinical psychologists, and so on—but it does not cohere. The notions do, however, sort themselves out into two piles.

The first heap is the view that comes out of the sciences. According to the sciences, we are basically organisms in environments, organisms who, over the millennia, have developed progressively more complex strategies for interaction. This view culminates with us—as humans—at the top of the heap; and our strategies have become pretty sophisticated.

Now, that is the heap of notions that we and our children are treated to five days a week. Then, on the weekend—Sabbath for Jews, Sunday for Christians—we hear from synagogues and church pulpits a very different heap of notions about who we are.

These notions go something like this: We were created by God with immortal souls; somewhere down the line we lost our way; suffered a catastrophe; and ever since, have been engaged in recovering ourselves—making our way back to our divine source.

Now, not only are these two notions different, they are diametrically opposed. According to the scientific view, we are the greater that has been derived from the lesser; whereas, according to the religious view, we are the lesser that has been derived from the greater. There is just no way that these two views fit together. Yet simply by virtue of being denizens of the contemporary West, all of us incorporate pieces of these two contradictory views. In this way you might say our contemporary society is schizophrenic.

Now, even those who think that they have tossed out the religious view entirely still argue for things like the dignity of the individual and inalienable human rights. But you cannot derive either of these from the scientific view. These are simply concepts unwittingly basking in the afterglow of the religious view.

That's the first part of my thesis: that we are not, as a culture, going to make much progress on this crucial issue of educating the human spirit until we find out who we are. And right now we don't have a clue to who we are. The second part of my thesis is this: there is no way of finding out who we are unless we understand the nature of reality. Because we are willy-nilly, no escaping the fact, creatures, denizens. We are a part of reality.

Now, on this score, too, we have a conflict. Until the rise of modern science, everywhere, across the world, all the major teachers and prophets saw reality as what has come to be called the Great Chain of Being. This view centers in absolute perfection; and from this perfection issues, because of its infinity, all manner of existences in lessening degree right down to the meagerest forms of existence that barely escape nonexistence. This view has been well articulated by Ken Wilber.

Now, as Wilber has said brilliantly, when we think of how ubiquitous that view has been—all cultures, all times, up until the rise of modern science—it is either the greatest mistake the human mind has ever made or it is true. He happens to think it's true; and I happen to think it's true. However, this view has been radically displaced by the scientific view. The new view has collapsed this Great Chain of Being all the way down to a single one-story universe, and produced, as Marcuse's book called it, a one-dimensional man.

In this single-story universe everything is material except for a few other things that may be, as the technical literature puts it, epiphenomenal. That is to say they're generated by the physical, but they have no independent existence. The epiphenomenal are something like the foam on the beer. You can have beer foam if you have beer, but you can't have the foam if you don't have the beer. So here again, we have these radically, diametrically opposed views.

Now, I think that the traditional view is the true view. But science, and our modern culture, doesn't. I believe that the reason that science doesn't accept this view is that its methodology, in principle, cannot connect with things that belong to these "higher registers." There are several areas, despite all of its power, that the scientific method cannot touch. As I go through this list, please ask yourself whether these things are important or not: values; meaning; purposes; quality; the invisible; and things (if they exist) that are greater than we are in all respects.

Science is great with quantity, but it can't deal with quality at all. The scientific method is a near-perfect method for understanding the material world; but for other reaches, if they exist, it is totally helpless. Yet we have been so ravished by its accomplishments in the material vein that we have been seduced and beguiled into thinking science can tell us about everything that exists. In fact, it cannot.

That is my bucket. Alfred North Whitehead said that the two greatest forces in human history are science and religion. I think this statement is true. Then he went on to add this: that more than on any other single factor, the future of humanity depends upon how these two most powerful forces settle into relationship with one another.

For four centuries, the relationship has been, as my Spanish friends would say, *muy malo*. Very bad. First, the Church had the power and it didn't use it well—it tried to strangle some of the sciences in their cradle. Now four hundred years later, the shoe is on the other foot: science has the power and, alas, it is not using it very well either.

Let me just add this: I don't want to conjure up any kind of conspiracy theory, or target white-jacketed bad guys. Five years ago, I was hit with prostate cancer. My PSA count was off the chart. My oncologist and urologist moved in with radiation. As a result, it's under control, and I've had five happy years, whereas without them I would have been in Tim Leary's shoes. So there is nothing wrong with science.

What's wrong is scientism. Scientism adds to science two things that are not supported by science at all. The two things are simply opinions. The first scientistic opinion is that the scientific method is, if not the only reliable method for getting at truth, at least the most reliable method. Well, that's an opinion, it is not a scientifically proven fact. The other opinion is that the things that science deals with—namely, those of the material world—are the most important things. That, too, is simply opinion.

The main obstacle we face to spirituality in education is that there is nothing in the world right now that has the power to stop scientism. And, therefore, it has just grown like Topsy, and become the orthodoxy of our day. This is most unfortunate because it is untrue, and it diminishes our understanding of ourselves.

RABBI ZALMAN SCHACHTER-SHALOMI: I'm glad that you mentioned Ken Wilber. And the question, "We won't be able to do anything until we know who we are." For me, the issue in spirituality and education is the issue of formation. Formation was the old word they used to use when a person joined a monastery: spiritual formation.

The question is, how do you take a person who comes off the street and turn him or her into a monk? It's a transformational method. I have the sense that this is where we have given up in education. We have pulled out of the area of formation. We want so much to give freedom and independence to people—so that they would become their own being—yet we haven't given them the tools to become allies to that which is striving for holiness, for wholeness in them. We as teachers and as a culture have fed a cynical attitude, and that has flattened it all out. As Ken Wilber talked about flatland—yes, things have become flatland.

So I ask, where should we focus the learning? What tools and means are available and necessary for just the next level of transformation? His Holiness the Dalai Lama spoke of how necessary it is to have such a thing as secular ethics. I think of this as generic spirituality: no-frills spirituality. This is the kind of stuff that really works for us. When I think about it, the real question is, what is it that I first would like to bring to myself and others? The answer is this: to become transparent to earth.

HUSTON SMITH: To earth?

RABBI ZALMAN SCHACHTER-SHALOMI: To earth.

HUSTON SMITH: I would say transparent to God.

RABBI ZALMAN SCHACHTER-SHALOMI: Well, I'm not so sure about the infinite. When I go way, way to the top, to the transgalactic, transcosmic, so far away—I'm happy to go just to the Gaian God. But other times, when we say the blessing, "Blessed art thou, Lord, king of the universe," the old way of saying it—I'm just willing to say "spirit of Gaia." That's the God—within the span of a lifetime, and my interaction with beings here on the planet—I can become in my experience transparent to. That's the one that is going to give me—right away—directions that are ethical; whereas, if I go to the cosmic, something that I can do conceptually only—way up to the top where nothing else exists and we are just maya—I don't get any ethics out of it.

HUSTON SMITH: Well, I applaud and bow to your humility, and it makes it seem like chutzpah for me to reach so much higher. Let me say, however, that I don't claim to have originated my views. I see myself—and think of my whole life work—as simply being a transmitter of what the great wisdom traditions have revealed. You can think of them coming from a him, a her, or that, itself; or you can think of them as emerging from the deepest unconscious of the spiritual geniuses of this human race.

But each of these different traditions have some version of *tat tvam asi*—the notion that the deepest element within us is the divine. In China, we are an uncarved block—and all the carvings of the society and so on have diminished us. And in Buddhism, wonder of wonders, all things are intrinsically the Buddha nature. We can go right on through Judaism—we were made in the image of God; Christianity took that over. The Koran tells us that we were made "in the best stature." So I just respond to the fact that this conclusion was reached virtually unanimously and independently in all of these cultures: it's like independent verification for me.

RABBI ZALMAN SCHACHTER-SHALOMI: I got that, but you know what? I'm more with Teilhard de Chardin. I think that this planet is now entering into a phase that we might call the divinization of the planet. And—to get into my bucket a bit—what I am thinking about is, where and how do I get the tools to become a better partner, a better cell of the global brain? To create for the next generation—taking into account all the individual differences, the cultural differences, and all that stuff—a way of becoming transparent to the next holon of which we are a part; that, I think, is the task of spiritual education.

When I go back and ask the question "What's tradition got to offer?" I'm not against tradition. Otherwise the Dalai Lama wouldn't have pulled my beard, would he? I notice he pulled yours, too! But when people say, "Zalman, what do you think about tradition?" I say, "Imagine a person who's getting older, about to die. He's made a pile of money. He goes to a Swiss bank, deposits the money, and learns the access code—the way by which he can retrieve it. He studies with a rinpoche so he shouldn't forget it, goes through the *bardos,* and thirty-five years later goes back to the bank to collect his stuff." That's how I think of tradition. Tradition is what we deposit in the bank of the global brain, the great RAM RAM RAM. And when we deposit there, we don't have to start from scratch.

HUSTON SMITH: Let me get this straight about tradition. Tradition is what we deposit in the bank?

RABBI ZALMAN SCHACHTER-SHALOMI: Right.

HUSTON SMITH: I think of tradition as what feeds me.

RABBI ZALMAN SCHACHTER-SHALOMI: Yes. When I come back and collect it, it feeds me. In other words, when people say, "I don't believe in tradition," I want to say, "Tradition is what you left behind the last time you were here."

HUSTON SMITH: I don't like the line of thought that you are pursuing. No. That's a very commercialistic, consumerist metaphor: tradition as a bank.

RABBI ZALMAN SCHACHTER-SHALOMI: But in the marketplace of ideas I think . . .

HUSTON SMITH: You are in the marketplace. That's right. The agora.

RABBI ZALMAN SCHACHTER-SHALOMI: William James says there's cash value for such ideas!

HUSTON SMITH: I think we both agree—we did agree—that tradition has resources that can feed us, on which we can build. But tradition, too, can be the dead weight of the past. So if someone is simply a slave to tradition, that wouldn't work; on that we both agree.

RABBI ZALMAN SCHACHTER-SHALOMI: Right.

HUSTON SMITH: On the other hand, we both agree that religions—at least when they reach the historical phase with writing—are always changing. If people close their eyes to what needs changing, that is wrong, too. I also concede that I tend to value the heritage of the tradition more; and am wary of innovations. I'm wary of tossing out the baby with the bath; whereas, you are afraid of being stuck in the rut of the past. Now, that seems to me to be a very legitimate difference, because I don't know if I'm right; and each side has points that can be made in its favor.

RABBI ZALMAN SCHACHTER-SHALOMI: I want to add just another point to the stew, another ingredient. It has to do with Hoyle's notion that when humanity will have seen the earth from outer space, a change will have happened in human consciousness that is totally new.

I have the sense that the earth was growing people in order to see herself. And if I ask the question, not so much in terms of etiology but of teleology—and this is where the future pulls me—I ask, "What is it that we are currently being deployed to do?" This question concerns me.

I'm afraid of people who paint a picture of a kind of *Saturday Evening Post*–cover religion. You know—how it used to be nice in the past, in the '50s or the '40s. I'd like to go to the place of imagination, to the question of "Who are we becoming?" I want to go to the transpersonal psychologies. I want to ask the question as to how do we get together. Because we have learned how to be individuals, but not to partner. Partnering is the hardest thing in life: if you have to partner with lots and lots of different people, it's very difficult.

The stories and myths of partnering—the ones that we have inherited from tradition, from the past—were such stories that set us apart from each other. In other words, Jews could partner with Jews—well, no, that's not even true! Maybe Ashkenazim with Ashkenazim, Sefardim with Sefardim, and so forth. But when it comes to partnering in a post-triumphalist way, we have neither the myth nor the ethics that are derived from that. And more than anything else, we don't have a devotional life anymore to open our hearts.

I don't see the stuff or tools at this point that allow us to do to-gethering. In the worship of the past, this devotional stuff would get us excited, bring us together: it would get us out of the limited part of our brain, together with our intuition, and inform our hearts, minds, and our ethics.

So here is where I feel it's really necessary to create a research-and-development setup for the spirituality of the future. To begin to ask those questions, like "How are we going to become conscious and willing members of the higher holon, which is a healthy planet?"

So that's what's in my bucket lately; these are the things I'm thinking about. As you were describing your PSA, I'm dealing with my stuff. What is happening is that I'm starting to ask, "What's the distillate of my life that I want to leave behind, that I'd like to upload, as it were, to the global brain?"

I'm not just for syncretism. I'd like to create a situation where we find out which special spiritual experiences will make us more ethical, more moral beings. So here is where we go to Kohlberg, where we go to Fowler, where we talk about growth. This is where we are today: the planet is moving into the next phase. The old cosmologies are fading; the institutions built on the old cosmologies are rotting away. Even our government can't keep it together! It's more than two hundred years old, and it's built on obsolete reality maps which aren't organismic.

So this is the stuff that's in my bucket, the stuff that worries me, the questions I ask myself at four o'clock in the morning. It keeps coming back to the question of spiritual formation: how do we train the *bodhisattva* for the year 2025? That's the question that agitates me.

HUSTON SMITH: That's my question, too. We certainly have some differences—though I would suspect they're differences in emphases rather than radical opposition. I suspect that we would come to some agreement if we talked long enough. Yes, we all desperately long for methods for self-transformation toward the next holon; or toward making our way back to God, as I would say. Our objectives are the same.

There comes the question of where we place the greatest confidence in developing these guidelines. Again, we have a difference in emphasis, and I'm sure it comes out of our different experiences. But my mentors, throughout my life, have all been very solidly rooted in their tradition: Mother Teresa, His Holiness the Dalai Lama.

These teachers come out of their traditions, and I'm not so sure that I see promising new methods. Take Ram Dass, for example (our hearts are very much with him now): but it was only upon meeting Nimkaroli Baba, a traditional sadhu and holy man, that he give his fortune away. Tradition engendered this compassion, dedication to *seva*, and so on.

RABBI ZALMAN SCHACHTER-SHALOMI: I'm not saying just drop tradition, because the traditions are such a wonderful treasure-house.

HUSTON SMITH: I understand.

RABBI ZALMAN SCHACHTER-SHALOMI: One of our masters, Abraham Joshua Heschel of Apt, put it this way: "If you want to learn how to pray, you can't learn it from books. Hang out with a praying person." Because you have to attune to that person. I think Mother Teresa attuned to her spouse. Ram Dass attuned to Nimkaroli Baba. And this attunement was as if to give him a calibration on the inside as to which direction to move in. It's not even conscious. It has to do with body, it has to do with ethics, with dream—the whole works. Knowing that in this direction he needed to attune was what made him become not just Professor Albert but Ram Dass. I think that that's very important. I'm not against that.

But I also find that there was a time when I had to make a break with my teacher, the Lubavitcher Rebbe. It was very clear that the kind of notions that separate Jew from Goy was something that in my innards I had to reject. It was as if my whole soul's immune system was saying, "That's poison. That's not good for me."

Along with that came a genuine interest in other methods—like what can I (and others) learn from Native Americans? Imagine me sitting for a night in a peyote meeting, experiencing something really amazing. What if I would have gone to the rebbe, and said, "Sir, may I attend the peyote meeting? Is it kosher for me?" The likelihood is that he would have said no.

Do you remember that joke about the Jesuit and the Dominican? They were walking around. Each one wanted to smoke a pipe while meditating. So the Dominican asked, "May I smoke while meditating?" He got the answer no. Whereas, the Jesuit said, "May I meditate while smoking?" and got the answer yes. That's the joke, but in my experience, I find that most traditional teachers aren't willing to open themselves to experiences and questions that come from collateral traditions, from other lineages. Nor do they ask questions like "What do the people who are doing brain/mind research think?"

In the synagogue that I would like to have, there might be, for instance, a thing to help get people into alpha state before the service begins. For some people, that would open them—make them more open to hearing the words with an open heart. I think that there are possibilities that we haven't explored, but the traditional teachers tend to say, "This is not the way my teacher gave it to me." I keep coming back to the business of what did you realize—never mind what the master said. That's the argument I have against tradition.

HUSTON SMITH: I would be lying through my teeth if I were, in any way, to appear as though I were championing the triumphalism of any one tradition. Multiculturalism, to the degree that we are experiencing it—and we will experience it as never before—is a genuinely new historical phenomenon. *Newsweek* had a field day in its review of my Bill Moyer series. They call me a "spiritual surfer." So there's no way that I am going to validate the triumphalism of any one of these traditions.

What Toynbee said fifty years ago I think still holds today: "There's nobody alive who can say that one religion contains more of the truth than another." But he added an interesting appendage: "Nor anybody alive can say that it doesn't," which leaves the matter open. But I certainly see no reason, out of my years of study, to prioritize any single tradition. Furthermore, the teachers that I went to were not hung up on the matter—perhaps because in Asia, triumphalism hasn't taken hold. So I don't think that is a difference between us.

RABBI ZALMAN SCHACHTER-SHALOMI: You know what? I think that business about "in Asia they didn't have triumphalisms"— I'm not so sure about that one either. Because Vaishnavis fight with the Shaivaites: they have their differences. Let me tell you a story. I went with a group of people to visit Swami Muktananda. We brought flowers, gifts, and all that kind of stuff. Before we get to meet him, he has a translator come and hang out with us—warm us up. Then he turns to me and says, "We are very universalistic; and you Jews are particularistic."

So I said, "That's great. Would you please translate a few words for me, just simple definitions." He replied, "Sure." "Dharma?" I said. "The teachings of righteousness," he replied. "Karma?" I asked. "The law of cause and effect." *"Mleccha."* And then he started to say, "That's our definition for non-Bharatic people." *Mleccha* means—translated straight—"excrement eaters." That's what they call the guys who are the goyim for them. See what I'm saying? I don't want to go and exalt the Vedanta-for-export that we have been getting, which says that we're all in the same soup, because in there, too, is a little bit that speaks of superiority.

We want to go to the next phase, as it were, of education for spirituality: to the opening up of what I think the Sufis call the *Alam al Mithal,* the "imaginative world." John Taylor Gatto said earlier today that we should not discourage a child from daydreaming. I would like to see that in courses: after we talk about a wonderful notion, we encourage the class, "Now daydream for five minutes about that." Measure yourself to this idea; see how it feels when you put it on. One of our masters said, "If a person doesn't spend fifteen minutes a day trying to be a perfect zaddik [righteous one], he hasn't begun to be awakened."

I would like to see a group of people take it as their task to find ways of increasing our consciousness; increasing our affective capacity; learning how to still the dinosaur inside of us; and learning how to collaborate more. When I look at the sophistication that we have in building a Stealth bomber, and then look at the lack of sophistication we have in conflict resolution, I feel really sad.

These are the thoughts that concern me. I want to reach out to all of you who are here and ask you to pay attention to the things that make a difference in your awareness and in your life. How can you reinforce these things? Talk with other people about it; see that we become part of the next holon, the next body, the next community: become the template that enables society to shift into something more benign, more loving, more of one body.

HUSTON SMITH: This question of growth and evolution is not just a question for you and me but for everyone. How much to treasure from our heritage, and how much to relinquish and replace it with something new? I feel that question, every day, and I think I've been hearing you say that you feel it, too. This is a question for all of us today.

RABBI ZALMAN SCHACHTER-SHALOMI: The ways in which we created the saints of the past was to sort of prune them: they didn't live life; they weren't householders; we kept on pruning everything so they only had one way to grow—up, up, up. When I think of those one-sided saints, I wouldn't want to live with any of them. They were paying attention to just this single aspect of growing to their heroic sainthood. I am looking for a saint who is a mensch.

Today, we want to have more holistic people, and that means that we need them more in their bodies. The kind of ascetics that we used to have were the ones who were not friendly to the body; now we need ascetics who are friendly to the body, who know how to taste taste, how to be grateful to the world, how to share with each other. A more sensual spirituality. I think this is very important. So that we don't become polarized: that if I enjoy food, that means that I am somehow denying God. That's how it was in the past. Once a guy came into our yeshiva, and as he came into our refectory, he said, "Good appetite, boys." I recall whispering under my breath "God forbid." Now I think it's time for a more feminized, earthy, body-centered spirituality.

14.

WHERE DO WE GO
FROM HERE?

Vincent Harding

Dr. Vincent Harding is professor of religion and social transformation at Illiff School of Theology in Denver, Colorado. He has had a long history of involvement in domestic and international movements for peace and justice, including the southern black freedom struggle. Vincent was the first director of the Martin Luther King, Jr. Memorial Center in Atlanta and served as director of the Institute of the Black World. Senior academic consultant to the PBS television series *Eyes on the Prize,* his books include *There Is a River; Martin Luther King: The Inconvenient Hero;* and *Hope and History.*

I wish I knew how it would feel to be free.
I wish I could break all the chains binding me.
—NINA SIMONE

B Y N O W, it should be clear that we do not need more words, or another speech. We have had a great number of magnificent presentations already. What seems more important now was hinted at by Jeremy Hayward, way back on Saturday, the first full day of our conference. He said, "It seems like everything has been said already. Why do we need to keep talking? Why don't we just go out and do it? And be it?"

I would like to reflect on some of the things that have been said, and consider what they have to do with our going out and being it, doing it, sharing it. In other words, I would like to reflect on where we go from here.

In the best of all possible worlds, I would not only share my reflections but also hear yours. However, while this is a wonderful world, it's not the best that we could have. So I'll just have to imagine what you are reflecting on as I share my reflections with you.

TO DO THE STRONG THING
THAT WE CAN DO

I almost didn't recognize Joan Halifax when we first saw each other. Then, as she explained the cutting of her hair, I began to see her in a different way. Joan shared with us the words her Buddhist teacher used to describe this matter of getting to the point where all of her hair would be gone. His words were: "It's a strong thing to do."

All through our time together, I've heard us being called to recognize the reality that what we are about, as we go back to our lives and places, is a strong thing to do. And people have also been saying to us, "You can do it. You can be it. Even though it might change the way you look, change your reputation, change what people think about you, it's a strong thing that needs to be done for our children and our nation: and you can do it." That has been the message.

So where do we go from here? To do the strong thing that we can do.

TO RETURN TO WHERE WE
CAME FROM, AS HEALERS

Joan kept speaking about rites of passage, and about how, in so many traditions, those rites call upon the participants to leave behind that which is familiar, well-known and lovely, so precious and good. For a time we must move out into the unknown, unclear, and uncharted, move on into the mystery of new creation. Joan suggested that even out there—in the sea of the unknown—the spirit of education must be fundamentally about preparing us to return into the world as healers.

So where do we go from here? To return to where we came from, as healers.

TO GET TO KNOW OURSELVES MORE FULLY

Then Joan said something else, as she talked about how hard it is to develop holistic, integrated education. "We have really underestimated who we are," she said. And of course, before long, the Dalai Lama was singing the same song: "We don't know who we are." And Huston Smith was saying the same thing: "We've got to become acquainted with ourselves." Not just with the shadows that we so often seem to specialize in—though not making believe that they aren't there—but becoming acquainted with the great light that is us, in us, through us. To nurture this light, develop it, value it.

So where do we go from here? To get to know ourselves a bit more, especially, most especially, our beauty.

To reintroduce ourselves to our beauty. Because unfortunately, so much in our life teaches us that this beauty isn't really there; or if it had ever been there, we had lost it a long time ago. Or we had some-how been penalized for having too much of it.

Where do we go from here? To reacquaint ourselves with beauty, in us, in others, around us all.

TO RECOGNIZE SPIRITUALITY AND HUMAN SERVICE AS ONE

Sometime in the midst of the conversation, in ways that I don't fully understand, we began talking about spirituality and human service as if they were two separate worlds. I would like to suggest that this is not the case. In one of the traditions that has shaped me, there is a magnificent story that Jesus tells. In essence, he says, "If you want to find me, if you really want to come close to me"—now what could be more spiritual than that?—"if you want to come close to me, then get close to the poor. If you want to find me, then find the prisoners. If you want to hold me and be held by me, then hold and be held by the outcasts."

Spirituality and human service are one thing in this tradition. It is not about getting ourselves ready, wonderfully spiritual, and then doing the other stuff. No, it's recognizing that there are all kinds of surprises for us, in so many unexpected places and among so many people. In people whom we never expected to be the source of such surprises—surprises like the presence of God.

So where do we go from here? To recognize spirituality and human service as one. And to be continually surprised, to expect the unexpected.

TO OUR STUDENTS

Where do we go from here? To our students. Imagine that! To our students. As I see it, one of the things we bring from here is a determination to make sure that we help them, as best we can, to find the way that avoids both underestimation and overestimation of themselves. And of course, we help them find that way because we're in that path ourselves—trying to avoid overestimation and underestimation of ourselves.

So we go from here in the movement of our own search into the midst of our students and their search: and by being in search ourselves, we recognize their search when we see it and feel it and hear it; and no matter what camouflage they put over it, no matter what words they shout out at us, we recognize from our search that they too are seekers, and we search together.

Where do we go from here? To the search, with our students, for that authenticity that they are looking for as intensely as we are.

TO OUR FEARS

Where do we go from here? To our fears. That's what people have been saying. Confront your fears, and recognize the power that is deep within you to overcome them.

That, as I understand it, is one of the most important components of spirituality: the power to overcome our fears. And by "overcome" I do not mean somehow canceling them all out and pushing them away. I remember vividly how often, as we were marching in some strange places in the South, we would be singing, "We are not afraid," and our legs would be shaking to beat the band.

What we were really saying was this: "We will not give in to the shaking. We will not let the fears overcome us." Not that the fears can somehow be banished but that we can find the strength, the courage, the vision, and the assurance to keep moving in the midst of the fears.

So we go from here recognizing that there is within us power to keep walking through the fears, including the fear of leaving the familiar, including the fear of moving out toward the mysterious, the liminal, and the unknown.

TO OUR LOVED ONES

Where do we go from here? We go—with all these struggles within us—to our loved ones. In some cases, we let them know for the first time that we, like them, are really struggling with all of this stuff that they assumed we had taken care of years ago.

We go to our loved ones, and we recognize in new ways how much of a part of each other's education we are. There is so much teaching already coming to us, if we are ready and willing to receive it, if we are prepared to admit to our dearest ones how much we need to be nurtured, taught, and held by them.

TO FACE HONESTLY THE MEANING AND CHALLENGE OF THE GREAT ABSENCE

Now, as I look at you, and as you look at me, it's clear that a significant part of where we go from here must be toward a disciplined and intentional search to understand why we are so overwhelmingly white here. We cannot simply accept this; we cannot be content with platitudinous statements like "Why, of course, we're in Boulder," or "We're Buddhists." No, this is not sufficient—not if we are serious about our spirituality and our teaching.

Where we go from here is to be deeply, painfully, embarrassingly honest with ourselves, and ask, "How could we have this conference on spirituality in education, when a whole sector of our nation—who have created great traditions of spirituality, and have believed in the power of education more than anybody else in the country—are not centrally present?"

We have to ask—without flailing each other or beating ourselves—honestly ask, "And why are they not here?" What is the source of this great absence of color? What does this say about us? What does this say about them? What does this say about Boulder? What does it say about Naropa? What does this say about anything we want to say anything about?

So we go toward a hard way. Cutting off our hair is not the only hard way—cutting off our excuses is even harder.

TO HUNGER AND THIRST AFTER RIGHTEOUSNESS

Where do we go from here? To face reality, to ask questions, and to know that they who hunger and thirst after righteousness shall be filled.

I consider the coming together of God's children as being one of the purest forms of righteousness that I can think of. And I want to be filled. I want to be filled under tents like this. I want to be filled at

Naropa. I want to be filled, and I want others to be filled, because I know what it's like to have that kind of filling.

So where do we go from here? To search out new and better ways to bring us into engagement with our separated sisters and brothers, because everything else becomes hollow if we are not avidly about that task.

TO EXPLORE LOCATION

Maybe that's part of what Jeremy Hayward was saying when he was talking about the world of scientific materialism and its power over us. Maybe that's what he was saying when he made this very fascinating statement: "Only in the strange is there any release from the trap of scientific materialism."

Part of the scientific materialism of our time, of our place, of our nation is the idea that we have different social locations. Some of us are located in Boulder, some of us are located at Naropa, and some of us are located in northwest Denver. It's just a matter of our locations, we say.

Some of us are located in all those fascinating African genes, and some of us just live in other ones, and other experiences. Yet all of the spirituality that we have been talking about here presses on us and says to us: "Aha, social location. Is that it? Social location is actually more powerful than spiritual location?"

Hmm. Is that what we spent all this time figuring out?

Where do we go from here? To try to figure out the relationship between spiritual location and social location.

TO DEVELOP NEW EYES

What I heard from my precious brother/father/teacher, His Holiness, was the constant Gandhi-like belief in the great possibilities of human beings to bring about human change. Some of us might think he has blinded himself to the irrationality of human beings, but all I know is that it is very likely true what he said: that unless we have a deep belief in the possibilities of bringing about these changes, they're not going to take place. One of the old community organizers, Saul Alinsky, used to say, "When you believe it, you'll see it."

Where do we go from here? To develop new eyes, eyes that start down in our guts. Lots of work. Lots of hard work. But I assume that this is what we came here for.

We go from here to nourish the belief in ourselves, in our friends, in our students, and in our family. We go from here to nourish the belief that change—humane, compassionate change—is actually possible, even in the world of the "free market." Now, that's—as the old folks used to say where I come from—that's more than a notion.

TO PAY MORE ATTENTION
TO TOUCH

Where do we go from here? His Holiness said something else that took hold of me. He was participating in what Jeremy was saying, and Jeremy was sharing the message of the Dalai Lama, a message that teaches us that when people are treated as mere objects—reductively, materialistically, mechanically—we push against their deepest nature as human beings. Our highest, truest nature is not materialistic, and when we define ourselves and each other materialistically, we are making for ourselves much trouble.

And then the Dalai Lama comes along and says, very simply, "Pay more attention to the human touch." Now, after having listened to him for many years, I don't think that he meant this as a metaphor. I think he was talking about the human touch as that which helps to encourage the human spirits in human beings.

Therefore, as a learner from all that I've been taught here these four days, I would say let's not wait until we go from here. Right now, would you please touch somebody in a human way? However you define that. Please, please. Yes. Yes. We'll set up some screens if we need to do that. Any way that is helpful to you.

TO BE INSANE IN
AN INSANE WORLD

The Dalai Lama was so beautiful to us, because he kept talking to us about how hard this way was in the light of the karma that we have developed nationally and personally. He said how tough and rough it was going to be for us, and at the same moment he said something crazy like, "You could just start with a little touching." We want seventy-three intricate formulae stretched out on boards long and wide, and he says, "Touch each other!"

Where do we go from here? To find some folks to touch. Go and touch.

More and more things in our culture are discouraging us from touching each other. It's dangerous. And that's how we become strange again. Touch. Strange? Crazy.

In the tradition that I know best there is an idea about being fools for Christ: fools for humanity's best possibilities, acting in ways that no sane, good American, middle-class, white or black person should act. Touching people.

Where do we go from here? To be insane in an insane world. To touch.

TO RIGHT HERE,
AT THE NEXT LEVEL

His Holiness challenged us to face the possibility that we don't have to go anyplace from here: we just have to be here, and do the work that's necessary to be done here. He was saying to us—and I think he gave me the permission to translate him—"Friends, you've got more power and more gifts and more beauties and more possibilities than you realize. Don't be satisfied with what you are, who you are, where you are, as you are. The best is yet to come."

And dear sister Judith Simmer-Brown spoke to us and asked the question in another way: Where do we need to go in order to take our practice to the next highest possible level? Now, of course, some of us believe that if we could just hold on to where we are, and not slip down too far, we're doing very well. And old Judith Simmer-Brown comes talking about moving to a higher level.

So where do we go from here? To right here, at the next level.

TO FLY

I have a dear friend by the name of William Sloan Coffin, who used to be chaplain at Yale University. He was there in the midst of the Vietnam War, and all of the turmoil that came from people trying to bring about change. Recently Bill was at Illiff School of Theology, and in his wonderfully practiced, pithy one-liners, gave us all kinds of things to think about.

Where do we go? Bill said, "Jesus offers us minimum protection and maximum support." How about that for those who take refuge? Minimum protection and maximum support. Just trying to get you out there, flying like a bird in the sky. Because if you're protected too much, you obviously can't fly.

So where do we go from here? To fly: to fly beyond where we thought we could go, maybe even to get some of our moribund institutions to begin to flap their bricks.

TO OUR ALL

I hope you still have the image of that trickster/saint/sister bell hooks talking to us about letting the life that is within us come forth. And the image of discovering the meaning of compassion in all of the strange places we operate. And bell hooks, from City College of New York, daring to talk about being guided by love. Now, if bell hooks can be guided by love walking around City College, just think of what we could do in Boulder!

I liked what bell hooks said to us very existentially. She asked us—not rhetorically—to ask ourselves, "What are the actions I will concretely do today to manifest the community that I seek? I have come here in search of community. What am I going to do to build it?" And then she said something that really threw me, because, again, you don't expect to hear this kind of language from accomplished, distinguished professors of English at the City College of New York or even at the University of Colorado. She said, "Surely the crisis of these times demands our all."

How do we get to our all? Everybody has been saying the same thing: Practice. Practice. Practice. Not with a large P, with a small p. Practice. Working at it. Working at it. Experimenting with it. Touching all kinds of crazy people. Constantly seeing what happens. Practice. Practice.

And then bell said, "And also remember we have to see the place of our pain as the place of our transformation and go right on."

Where do we go from here? To our all. To practice, to pain, and to transformation.

FURTHER THAN WE EVER DREAMED POSSIBLE

This is a tough agenda. Bell hooks said the demands are all. Ron Miller said it's a long rough road. Some of us have so much frustration and fear in our faces that just upon hearing these words we need to remember that this is why we take refuge in the Buddha, or in Christ. Not to make the path easier but to make us stronger. And maybe—now, I don't know about the Buddha, but I do know about some other marvelous manifestations of the love of the universe—when they make people stronger, the path gets rougher again, because they want us to practice, to build up our muscles. Practice. Practice. Practice.

And that's why some people where I come from used to sing, "Nobody knows the troubles I've seen." "Glory, hallelujah." That's why we say, "Precious Lord, take my hand." If you're not going any-place new, strange, odd, or uninhabited, you don't need anybody to take your hand! You just skip along. But to go where we never dared to go before, on the rough, rough road, then, precious Lord, take my hand.

So where do we go from here? I think some of us are going to go further than we ever dreamed possible. Don't stop yourself. Don't stop yourself.

TO PARTICIPATE IN THE BUILDING
OF A NEW WORLD

To close, I want to read to you something—though attributed to the Venerable Nelson Mandela Rinpoche—that comes to us as a gift from Marianne Williamson.

> *Our deepest fear is not that we are inadequate. Our deepest fear is that we are powerful beyond measure. It is our light, not our darkness that most frightens us. We ask ourselves, "Who am I to be brilliant, gor-geous, talented, and fabulous?" Actually, who are you not to be? You are a child of God. Your playing small doesn't serve the world. There's nothing enlightened about shrinking so that other people won't feel in-secure around you. We were born to make manifest the glory of God that is within us. It's not just in some of us. It's in everyone. And as we let our own light shine, we unconsciously give other people permission to do the same. As we are liberated from our own fear, our presence au-tomatically liberates others.*

Where do we go from here? Wherever we go from here, I want to suggest that we go singing a new song. I'd like to teach you a song that you can go with. This song comes out of the black American slavery tradition. It is the music of "We Are Climbing Jacob's Ladder," but with new words for this time.

We are building up a new world.
We are building up a new world.
We are building up a new world,
builders must be strong.

Courage, sisters, don't get weary.
Courage, brothers, don't get weary.
Courage, people, don't get weary,
though the way be long.

Rise, shine, give God glory.
Rise, shine, give God glory.
Rise, shine, give God glory,
children of the light. (repeat)

Where do we go from here? We go out to participate in the building of a new world. It's a tough assignment. But we are tough people: moving from within, beginning a thousand foolish projects, training bodhisattvas for the year 2025. Be strong!

CONCLUSION:
THE HEART OF LEARNING

THERE IS NO THING to be done; there is also no shortage of things to be done. Just as spirit pervades everything, spirituality in education is about everything. It is about bringing ourselves more fully to each moment, learning, acting, and teaching not merely as if *our* life depended on this but *all* of life.

Spirituality in education begins with openness: opening up to ourselves, feeling our experience, and exploring the inner landscape of our lives. We must take on the work of facing our fears, opening to intimacy and vulnerability, and opening to the unknown, to surprise. We can learn to open to situations simply, without aggression or defensiveness; and open to the inside as well: the depths beyond the surfaces of all life.

While openness begins as an inner, personal discipline, it very quickly evolves into a dynamic, interactive experience. Our own openness actually collapses boundaries between ourselves and others and the world. Indeed, our openness enables us to create open, spacious environments. Through our personal efforts—discipline, sincerity, and embodiment—these environments can be carried out and manifested in our lives: touch our relationships, our classrooms, our schools, and communities. Indeed, we ourselves can give open, spacious environments to our schools.

Spirituality in education then proceeds—with our individual willingness and commitment to awareness: care and carefulness; facing and engaging fully with situations; heartfelt curiosity. And also our willingness to change: modify our beliefs, actions, and strategies as much (and as often) as necessary. Here again, what begins as a personal engagement can quickly manifest in the world as a very real quality:

one that can be seen, felt, heard, remembered. We know—and others do too—what a real sense of presence feels like. We have felt the sense of possibility—or perhaps even the sense of vastness—that can arise for us in specific situations or environments. Presence is something that we can cultivate in our lives. A sense of presence is a gift. Presence is a gift that we can give to our students and schools.

By sharing with our students this quality of presence, we play an extremely important role in combating the materialism of contemporary culture. Through the offering of genuine engagement to our students, they can begin to experience interconnection and wholeness, and experience the interior, energetic, nonmaterial quality of life. This allows them, in turn, to cocreate environments where they interact with their peers in this same way. Then, as communities, we can begin to teach and model together the practices of openness, awareness, respect. Within our communities, we can begin to engender, model, and feel a sense of wholeness.

Wholeness can be cultivated, as well, by tearing down the artificial boundaries that divide us: divide us from each other; divide our schools from our communities; divide our schools from the world. The schoolyard can become curriculum, the regional landscape, the local culture, and city politics, too. All of these and more can be folded into a transformed notion of education and educational journey.

In short, spirituality in education is about transformation. Not just hoping for transformation, or wishing for transformation, or believing in transformation, or even talking about it, but actual transformation. Transformation is not necessarily hard; in fact it is quite easy. Things are changing all the time, even moment to moment. Can't we?

The list of what's wrong, what needs to be fixed, seems endless. It's daunting; it seems like there is nowhere to begin. But there is a place: just now. Right now is not too late—it is the right moment. We can begin openness, awareness, and wholeness right now, in our immediate situations.

What keeps us from right now? Fear. The same place we are all so afraid of is just out there, is the coming unknown. We have fear: fear of what might be; of exposure; of danger to ourselves, or to our loved ones. But the coming unknown, the next moment, is all there is. It presents itself to us, again and again, throughout our lives. Paying attention, this is what our basic experience is: a flickering of awareness, turning to experience, and then turning into history, again and again.

Phenomena are elusive and endless (and sometimes even exhausting for us)! Phenomena are woven and entwined all the way up, down, and across—whether we like it or not. In the face of the shifting textures and groundlessness, we can either hold on to our anxiety, hold on to some false sense of safety, or let go into the free play of what is next.

This is spirituality in education. Attending to the present; attending to what presents itself; taking things firsthand. Taking care, and bringing care. Seeing in each moment—this very moment—the opportunity for transformation.

By letting all phenomena—all our experience—be our teacher, school is never out. Education never stops, learning never stops. We learn from our bodies, our emotions, our awareness, our experience. We greet life: we meet it face to face. In meeting the unknown we find everything we're looking for: spirit, our selves, a sense of community, and a sense of place—indeed wholeness.

This may be simple for us, or it may take hard work, but it's the work of our lives. We all have choices: to learn or not, to grow or not, to live or not, "to be or not to be." We can deny or expose, we have the choice of learning or forgetting. Unfortunately, contemporary education is choosing denial, choosing forgetting. Contemporary education is teaching us to succeed in this world as it is, rather than to heal this world into what it might become. Yes, we are learning to read, to write, to program computers, to find jobs; but the way we are teaching and learning—the way we are learning to see, to act and behave—is undermining the life and life force that ultimately sustains us all. Our materialism is undermining the spirit of the world.

We can no longer close our eyes to the lessons that the world is teaching us day in and day out. We need to step out of abstraction—

beyond the isolation of the subject, the discipline, and the class-room—into the full experience of life as it is happening to us, in us, with us. We need to step beyond a surface material view to a view of wholeness. With this step comes not merely a new view but also a new ethic: an ethic of engagement and responsibility.

A raging stream of information—teachings about everything, all possible subjects—is flying towards and through us, at the speed of life, in each and every moment. Are we willing to see this? To open to this opportunity? To learn from life? We can bring spirituality into education by seeing life—exactly as it presents itself to us—as the classroom. We can bring spirituality into education by seeing our experience, actions, and interactions as the curriculum.

The heart of learning is returning always to the heart of all life. The heart of life is openness, awareness, and wholeness inseparable. It is the Great Chain of Being: the joining of form and the formless, the joining of matter and spirit, the joining of sacred and profane. The heart of learning is learning to see ourselves and this living world as totally, utterly, and completely inseparable—as whole. The heart of learning is, finally, learning from and attending to the life thread of spirit pervading and connecting all things.

ACKNOWLEDGMENTS

THIS BOOK would never have been possible without the wisdom, kindness, and patience of so many. Though the beings are countless (and the list of names endless), I do wish to acknowledge the following:

Thank you to everyone involved in putting together the Spirituality in Education conference. Especially Debra Horowitz, co-dreamer, heart collaborator, and conference administrator extraordinaire! Thank you to the conference participants, for sharing both their time and timeless wisdom: His Holiness the Dalai Lama, John Taylor Gatto, Joan Halifax, Vincent Harding, Jeremy Hayward, bell hooks, Ron Miller, David Orr, Parker Palmer, Dzogchen Ponlop Rinpoche, Rachel Naomi Remen, Rabbi Zalman Schachter-Shalomi, Judith Simmer-Brown, Huston Smith, and Diana Chapman Walsh. Thank you to the core conference staff, for giving many months of your lives (and the entirety of your hearts) to this magical event: Cassandra Terman, Lisa Trank, Kristyn Demko, Max Regan, Dana Ming, Mark McCaffrey, Deb Bowman, and Richard Brown. Thank you to the jump-start performers, panel moderators, and conference weavers: for molding the event into a living whole. Kudos to the conference registration staff, support staff, discussion group leaders, experiential form leaders, and volunteers. Brilliant work!

Thank you to my many friends and colleagues at The Naropa Institute. John Cobb and Phil Jacobson: thank you for believing in me, in this dream, and helping make it manifest. Much love to Lex Hixon and Jay Peter Chipmann, for vision and generosity in supporting the founding of The Naropa Institute School of Continuing Education. Endless gratitude to the staff of CE: Kate Beal, Jan Berger, Kristyn

Acknowledgments

Demko, Betsy Gill, Sue Hammond, Michele Hartley, Cat Kowalski, Nancy Levin, Frank MacOwen, Joanna McKenzie, Summer Morrell, Charlotte Rotterdam, Barry Townsend, Rima Wilson, and Mark Wolff. Bob Morehouse and the Vermilion folks, too! A bow of respect to my inspirational Naropa family: Ralph Basch, Barbara Dilley, Emily Hunter, Saul Kotzubei, Pamela Krasney, Cynthia Moku, Audrey Romeo, Lucien Wulsin, and Reb Zalman. Whatever small bit I understand of the so-called "founders' vision," I understand due to endless conversation with you.

Thanks to Living Education: Chip, Carol, Stacey, Saul, Debra, Audrey, Emily, and Lloyd. An outrageous, beautiful, rare, and sometimes frustrating thing that we have with each other. Imagine it: education that has to do with our direct experience of this place and moment. Just what we need to learn from now! Gratitude to Chip and Carol for supporting Stacey, Kayla, and me with a lovely home during the writing of this book.

Thank you to my teachers: Elaine Moore Hirsch, founder of the visionary School of Sacred Arts. SOSA was a decade before its time, but its values and approach became entwined in my heart and life. Much love and gratitude to you, Elaine, for starting me out on this path. Thank you, Pema Wangyal. You taught me so much—though not using so many words. And certainly with a unique style all your own! Hardly a day passes that I do not remember a lesson. Thank you, Lex and Sheila Hixon: you have been spiritual family. Always serving—whether for shelter, a cup of tea, or encouragement. You inspired me towards spirituality in education by not only sharing the path but also its fruits. Thank you especially, Chagdud Tulku Rinpoche, for opening in my life the doorway to Buddha nature. From the beginning you have cared for me gently as your child. Your teachings continue to arise in my life as just what I need in this moment. May they continue to open wider and wider my heart.

This project required time and energy—but especially the support of good friends. (So many of you are mentioned above, but I won't repeat myself. Okay?) Thanks to the folkers—James Barnett, diane bartko, Eric Feingold, and Michele Adam—for always believing in me. Thanks to the A boys, Paul and Ray Agostinelli, for support and caffeine. Thanks to Uncle Beardsley, for unwavering friendship, and Blake Spalding, for the brilliant sunshine of your heart.

Gratitude to Mark Beaver, Clarke Strand, Janine Benyus, Lisa Leghorn, Charles Jakiela, Christie Green, and Mitchell Zucker for help in the early stages of the proposal and book. My thanks to Jim Levine, my agent, for helping this book find a good home, and to Mitch Horowitz at Tarcher/Putnam, for his fine eye and hand in editing.

Thanks and so much love to Stacey, my companion in this outrageous thing called life: for your daily friendship and endless encouragement towards my pursuit of crazy dreams. Thank you, Kayla Beth, for bringing me out of the sky and down to the earth. Much love and thanks to my family—Mom, Bob, Meg, Russ, Doug, Maria, Jeff, Susan, Rita, Alan, Stephen, Sharon, Andy, Gail, Nana, et al.—for your love and patience in watching the river of my life meander.

The brilliance of many wonderful teachers, thinkers, and saints—past and present—form the inspirational vision of this book. So for the gift of the vision, I bow in gratitude to them. In terms of the details of this book, however, any flaws, shortcomings, and inconsistencies are but a reflection of me: my own small mind and its inability to contain, sustain, and synthesize the vast expanse of wisdom. My hope and prayer is that this small volume may be of great benefit.

NOTES AND REFERENCES

CHAPTER 1: THE GRACE OF GREAT THINGS

1. This essay is an edited transcription of the keynote talk at the May 1997 Naropa Institute conference on Spirituality in Education in Boulder, CO.

2. *The Transformation of Allen School*. Dayton, OH: Patrick and Joey O'Donnell Productions, 1996.

3. T. H. White, *The Once and Future King*. NY: Ace Books, 1987, p. 183.

4. Rudolf Otto, *The Idea of the Holy*. London: Oxford University Press, 1952.

5. Rainer Maria Rilke, "Archaic Torso of Apollo," in Robert Bly, ed., *Selected Poems of Rainer Maria Rilke*. NY: Harper & Row, 1981, p. 147.

6. Dr. James Shapiro, University of Chicago, quoted in "Dr. Barbara McClintock, 90, Gene Research Pioneer, Dies," *The New York Times*, September 4, 1992, p. C16.

7. Evelyn Fox Keller, *A Feeling for the Organism: The Life and Work of Barbara McClintock*. New York: W. H. Freeman and Company, 1983.

8. Evelyn Fox Keller, *Reflections on Gender and Science*. New Haven: Yale University, 1985, p. 164.

9. David Denby, *Great Books*. New York: Simon and Schuster, 1996.

10. Thomas Merton, "Hagia Sophia," in Thomas P. McDonnell, ed., *A Thomas Merton Reader*. New York: Doubleday, 1989, p. 506.

11. Rainer Maria Rilke, *Rodin and Other Prose Pieces*. London: Quartet Books Limited, 1986, p. 4.

12. Transcript of *The Day After Trinity: J. Robert Oppenheimer and the Atomic Bomb*. Kent, OH: PTV Publications, 1981, p. 30.

13. James D. Watson, *The Double Helix*. New York: Atheneum, 1968.

14. Leon Jaroff, "Happy Birthday, Double Helix," *Time* 141 (11) March 15, 1993, pp. 58–59.

Notes

CHAPTER 4: UNLEARNING TO SEE THE SACRED

Karen Armstrong, *A History of God: The 4000-Year Quest of Judaism, Christianity and Islam.* New York: Ballantine Books, 1992. A journey through the evolution of the Western world's relation to the idea of one God.

Jeremy Hayward, *Letters to Vanessa on Love, Science, and Awareness in an Enchanted World.* Boston: Shambhala, 1997. The stories of the one-dimensional, dead world and the enchanted world told through the language of science and Buddhism, for ages eighteen to eighty.

Jeremy and Karen Hayward, *Sacred World, The Shambhala Way to Gentleness, Bravery and Power,* 2d ed. Boston: Shambhala, 1998. The Shambhala path of spiritual warriorship, its teachings on awareness practice, sacredness, and drala.

Robert Jahn and Brenda Dunne, *Margins of Reality: The Role of Consciousness in the Physical World.* New York: Harcourt Brace Jovanovich, 1987. An account of the experiments at the PEAR laboratory and the wave-particle theory of consciousness.

Ervin Laszlo, *The Whispering Pond: A Personal Guide to the Emerging Vision of Science.* Rockport, MA: Element Books, 1996. A careful examination of the leading edge of the sciences powerfully arguing for the theoretical need for a "psi-field," a psychic field pervading all of space.

Dean Radin, *The Conscious Universe: The Scientific Truth of Psychic Phenomena.* New York: HarperEdge, 1997. A careful, critical review of the clear and certain evidence for phenomena such as remote viewing and psychokinesis, together with a fierce indictment of the deliberate blindness and deception of self-styled "skeptics."

Huston Smith, *Forgotten Truth: The Common Vision of the World's Religions.* New York: HarperCollins, 1992. The inner teaching of multileveled reality common to all the world's spiritual traditions.

CHAPTER 6: COMMITMENT AND OPENNESS

1. Richard Hughes Seager, ed., *The Dawn of Religious Pluralism: Voices from the World's Parliament of Religions* (1893). LaSalle, IL: Open Court Press, 1993.

2. Raimundo Panikkar, "The Myth of Pluralism: The Tower of Babel," *Invisible Harmony: Essays on Contemplation and Responsibility.* Minneapolis, MN: Augsburg Fortress Press, 1995, p. 59.

3. Diana Eck, *Encountering God: A Spiritual Journey from Bozeman to Benares.* Boston: Beacon Press, 1994.

4. For more detailed examination of the notions of sameness and difference from a Buddhist perspective, see the author's "Pluralism and Dialogue: A Contemplation of the Dialogue Relationship," in Roger Jackson and John Makranski, eds., *Buddhist Theology.* Curzon Press, 1998.

5. Eck, *Encountering God,* p. 195.

6. Petrul Rinpoche, *The Special Teaching of the Wise and Glorious King and Its Commentary.* Vajravairocana Translation Committee, 1989, p. 2.

7. Thomas Merton, *Asian Journals*.

8. Nyoshul Khen Rinpoche, *Natural Great Perfection*. Ithaca, NY: Snow Lion, 1995, pp. 112–14.

9. In the Tibetan tradition, the feminine principle is Prajnaparamita herself, the penetrating insight which is the basis of all enlightenment. See forthcoming, Judith Simmer-Brown, *Dakini's Warm Breath: Feminine Principle in Tibetan Buddhism*.

10. Herbert Guenther, *The Life and Teachings of Naropa*. London: Oxford University Press, 1963, p. iii.

11. Guenther, 1963, p. 24. For the rest of the account, see Chap. 3.

12. The event described here is taken from the long biography of Guru Rinpoche, written by his dakini-consort Yeshe Tsogyal, discovered by Terchen Urgyan Lingpa, translated from the Tibetan into French by Gustave-Charles Toussaint, and translated into English by Kenneth Douglas and Gwendolyn Bays, *The Life and Liberation of Padmasambhava: Padma bKa'I Thang*. Berkeley, CA: Dharma Publishing, 1978, pp. 219–20.

CHAPTER 11: HOLISTIC EDUCATION FOR AN EMERGING CULTURE

Dee Coulter, "Montessori and Steiner: A Pattern of Reversed Symmetries," *Holistic Education Review*, vol. 4, no. 2, 1991, pp. 30–32.

Rachael (Shelley) Kessler, "The Teaching Presence," *Holistic Education Review*, vol. 4, no. 4, 1991, pp. 4–15.

Ron Miller, "Two Hundred Years of Holistic Education," *Holistic Education Review*, vol. 1, no. 1, 1988, pp. 5–12.

Ron Miller, *What Are Schools For? Holistic Education in American Culture*. 3d ed. Brandon, VT: Holistic Education Press, 1997.

Bernie Neville, *Educating Psyche: Emotion, Imagination and the Unconscious in Learning*. Blackburn, Australia: Collins Dove, 1989.

Kate Silber, *Pestalozzi: The Man and His Work*. 2d ed. London: Routledge & Kegan Paul, 1965.

Rudolph Steiner, *The Spirit of the Waldorf School: Lectures Surrounding the Founding of the First Waldorf School*. Hudson, NY: Anthroposophic Press, 1995.

Ken Wilber, *The Eye of the Spirit: An Integral Vision for a World Gone Slightly Mad*. Boston: Shambhala, 1997.

BIBLIOGRAPHY

Alexander, Christopher. 1979. *The Timeless Way of Building*. New York: Oxford University Press.

———. et al. 1977. *A Pattern Language*. New York: Oxford University Press.

Almaas, A. 1986. *Essence*. York Beach, ME: Samuel Weiser.

———. 1988. *The Pearl Beyond Price*. Berkeley: Diamond Books.

Andruss, Plant, Plant, and Wright. 1990. *Home: A Bioregional Reader*. Philadelphia: New Society.

Berry, Wendell. 1984. *Collected Poems*. New York: North Point Press.

———. 1977. *The Unsettling of America*. San Francisco: Sierra Club.

Bowers, C. A. 1995. *Educating for an Ecologically Sustainable Culture*. Albany: State University of New York.

Cajete, Gregory. 1994. *Look to the Mountain: An Ecology of Indigenous Education*. Durango, CO: Kivaki.

Carse, James P. 1994. *Breakfast at the Victory: The Mysticism of Ordinary Experience*. San Francisco: HarperSanFrancisco.

Coles, Robert. 1990. *The Spiritual Life of Children*. Boston: Houghton Mifflin.

Cooper, David A. 1992. *The Heart of Stillness*. New York: Bell Tower.

Csikzentmihalyi, Mihaly. 1990. *Flow: The Psychology of Optimal Experience*. New York: Harper & Row.

Devall, Bill, and George Sessions. 1985. *Deep Ecology*. Salt Lake City: Gibbs Smith.

Fine, Melinda. 1995. *Habits of Mind: Struggling over Values in America's Classrooms*. San Francisco: Jossey-Bass.

Fox, Matthew. 1991. *Creation Spirituality*. San Francisco: HarperSanFrancisco.

———. 1983. *Original Blessing*. Santa Fe: Bear & Co.

———. 1994. *The Reinvention of Work*. San Francisco: HarperSanFrancisco.

Gardner, Howard. 1991. *The Unschooled Mind*. New York: Basic Books.

Gardner, John Fentress. 1996. *Education in Search of the Spirit*. New York: Anthroposophic Press.

Gatto, John Taylor. 1992. *Dumbing Us Down: The Hidden Curriculum of Compulsory Schooling*. Philadelphia: New Society.

———. 1993. *The Exhausted School*. New York: Oxford Village Press.

Global Alliance for Transforming Education. 1991. *Education 2000: A Holistic Perspective*. Grafton, VT: GATE.

Goldsmith, Edward. 1992. *The Way: An Ecological World-View*. Boston: Shambhala.

Goldstein, Joseph. 1983. *The Experience of Insight*. Boston: Shambhala.

Gyatso, Tenzin. 1988. *The Dalai Lama at Harvard*. Ithaca: Snow Lion.

———. 1995. *Dialogues on Universal Responsibility and Education*. Dharamsala: Library of Tibetan Works and Archives.

———. 1994. *A Flash of Lightning in the Dark*. Boston: Shambhala.

———. 1990. *Freedom in Exile: The Autobiography of His Holiness the Dalai Lama of Tibet*. London: Hodder & Stoughton.

———. 1996. *The Good Heart: A Buddhist Perspective on the Teachings of Jesus*. Boston: Wisdom.

———. 1984. *Kindness, Clarity and Insight*. Ithaca: Snow Lion.

———. 1980. *Universal Responsibility and the Good Heart*. Dharamsala: Library of Tibetan Works and Archives.

Halifax, Joan. 1982. *Shaman: The Wounded Healer*. London: Thames and Hudson.

———. 1979. *Shamanic Voices: A Survey of Visionary Narratives*. New York: E. P. Dutton.

Halifax, Joan, and Stanislav Grof. 1977. *The Human Encounter with Death*. New York: E. P. Dutton.

Hannum, H. 1997. *People, Land, and Community*. New Haven: Yale University.

Hansen, David T., Philip W. Jackson, and Robert E. Boostrom. 1993. *The Moral Life of Schools*. San Francisco: Jossey-Bass.

Harding, Vincent. 1990. *Hope and History*. Maryknoll, NY: Orbis Books.

———. 1996. *Martin Luther King: The Inconvenient Hero*. Maryknoll, NY: Orbis Books.

———. 1981. *There Is a River*. New York: Harcourt Brace Jovanovich.

Hayward, Jeremy. 1997. *Letters to Vanessa: On Love, Science, and Awareness in an Enchanted World*. Boston: Shambhala.

———. 1984. *Perceiving Ordinary Magic: Science and Intuitive Wisdom*. Boston: Shambhala.

———. 1995. *Sacred World: A Guide to Shambhala Warriorship in Daily Life*. New York: Bantam.

Hixon, Lex. 1995. *Coming Home*. New York: Larson.

―――. 1992. *Great Swan: Meetings with Ramakrishna*. Boston: Shambhala.

―――. 1988. *Heart of the Koran*. Wheaton, IL: Quest.

―――. 1995. *Living Buddha Zen*. New York: Larson.

―――. 1993. *Mother of the Buddhas*. Wheaton, IL: Quest.

―――. 1994. *Mother of the Universe: Visions of the Goddess and Tantric Hymns of Enlightenment*. Wheaton, IL: Quest.

hooks, bell. 1981. *Ain't I a Woman: Black Women and Feminism*. Boston: South End Press.

―――. 1995. *Art on My Mind: Visual Politics*. New York: New Press.

―――. 1992. *Black Looks: Race and Representation*. Boston: South End Press.

―――. 1996. *Bone Black: Memories of Girlhood*. New York: Henry Holt.

―――. 1991. *Breaking Bread: Insurgent Black Intellectual Life*. Boston: South End Press.

―――. 1995. *Killing Rage: Ending Racism*. New York: Henry Holt.

―――. 1994. *Outlaw Culture: Resisting Representation*. New York: Routledge.

―――. 1989. *Talking Back: Thinking Feminist, Thinking Black*. Boston: South End Press.

―――. 1994. *Teaching to Transgress*. New York: Routledge.

―――. 1990. *Yearning: Race, Gender and Cultural Politics*. Boston: South End Press.

Huxley, Aldous. 1944. *The Perennial Philosophy*. New York: Harper & Row.

Illich, Ivan. 1971. *Deschooling Society*. New York: Harper & Row.

Jackson, Wes. 1994. *Becoming Native to This Place*. Washington: Counterpoint.

Jensen, Derrick. 1995. *Listening to the Land*. San Francisco: Sierra Club.

Keats, John. 1958. *The Letters of John Keats*. Cambridge, MA: Harvard University.

Kilpatrick, William. 1992. *Why Johnny Can't Tell Right From Wrong: Moral Illiteracy and the Case for Character Education*. New York: Simon and Schuster.

Kunstler, James Howard. 1993. *The Geography of Nowhere*. New York: Simon and Schuster.

―――. 1996. *Home From Nowhere*. New York: Simon and Schuster.

Kushner, Lawrence. 1994. *Honey from the Rock*. Woodstock, VT: Jewish Lights Publishing.

Langer, Ellen. 1997. *The Power of Mindful Learning*. Reading, MA: Addison-Wesley.

Lasch, Christopher. 1991. *The True and Only Heaven: Progress and Its Critics*. New York: W. W. Norton.

Bibliography

Lasley, Thomas J., II. 1994. *Teaching Peace*. Westport, CT: Bergin and Garvey.

Leach, William. 1993. *Land of Desire*. New York: Vintage.

Lingpa, Dudjom. 1994. *Buddhahood without Meditation*. Junction City, CA.: Padma Publishing.

Longchenpa. 1977. *Kindly Bent to Ease Us*. Emeryville, CA: Dharma.

Loori, John Daido. 1992. *The Eight Gates of Zen*. Mt. Tremper, NY: Dharma Communications.

Lovejoy, Arthur. 1964. *The Great Chain of Being*. Cambridge: Harvard University Press.

Mander, J., and E. Goldsmith. 1996. *The Case Against the Global Economy*. San Francisco: Sierra Club.

Mander, Jerry. 1991. *In the Absence of the Sacred*. San Francisco: Sierra Club.

McKibben, Bill. 1992. *The Age of Missing Information*. New York: Plume.

Miller, Alice. 1983. *For Your Own Good*. New York: Farrar, Straus Giroux.

Miller, J. P. 1981. *The Compassionate Teacher*. Englewood, NJ: Prentice Hall.

———. 1988. *The Holistic Curriculum*. Toronto: OISE Press.

Miller, Ron. 1993. *The Renewal of Meaning in Education*. Brandon: Holistic Education Press.

———. 1992. *What Are Schools For? Holistic Education in American Culture*. Brandon: Holistic Education Press.

Mitchell, Stephen, ed. 1989. *The Enlightened Heart*. New York: Harper & Row.

Moffett, James. 1994. *The Universal Schoolhouse*. San Francisco: Jossey-Bass.

Moore, Thomas. 1992. *Care of the Soul*. New York: HarperCollins.

Nabhan, G. P., and S. Trimble. 1994. *The Geography of Childhood*. Boston: Beacon Press.

Nabhan, Gary Paul. 1997. *Cultures of Habitat*. Washington, D.C.: Counterpoint.

Nachmanovitch, S. 1990. *Free Play: Improvisation in Life and Art*. Los Angeles: Jeremy P. Tarcher.

Noblit, George W., and Van O. Dempsey. 1996. *The Social Construction of Virtue: The Moral Life of Schools*. Albany: Southern University of New York.

Norberg-Hodge, Helena. 1991. *Ancient Futures: Learning from Ladakh*. San Francisco: Sierra Club.

Norbu, Thinley. 1981. *Magic Dance*. New York: Jewel Publishing House.

———. 1977. *The Small Golden Key*. New York: Jewel Publishing House.

———. 1992. *White Sail*. Boston: Shambhala.

Occhiogrosso, Peter. 1991. *Through the Labyrinth*. New York: Viking.

Orr, David W. 1994. *Earth in Mind: On Education, Environment, and the Human Prospect*. Washington, D.C.: Island Press.

————. 1992. *Ecological Literacy*. Albany: Southern University of New York.

————. 1979. *The Global Predicament*. Chapel Hill: University of North Carolina.

Palmer, Parker. 1990. *The Active Life*. San Francisco: HarperSanFransicso.

————, ed. 1990. *Caring for the Commonweal*. Macon, GA: Mercer University Press.

————. 1991. *The Company of Strangers*. New York: Crossroad.

————. 1997. *The Courage to Teach*. San Francisco: Jossey-Bass.

————. 1983. *To Know as We Are Known*. San Francisco: HarperSanFrancisco.

————. 1993. *The Promise of Paradox*. Washington, DC: Servant Leadership Press.

————. 1980. *The Recovery of Spirit in Higher Education*. New York: Seabury.

Patrul Rinpoche. 1994. *The Words of My Perfect Teacher*. San Francisco: HarperSanFrancisco.

Pearce, Joseph Chilton. 1971. *The Crack in the Cosmic Egg*. New York: Pocket Books.

Postman, Neil. 1995. *The End of Education*. New York: Vintage.

Rabjam, Longchen. 1998. *The Precious Treasury of the Way of Abiding*. Junction City, CA: Padma Publishing.

Remen, Rachel Naomi. 1996. *Kitchen Table Wisdom: Stories That Heal*. New York: Riverhead.

Richards, M. C. 1964. *Centering: In Pottery, Poetry and the Person*. Middletown: Wesleyan University Press.

————. 1973. *The Crossing Point*. Middletown: Wesleyan University Press.

————. 1980. *Toward Wholeness: Rudolph Steiner Education in America*. Middletown: Wesleyan University Press.

Rockefeller, Steven C., and John C. Elder. 1992. *Spirit and Nature*. Boston: Beacon Press.

Saint-Exupéry, Antoine de. 1971. *The Little Prince*. San Diego: Harcourt Brace & Company.

Sale, Kirkpatrick. 1985. *Dwellers in the Land: The Bioregional Vision*. San Francisco: Sierra Club.

Schachter-Shalomi, Zalman M. 1993. *Gate to the Heart*. Philadelphia: ALEPH.

————. 1991. *Spiritual Intimacy*. Northvale, NJ: Jason Aronson, Inc.

Schumacher, E. F. 1979. *Good Work*. New York: Harper Colophon.

————. 1973. *Small Is Beautiful*. New York: Harper & Row.

Bibliography

Shantideva. 1979. *A Guide to the Bodhisattva's Way of Life*. Dharamsala: Library of Tibetan Works and Archives.

Sichel, Betty A. 1988. *Moral Education: Character, Community and Ideals*. Philadelphia: Temple University.

Sivaraksa, Sulak. 1992. *Seeds of Peace*. Berkeley: Parallax.

Sloan, Douglas. 1983. *Insight-Imagination: The Recovery of Thought and the Modern World*. Westport, CT: Greenwood.

Smith, Huston. 1982. *Beyond the Post-Modern Mind*. New York: Crossroads.

———. 1965. *Condemned to Meaning*. New York: Harper & Row.

———. 1976. *Forgotten Truth*. New York: Harper & Row.

———. 1989. *Primordial Truth and Postmodern Theology*. Albany: State University of New York.

———. 1955. *The Purposes of Higher Education*. New York: Harper & Brothers.

———. 1958. *The Religions of Man*. New York: Harper & Row.

Snyder, Gary. 1969. *Earth House Hold*. New York: New Directions.

———. 1995. *A Place in Space*. Washington, D.C.: Counterpoint.

———. 1990. *The Practice of the Wild*. San Francisco: North Point Press.

———. 1980. *The Real Work*. New York: New Directions.

Sobel, David. 1993. *Children's Special Places*. Tucson: Zephyr Press.

Steiner, Rudolf. 1996. *The Child's Changing Consciousness and Waldorf Education*. Hudson, NY: Anthroposophic Press.

———. 1996. *The Education of the Child, and Early Lectures on Education*. Hudson, NY: Anthroposophic Press.

———. 1994. *Intuitive Thinking as a Spiritual Path: A Philosophy of Freedom*. Hudson, NY: Anthroposophic Press.

———. 1967. *Stages of Higher Knowledge*. Spring Valley, NY: Anthroposophic Press.

Thomashaw, Mitchell. 1995. *Ecological Identity*. Cambridge, MA: MIT.

Trungpa, Chogyam. 1991. *Crazy Wisdom*. Boston: Shambhala.

———. 1996. *Dharma Art*. Boston: Shambhala.

———. 1981. *Journey without Goal*. Boulder, CO.: Prajna Press.

———. 1976. *The Myth of Freedom*. Boston: Shambhala.

———. 1984. *Shambhala: The Sacred Path of the Warrior*. Boston: Shambhala.

Tulku, Chagdud. 1993. *Gates to Buddhist Practice*. Junction City, CA.: Padma Publishing.

————. 1987. *Life in Relation to Death*. Cottage Grove, OR: Padma Publishing.

————. 1992. *Lord of the Dance*. Junction City, CA.: Padma Publishing.

Vitek, W., and W. Jackson. 1996. *Rooted in the Land*. New Haven: Yale University.

————. 1998. *The Marriage of Sense and Soul*. New York: Random House.

Wilber, Ken. 1995. *Sex, Ecology, Spirituality*. Boston: Shambhala.

ABOUT THE EDITOR

Steven Glazer has been a substitute teacher, elementary educator, arts administrator, development officer, and school director. The co-founder of two educational organizations, The Naropa Institute School of Continuing Education and Living Education: Place-Based Living and Learning, he lives with his wife, Stacey, and daughter, Kayla, in Patagonia, Arizona.

This book was born out of the Spirituality in Education *conference, held at the Naropa Institute, in Boulder, Colorado, during the summer of 1997. For more information about the Institute, please write: The Naropa Institute, 2130 Arapahoe Avenue, Boulder, Colorado 80302.*